EARL LOUIS
"CURLY"
LAMBEAU

★ ★ ★ ★ ★ ★

To Tony Canadeo, one of the greatest Packers ever,
and a fine man I consider a privilege to call a friend.

Eagle Books
P.O. Box 253
Hales Corners, WI 53130

Printed by Graphic Innovations, Inc.
United States of America
First Edition

ISBN 1-882987-08-X

LAMBEAU

★ ★ ★ ★ ★ ★

The
Man Behind
The Mystique

DAVID ZIMMERMAN

EAGLE
BOOKS

TABLE OF CONTENTS

Foreword

APacker player said after winning a close game: "It's the ghost of Lambeau." A visiting player said after losing a close game: "It's part of that whole Lambeau thing. Teams come in here and self-destruct."

Those two references to somebody named Lambeau were delivered after the Packers' 1,095th game in their 82nd National Football League season – against the Buffalo Bills at Lambeau Field on December 22, 2002, a 10-0 Packer victory.

Lambeau? The time has come to put aside all those books on Vince Lombardi and others and present Earl Louis (Curly) Lambeau in book form, namely, *Lambeau: the Man Behind the Mystique.*

Strangely, the fascinating life of Curly Lambeau has never been published until now. Also strange is the fact that if this 21-year-old Green Bay youngster did not have the urge to start a football team in 1919 there never would have been a team known as the Green Bay Packers.

Can you imagine the NFL without this Lambeau offspring from a dinky little town in northeastern Wisconsin? In fact, Curly often heard jokes from the big city press about "the Indians still in the backyard out there."

Just think what the Green Pay Packers inherited from Lambeau's desire to kick and throw a football. The list is fabulous and endless, including: Twelve NFL championships, including three in a row twice; the Ice Bowl; players like Don Hutson, Tony Canadeo, Bart Starr and Brett Favre to mention a few; yes, Vince Lombardi whose five championships fell one short of Lambeau's; a really huge underground of Packer fans nationwide; and a special soft spot in the hearts of everyone who loves football.

Perhaps, Curly was too successful too early since he was only 33 when he already had won three straight championships. Curly-haired, handsome and always dressed to kill, Lambeau was a big attraction, especially to the opposite sex, as the Packers traveled to the big cities.

I've always felt Lambeau outgrew the peaceful, family life of Green Bay to some extent as he went through three divorces, including the first from his high school sweetheart. He was often accused of "going Hollywood" since he spent considerable time there and his second and third marriages were with women involved in the California cinematic world.

My association with Lambeau started in late 1941 and I soon discovered that he was an "incurable optimist" and that he could stretch the truth a tad. He always thought he'd win every game, never taking the blame if he lost one and often blaming it on an individual player.

Lambeau could be a lot of fun, noting once that, "You should never take a drink until after five o'clock and surround yourself with a lot of pretty girls." He often had a cigarette dangling from his mouth during the games, but somebody once said, "He never inhaled."

Yes, Curly Lambeau's football achievements are historic and his life spread from great popularity, some shame and final redemption before he died at 67, hoping to wed a girl half his age.

Now, Earl Louis Lambeau comes to life again in this amazing book by David Zimmerman, who also penned *In Search of a Hero: The Life and Times of Tony Canadeo*, one of Curly's star players.

Art Daley
Former sports editor
Green Bay Press-Gazette
1946-1970

Introduction

My daughter, Christy, suggested the subtitle of this book, *The Man Behind the Mystique*. In fact, her persuasive pleas convinced me to write a biography on Lambeau since none had ever been written. What gave me the final push into the project was her offer to assist in the research process. Tom Murphy, director and archivist for the Green Bay Packer Hall of Fame, and Tony Canadeo, longtime Packer star and board member, also had been encouraging me for some time to tell the Lambeau story.

Christy's idea for the subtitle came from our frequent conversations about how I would treat a Lambeau biography. I wanted to dig deep enough into the past to discover the true essence of the man, as much as possible, nearly 40 years after his death. Peeling back the pages of time would hopefully reveal the nature and character of the person primarily responsible for the most unique story in professional sports, the Green Bay Packers.

Reliving Lambeau's life was like discovering an attic of lost treasures. From old newspapers to revealing conversations, I managed to go back in time to the golden age of sports in the 1920s. I relived the nation's period of financial hardship during the Depression of the 1930s and witnessed the incredible impact of World War II; and the 1950s – when professional football emerged as the number one fan favorite.

While the book is intended to be a biography, I could not exclude a generous amount of the glamorous and romantic first 31 years of the Packers. I discovered how Lambeau became one of the most famous and powerful football coaches of his era and an American success story. While some of his human frailties would eventually pull Lambeau from his lofty pedestal, during a 30-year stretch from 1929 to 1959 he was one of the most well known personalities in the nation.

Lambeau's greatest gift was not in the basic X's and O's of football, but, rather, his understanding that with the Packers from tiny Green Bay in the fledgling National Football League, he was part of something that would capture the imagination and interest of sports fans everywhere.

It took more than a year to write and research this book. Pulling together the background materials took four of us nearly seven months of dedicated, non-stop investigation. It was a wonderful opportunity to sift through information and photographs in the archives in the basement of the Packer Hall of Fame in Green Bay, the Packer files at the Pro Football Hall of Fame in Canton, Ohio and materials provided by Packer historian Marv Niec of Packer City Antiques.

We poured through newspaper articles from the 1920s through the 1960s from the Green Bay *Press-Gazette, Milwaukee Journal, Milwaukee Sentinel, Chicago Tribune, Chicago Sun-Times, Washington Post* and various other newspapers and magazines from that time period. We also reviewed over 50 books covering any aspect of professional football and several on Notre Dame football in the early 1900s. Particularly helpful was the unpublished manuscript by Ralph Hickok on Johnny Blood. The idea for the opening chapter, recounting Lambeau's death, came from an interview with Larry Names, who has written four books on the first 41 years of the Packers. We also had the opportunity to see letters written by Lambeau to several people, and to view films of taped interviews with numerous Packers who played for Lambeau, but are now deceased.

I owe a great deal of gratitude to those who assisted in this project: my long-time assistant, Chris Mroz, who helped me in so many ways that I could not have completed the book without her assistance; Christy Cool who was a big help with the research; Katie Grueneberg for her astute editing; and Tom Murphy and Fritz Van for their valuable editorial contributions. We also got help from research assistant Diane Tunis, who provided valuable material from Lambeau's time on the west coast.

Numerous former Packers who played for Lambeau, as well as some who were with the Chicago Cardinals and Washington Redskins when he coached them in the early 1950s, were kind enough to grant interviews. I also spoke with journalists who covered the Packers during Lambeau's time plus relatives, friends and several historians. The information and photos provided by Mary Lu Hoyt Gough, the granddaughter of Grace Garland, Lambeau's third wife, gave me extremely helpful insight on his life in California during the 1940s and 1950s. My lengthy conversations with Mary Jane Sorgel provided a revealing look at Lambeau's character in the later years of his life.

Having people trust you enough to confide intimate recollections is an intoxicating, but dangerous brew. What I tried to do was disengage from what can be very personal conversations, probe rather than parrot what was said, and then write the truth about Lambeau, the people and circumstances around him during his life, as I saw it.

David Zimmerman
January 2003

1

Requiem For An Original

It was a warm, late summer afternoon with the sunlight glistening across the water in the bay when he locked the door to his carriage house and walked across the gravel drive, humming a familiar Ray Conniff tune.

Sliding into his new red Cadillac convertible, he pushed a button on the dashboard and waited for the top to fold back. He drove out of the circular drive, past the huge pine trees and out the front gate of his eight-acre estate. People waved to him from the front porch of the old Thorp Hotel as he drove past and down the main street of the tiny village of Fish Creek, his home for the past five summers.

He passed the small shops clustered together and the C & C Club, his favorite hangout. It was tourist season and the sidewalks were busy with summer visitors. Some stopped to stare as he drove by slowly. "Maybe they recognized me," he thought. "The locals all know me, but the tourists may think they do," he mused. A familiar face from the past. The glorious past. Those wondrous years of glory and adulation. "Ah, those were the times, but this time right now is very good too," he murmured out loud as he waved to Ray, who was giving him the high sign from his gas station. He turned up the hill that headed out of town, and drove down Highway 42, south along the bay.

As his foot pushed down on the gas pedal, he could feel the

Caddy's power and was pleased at how quickly it could get to 60 miles an hour. Down the highway he sped, past the pine, poplar and birch trees. Occasionally, a gap in the trees allowed him to see the sun sparkling off the bay to his right.

He turned on the radio and dialed for just the right music to match his mood. "I'm feelin' good tonight!" he thought. And why not? He had a date with a beautiful young woman, felt great and couldn't wait to put the new boat into the water. He had just received a clean bill of health from the doctor, clearing the anxiety he had felt the last couple of months from that nagging upset stomach. Today he felt pain-free, and was looking forward to the next few days.

He began to hum with the music as he drove slowly through Egg Harbor, another little Door County town. He thought of Mary Jane and how much he enjoyed being with her. Even though she was half his age it didn't seem to matter to the two of them. She was so uncomplicated, down-to-earth in many ways, so different than he was, yet they seemed to have a great time when they were together. "She doesn't care one hoot about my past — the good and not so good — she just cares about the me of now," he reasoned. "You've got it made, old timer," he said to himself. "Hey, I'm only 67 — in the prime of my life. I'm going to have some real fun now. This could be the best of times for me. I'm not an old man and I'm not going to act like one," he told himself as he pushed the speedometer to 65 miles an hour. He didn't want to be late. He prided himself in never being late. The flavor of Wisconsin was all around him. Millions of cherry blossoms. Farmhouses that had been there for years. "It hasn't changed much since I first came here on vacation with my parents when I was a kid," he thought.

He slowed down at the city limits of Sturgeon Bay where Mary Jane lived with her parents, Francis and Gertrude Van Duyse. He felt part of that family now. Mary Jane, her two brothers, Fritz and Bob, her parents — they made him feel so welcome every time they were together and they didn't pry into his past. It wasn't that he was trying to forget it all. There were just parts of his past he didn't want to have to explain over and over. Some of it he wasn't very proud of and there was no sense getting into it. They never pried and for that he was grateful. Maybe they reminded him a little of his own close family when he was younger. Mom and Dad with their strong Belgian heritage, his brothers, Rummy and Ollie, and sister, Vee, all growing up together on Cherry Street in nearby

Green Bay. "We were all close once," he reflected. "What happened?" he wondered. "I guess it was all the stuff with the team — I was too absorbed to notice how we drifted apart through the years." Now it seemed too late. Mom, Dad and Rummy were gone now and the others, including Donald, seldom came around any more. Too many years. Too many scars. "Too bad," he muttered to himself as he pulled into the Van Duyse driveway.

Francis was cutting the grass in their small front yard with an old push mower. Seeing that big wave and familiar smile, he waved back and brought the car to a stop. Six forty-five — he was early for the date. He stepped out, ran his hand through his hair, took off his white sports coat and laid it carefully over the front seat. As he walked swiftly toward Francis, he rolled up his sleeves and said, "Hey, Francis, let me take a turn at that. I need some exercise." Francis stepped aside with a big smile and allowed him to take the handles of the mower. Up and down the lawn he went. It felt good. He felt good. After a few swipes at the lawn, he stopped to wave at a neighbor coming down the street. "Hey, Herb, come here for a minute," he shouted. "Look at this new dance I've learned in California," and began to do the twist while holding onto the mower's handles. Francis, standing nearby, said "Curly — don't do this."

With sweat rolling down his face and his shirt now damp with perspiration, he stopped, reached for his handkerchief in his back pocket and began wiping his face. Suddenly, he felt dizzy, disoriented and sick to his stomach. "I feel kind of sick," he mumbled. Then he fell backwards into Francis' arms. He lay there motionless on the freshly cut grass.

Francis, neighbor Herb, and now Mary Jane came and knelt at his side. Within minutes they knew. He was gone. Earl Louis "Curly" Lambeau was dead. It was June 1, 1965.

Soon a small crowd gathered on the front lawn. A doctor, a priest and an ambulance. It was too late for the doctor and the priest. The ambulance drove him to a nearby funeral home.

The next day, flags hung at half-mast while newspapers around the entire nation covered his sudden death and his illustrious career. Five days later he was laid to rest in nearby Green Bay at a cemetery near the Fox River, next to his mother, father and brother, while hundreds of former companions and relatives looked on. Church bells rang out two days after that, heralding a requiem Mass at the Catholic cathedral in downtown Green Bay. It was a requiem for an original.

Earl "Curly" Lambeau was truly one-of-a-kind. He was an individual who comes around once in a great while to make a profound difference. The kind that makes an impact and leaves an imprint for generations to come.

Lambeau, as a youth, played football with such passion and devotion that it eventually parlayed him and his hometown of Green Bay, Wisconsin into the national spotlight. With Lambeau's unbridled enthusiasm and wholehearted dedication to his football team, both those who played the game and the citizens of the city formed a bond so uncommon that it has also been called "one of a kind."

As the years went by, men and boys, businessmen and players, would unite to constitute one of the most unique and heartwarming stories in sports: the undying vision of Lambeau, the hometown boy who didn't want to stop playing the game, the industriousness and courageous men of Green Bay who supported him, the passionate civic loyalty of Green Bay and the entire state of Wisconsin who have melded together over eight decades to produce the wondrous mystique known as the Green Bay Packers.

No one person owns the Green Bay Packers. Not then. Not now. Instead, thousands do. Today, 111,000 stockholders own a total of nearly five million shares. In its infancy, the Packers became a non-profit organization that still ranks as the only publicly owned franchise in major league sports. The thousands of stockholders are the average fans, the average working Joe, the guy next door. As a result, the people of Green Bay and all of Wisconsin embrace *their team* as do no fans anywhere else.

How can this be? These people see the Packers as one of their own — much like a father with his son or grandson. Packer football is not just a sport to these folks. To outsiders they seem to have a devotion to the Packers that borders on worship. Clearly, those avid early followers and their descendants have created a special kind of bond with the team that has not been duplicated anywhere the game of football is played.

The smaller city competing against teams from much larger cities created the compelling "David and Goliath" story over and over again through these many years. The faith that rallied the Packers in their early years in the NFL and supported them in other trying seasons is a wondrous quality. It made it possible for the Packers to advance from the scrubby turf of an open field in 1919 to the best-known outdoor sports stadium in the nation — Lambeau Field.

The stadium where the Packers play today is named after the man who organized the team at age 21 and then led it as captain and coach for the first 31 years of its existence. Starting the team as a city club for two years (1919 to 1920), he took the Packers into what would become the National Football League.

Lambeau was a solid player from 1919 until he retired from playing after the 1928 season. As head coach from 1919 through 1949, he compiled an amazing record. His Packer teams won six National Football League titles — three in a row from 1929 through 1931— then again in 1936, 1939 and 1944. He compiled a 31-year record of 248-108-23 for a fantastic .685 winning percentage. Piling up 209 wins from 1921-49, Lambeau had more victories in that period than any other NFL coach.

Lambeau coached in the NFL for 33 years, including 29 with the Packers. Only George Halas coached longer. His NFL record of 226-132-22 trails only Don Shula and Tom Landry and his six NFL championships are second to none.

In the nine-year stretch between 1936 and 1944, Lambeau's Packers would win 75 percent of all their regular NFL season games, win the Western Division Championship four times, place second for five seasons and capture three world championships. The Packers' record during this remarkable span of time was 73-21-4. No other NFL coach came close to matching Lambeau's success during this period.

After each of the six world championships, the Green Bay citizens treated Lambeau like a conquering hero, their knight in shining armor. He was the city's favorite son, the hometown boy who made good. On cold December nights, tens of thousands would greet the team for exuberant title celebrations. Parades and all-night parties would cap off each of the triumphs. It was an unbelievable time of adulation and jubilation. Lambeau became a national celebrity throughout the 1930s and 1940s. His accomplishments, charming personality and the "David vs. Goliath" theme caught the fancy of journalists in all the major newspapers and magazines of the time. The *Saturday Evening Post, Look, Life* and numerous other national publications carried feature stories on Lambeau, and he was interviewed hundreds of times.

Lambeau was inducted into the Pro Football Hall of Fame in 1963, its first year in existence, and was later inducted into the

Packer Hall of Fame (1970) and the Wisconsin Hall of Fame. The contributions he made to the game of football, the NFL, the city of Green Bay and the state of Wisconsin were major. He gave the team and the city of Green Bay unequaled national prominence between 1921 and 1949.

Earl "Curly" Lambeau *was* the Green Bay Packers the first 31 years of their existence. It was his team representing the town where he grew up. He started it, picked the players, provided the drive, motivation and ran it with an iron hand until near the end of his tenure with the Packers in 1949. He alone found the players he wanted, negotiated their contracts, handled team travel and designed team uniforms.

No one close to the situation questions the fact that without Lambeau there would be no Green Bay Packers today. That is some legacy. But who was this man? What were his real personality, character, nature, disposition and temperament?

As with all of us, he underwent changes throughout his lifetime. His character featured the good, the bad and the ugly. But immense celebrity has a way of making one's good and bad qualities much more pronounced than those of the average person.

In his early years, Lambeau was an energetic and gifted athlete with a charming personality that captured the hearts of his teachers and classmates alike. Blessed with good looks and a strong body, Lambeau stood out among his peers. He was bright and an extreme extrovert. As he assembled his successful Packer teams in the 1920s, he demonstrated his natural leadership skills along with a knack for selling. He successfully sold his hometown, his players and fans on his Packers throughout the beginning stages of the fledgling team.

After his first world championship in 1929 and through the glory years of six world championships up until the mid-1940s, his personality and character would undergo gradual changes. As the team grew more successful and his image developed into a larger-than-life character, his passion for winning grew even stronger. He became more intense, impatient and impulsive. At the same time, Lambeau would be more creative, disciplined and focused than at any time in his life. Winning became an obsession. Continued success also inflated his ego, which in turn had a tendency to give him a distorted view of his own importance. He displayed nearly vol-cano-like emotions at times. His time in California increased through the years, affording Lambeau numerous opportunities to socialize with movie directors, producers, actors and actresses.

During this period, Lambeau, although married to his high school sweetheart, became sexually restless and promiscuous. It eventually cost him three marriages and earned him a notorious playboy reputation. It would become a stigma that tarnished his golden image for years. Even into his 60s, Lambeau remained a handsome man with a fine, athletic physique. Always impeccably dressed when in public, his appearance was of paramount importance to him through his entire life. Women were enamored by his manly charm and were easily smitten and many fell victim to his magnetic personality over the years. While he amassed a small fortune, Lambeau never threw his money around. Of frugal Belgian stock, he liked to tell how his father had ordered him never to bank less than ten percent of his pay, no matter how small it was. "And I banked that ten percent every month of my life," Lambeau would relate. When he died, his estate would total a value of nearly one million dollars, made up mostly of property in California and Wisconsin.

In the inglorious years following World War II when the Packer teams descended from mediocre to lousy, Lambeau's personality evolved into the unsavory figure of a fallen champion. With the winds of fate howling without mercy in the late 1940s, Lambeau saw his beloved Packers come apart, the team's finances crumble and his supporting cast of local Green Bay businessmen turn against him. Now spending more time every winter in California, he had become visibly more vain, often displaying extreme pride when dealing with his team and the Packer board of directors. It was during this time when people said he had "gone Hollywood." He became more emotional, rash and often blamed others for the sorry state to which the Packers had descended to by 1949. He had a most ignominious departure from the Packers after the 1949 season, resigning after a long and ugly battle with some members of the Packers' board. It was a shameful departure that never should have happened. The Packers continued their decline until Vince Lombardi arrived on the scene ten years later.

After he left the Packers, Lambeau would coach two other NFL teams, the Chicago Cardinals and Washington Redskins, for two years each. His passion for the game, however, was gone when he left the Packers. What's more, his hometown felt he betrayed them and his popularity sunk to an all-time low. In the mid-1950s, his third wife, a California socialite, would divorce him for adultery.

No longer coaching or in the limelight and with his popularity and reputation now tarnished, Lambeau resembled a character in a Greek tragedy: the fallen hero of a bygone era who had become a shadow of his former self.

Years later, Lambeau would manage to redeem himself with his hometown of Green Bay. He reversed his previous conceited manner by working to change his image. In a rather heartwarming finish to his life, Lambeau lived a more private, unassuming and simple life. He did not suddenly turn into a shy, timid and meek shell of the former Lambeau, but there were succinct changes. Fittingly, toward the end of his life he also received the honors and recognition he deserved as founder and leader of the Packers for more than 30 years.

During my research and interviews, I found no one who got to know Lambeau well. He never really revealed himself to many people. He had many superficial acquaintances, but few, if any, close friends. He had many more women who were friends than men through his lifetime. Don Hutson was one of the few men who remained a close friend after his retirement as a Packer and until Lambeau's death. Francis Van Duyse, his girlfriend's father, was probably Lambeau's closest male friend in the later years of his life. It's possible no one really knew Lambeau well. He revealed little of his inner self. In many ways, he was a very complex individual with a wide range of personalities.

While Lambeau made it a practice to never get too close to his players, the men who played for him may have known Lambeau best. Yet, even their reflections are mixed. Cliff Christl, a long-time Wisconsin newspaper reporter with the *Press-Gazette* and *Milwaukee Sentinel* and a historian of Packer lore, has studied Lambeau extensively, interviewing the men who played for him through the years. Christl wrote: "Lambeau wasn't so much a tyrant, but he could be arrogant and uncompromising. Players were forever complaining about his strict rules and ironhanded enforcement of them. He would slap players with steep, unreasonable fines in an age when they made meager wages. He threatened their jobs. He placed the blame for mistakes and defeats squarely on their shoulders."

One of his best players, Clarke Hinkle, said he never really respected Lambeau, but played his heart out for him. Some of his players spoke highly of Lambeau. "Curly was a great coach," according to Buckets Goldenberg, who played for Lambeau from

1933-1945. Tony Canadeo, a star halfback for Lambeau in the 1940s, said, "When you think of Green Bay, you think of Curly. All I know, he was boss when I played and I'm proud of it." A twelve-year veteran (1934-1946) halfback Joe Laws said, "Curly was tops with me. If you played ball for him, he played ball with you." Most of the former players interviewed said Lambeau was not considered a football strategist, but was "one hell of a motivator." Charlie Brock, a Packer from 1939 to 1947, offered, "Maybe the fellows didn't always like him because he was a driver for condition, but we knew he had a job to do and we put out for him." Coaching through fear is a theme often heard about Lambeau. He had a volatile temper and players often felt his wrath. Bob Snyder, an assistant coach for Lambeau in 1949, said players played more out of fear than respect for Curly. Former players from the 1950s Chicago Cardinals and Washington Redskins had few compliments for Lambeau. However, many credit Lambeau for his role in the NFL. His archrival on the field, George Halas of the Chicago Bears, once said he doubted if the NFL would exist without the likes of Lambeau.

While his former players had mixed feelings about Lambeau, their wives were consistently praising. One wife said, "Curly would smile at you with those dimples — there was just something about him." They called him, "Handsome, charming, personable and caring." Mary Jane Van Duyse, Lambeau's girlfriend the last five years of his life found him to be "warm and sensitive with a heart of gold." Others we interviewed who knew him later in life called him, "A real nice, regular guy, who was easy to talk to and 'down to earth.'"

Lambeau's relationship with the press for the most part was cordial. His coverage from newspaper sportswriters between 1930 and 1955 was extensive not only in Green Bay and Milwaukee, but around the nation. Art Daley of the Green Bay *Press-Gazette* covered the Packers in the 1940s, respected and feared Lambeau at the same time. He could never get too close to him. Lee Remmel, who also covered the Packers for the *Press-Gazette* in the 1940s and is now executive director of public relations for the Packers, called Lambeau an, "imaginative, impatient visionary with vast energy who had an indomitable will to win." Christl, who has covered the Packers for years, was very direct when he called Lambeau a "philanderer, compulsive liar, manipulator, while at the same time a fascinating, enigmatic individual with an insatiable appetite for power, women and riches who had few peers as a salesman and motivator."[1]

Sportswriter Lloyd Larson of the *Milwaukee Sentinel* said at one time, "Lambeau had a great knack of spotting potential stars and selling them on coming to Green Bay." Bud Lea, long time sportswriter for the *Milwaukee Sentinel* said, "It was Lambeau's persistence that kept the Packers alive."

Reflections of Lambeau came from many other reporters, too. Arthur Daley, well known sportswriter for the *New York Times* wrote, "Curly Lambeau was the Packers." Arch Ward, sports editor of the *Chicago Tribune* and long time acquaintance of Lambeau once said, "My association with Lambeau, which spans more than two decades, has been one of unbroken pleasantness." Oliver Kuechle, one time sports editor of the *Milwaukee Journal* who covered the Packers during most of Lambeau's tenure at Green Bay once wrote, "Lambeau dominated his teams, bent them to his will. He was a genius in the way he inspired and led his teams." He added at the time of Lambeau's death a statement that carries a great truth: "Few men anywhere have ever done as much for their hometown as Lambeau for his."

Lambeau was truly an enigma. His persona was "all in the eyes of the beholder." Regardless of how he was seen by others, the Lambeau story unfolds like a novel. It has all the ingredients of good fiction: courage, valor, conquest, infidelity, honors, greed, pride, envy, joy, sorrow, shame and redemption. The story of Curly Lambeau is really about a small town boy who rises up along with his hometown to gain national fame only to fall from grace. After years of disgrace and wandering, he returns home to regain his lost fame and dignity.

As the story begins, however, Lambeau himself, little more than a boy, has a premonition of his own destiny.

2

"Conquer the World"

"*When I get through with athletics, I'm going out and conquer the rest of the world,*" read the boastful statement printed next to Earl Lambeau's picture in his high school yearbook. At 19 years old, a head taller and a year older than many of his senior classmates, young Earl was full of himself and brimming with self-confidence. And why not? A ruggedly handsome athlete, he had been a high school star in football and track. Lambeau possessed a captivating personality that adults and teenage companions alike found seductively charismatic. His teachers fell unashamedly under his charm. An easy smile, punctuated with deep dimples, seemed to light up his entire face. His buddies adored him and would follow his inspiring leadership anywhere, anytime, for any cause. Known by everyone in town as "Curly" because of his pitch black, naturally curly hair, Lambeau seemed mature for his age. He was known as somebody meant for something grand in the years ahead.

Earl Louis Lambeau was born in Green Bay on April 9, 1898, the firstborn of Marcel and Mary Lambeau. Their parents had come to Wisconsin some 20 years earlier and settled in the Belgian neighborhood of the city. Marcel Lambeau's parents came from Belgium while Mary's family originated in southern France. Marcel and Mary had learned firsthand to be frugal and independent, character traits they would pass onto their children. Marcel had just begun to build a name for himself with his own construction business that would eventually become one of Green Bay's best-known. As fate would have it, he would become one of the leading contractors on the Green Bay City Stadium — the very spot where the Packers would play for over 30 years and where his son Earl would develop his reputation.

Earl was the oldest of four children in the Lambeau household. His brothers Raymond (Rummy) and Oliver (Ollie) were two and four years younger, while his sister Beatrice (Vee) was the youngest. While the Lambeaus weren't poor, they certainly were not wealthy, either. They grew up in a conventional, modest residential area on the northeast side of Green Bay. "Home" was an unpretentious two-story bungalow at 1205 Cherry Street, just blocks from the 'downtown' main street and the Fox River that wound its way through the middle of the city.

With living space at a premium, the three boys shared a bedroom, while Vee had her own room. The Lambeau home stood on a small lot, just a few feet off the sidewalk where modest houses lined up, crowded together with small front yards and very little space in the rear. Maple trees lined the street, spaced out in front or between the houses for blocks on end.

Raised as devout Catholics, the family attended St. Willebrord Church for Mass on Sundays and St. Francis Cathedral on special Feast days, both only a few blocks from their house. In fact, most if not all of the activities Curly would participate in during his youth would take place within a ten to twelve-block radius of their house. Sports, school, church, movie houses and shopping were all within walking distance. Even the girl Curly would one day marry lived only a few blocks away. To play baseball or football, the Lambeau boys and their friends would ride their bikes about eight blocks to St. Clair Street, which in those years was a sandy, unpaved thoroughfare. The few times they would leave the neighborhood were the times when Curly was a young teen and the family would vacation in nearby beautiful Door County.

Wisconsin is shaped like a child's mitten on the right hand, palm up with the city of Green Bay between the hand and thumb. The thumb would be Door County, about an hour's drive from Green Bay. The Green Bay area has a long and rich history and it's not all tied to the Packers. With the end of the American Revolution in 1783, the Northwest Territory became part of the United States and Green Bay was incorporated in 1854. By 1920, nearly 20 percent of all the labor force in Green Bay was somehow involved with papermaking, turning the logging business into Wisconsin's number one industry for years. In addition, Green Bay, where winter's cold comes early, had become the largest cheese manufacturing and shipping center in the world. During that same period, the city had 13 religious sects organized into 30 congregations, of which most (nine) were Roman Catholic, five Lutheran, three Methodist and one Jewish.

Turn-of-the-century Green Bay was a bustling little city for its size. Downtown streets were named after the American presidents, starting with Washington, and a glut of hotels, five banks and four movie theaters dominated activity. The city had an excellent education system for more than 18,000 pupils. St. Norbert College boasted a student body of 251 and a faculty of 26, with nearly all the latter members of the Premonstratensian Order. The Norbertines, as the order is more widely known, also maintained a seminary.

With a population of nearly 30,000 Green Bay at that time was (and still is) heavily Catholic, considered more than a little conservative, with ethnic groups made up primarily of Germans, Poles, Belgians and Irish. Names like Anderson, Dahlke, Hanson, Jacobs, Kabacinski, Kelly, Murphy, O'Brien, Schroeder and Webster were numerous. And while not usually touted at the time, Green Bay had more than its share of taverns, pubs and speakeasies during the prohibition years of the 1920s.

Lambeau's favorite family vacation area in Door County has not changed much since the time Curly was a boy. Beautiful rural farm country, rocky beaches on 250 miles of shoreline, old lighthouses, fishing boats, pretzel bent streets, mind-boggling switchbacks and exhilarating roller-coaster roads climb through towns and villages with names like Egg Harbor, Ephraim, Sister Bay, Ellison Bay, Washington Island, Baileys Harbor and Sturgeon Bay. One village in particular, Fish Creek would be Lambeau's home in the later stages of his life. He often said the fond memories of vacationing with his family in Door County every fall created his lifelong desire to one day make the area his home. Wisconsin has never received the kind of national reputation for fall foliage that New England has enjoyed, but if you have ever experienced a northern Wisconsin autumn day, breathing the crisp, fresh air under deep blue skies surrounded by blazing foliage of red, orange, yellow and brown, you'll never forget it.

It was in the crisp fall days of the year that Curly could relish his first love, football. A leader in his neighborhood even as a youngster, he, his two brothers and their buddies would gather almost every day in the fall and get up a game. The nearest empty lot would do just fine, thank you. Sometimes they'd make their way to their favorite playground on St. Clair Street, a stone's throw from where City Stadium would be built and where he would later coach the Packers to greatness. Lambeau, his younger brothers and neighborhood kids would play football there until it got too cold or the snow got too deep. In his later years, Lambeau would tell Arch Ward, the well-known sports editor of the *Chicago Tribune* that when he was a youngster, he didn't own a real football. Instead, he made his own out of an old salt sack, stuffing it with leaves, pebbles and sand before heading into battle on the vacant lots around Cherry Street.

Lambeau started playing organized football when he was an eighth grader at Whitney Grade School. His tough Whitney team gained early recognition when they beat the older East High School freshman team, 18 to 0. Unfortunately, he broke his ankle playing football that year, a mishap that would be the only serious injury he would suffer in his 16 seasons as a player.

Lambeau would become a celebrated triple threat back for Green Bay East High School where he lettered in football all four years. Since he was a year older than most of his teammates and the other teams' players, Lambeau was stronger and faster than the others. In his senior year, at 5 feet 10 inches and 185 pounds, with unusually broad shoulders and thick thighs, he could run over, around and through smaller tacklers. He also became adept at drop kicking the football, the technique used to kick field goals and extra points in those years. Lambeau became so proficient in this art he could accurately drop kick a field goal nearly 40 yards.

While his running and kicking were impressive, it was his infatuation with throwing the football that really made Lambeau different from other players of that era. Dating all the way back to his sandlot days, Curly simply loved to pass. Trouble was, the round footballs of the day, looking more like basketballs, made throwing an adventure. Conventional wisdom said the game was meant to run, run and run again. Grind out the yardage and wear your opponent down. It would have been unusual for a team to pass more than two or three times an entire game, whether it was a high school or college game. While most of the plays run by East High

School during Lambeau's four years centered on the run, they still passed far more than their opponents and Curly did all of the throwing.

East High School, located on the corner of Chicago and Webster Streets, about ten blocks from the Lambeau family home, was built in 1893. Because the building was located on top of a hill, the students were nicknamed the "Hilltoppers." On the other side of town was West High School. The two schools became bitter rivals with city bragging rights to the winner of every fiercely fought contest between them. Through the years, West High School held the upper hand in football and usually defeated East High School in their traditional Thanksgiving Day game. For seven straight seasons, East found itself on the wrong side of the scoreboard.

Lambeau, now in his senior year, was determined to end the bitter losing streak. He was named captain of the team that 1916 season and even shared some of the coaching responsibilities. He would later say of that year, "Our coach the year before, Carroll Nelson, didn't come back. A teacher was assigned to coach us, but he had never played football. They had elected me captain since I was bigger than they were. I went to him and asked him what he wanted to do. He said that he wanted to read a book on football, so go ahead and do what you want to."

In truth, according to the East High School yearbook of that year, Lambeau had considerable help coaching the squad. Ralph Cavright, the teacher who replaced the regular coach, had never played football. He left the team after a few practice sessions and told Lambeau to take over. Within a few days, however, local fans of the team, Joseph Hoeffel, Dr. DeBoth and Walter Eckhardt, offered to help with the coaching and did so for the balance of the season. But it was Lambeau, who in addition to providing input to the design of plays, called all of the plays during the game. He led his East High School team to an undefeated season his senior year, including a satisfying 7 to 6 win over rival West High School on a cold, snowy Thanksgiving Day before a large crowd of locals.

During the season, Lambeau scored most of the team's touchdowns, including long touchdown runs of 40, 55 and 75 yards. He also did most of the team's passing, punting and kicking. But Lambeau's talents didn't end there. He was also the captain of the track team in 1916 where he performed the shot, the hammer, the discus and the broad jump. Putting his strength and agility on display, Curly won the first individual honors at the Northeast Wisconsin Interscholastic meet in Appleton that year. He was undeniably the best and most versatile athlete to graduate from either Green Bay high school up to that time, with a reputation that had spread throughout Wisconsin. The praises and accolades flowed in from all directions. From his fellow students to the townsfolk he'd run into on the streets and in the shops of Green Bay, Lambeau was a legend in the making. His name constantly found its way into the sports section of the local paper, the *Press-Gazette*. Curly Lambeau had definitely emerged as the darling of Green Bay.

Shortly before his graduation from East High School along with 64 other seniors, the United States officially entered World War I. The government, under President Woodrow Wilson, had tried keeping the country neutral while maintaining freedom of trade on the high seas after the war began in August 1914. Unfortunately, the United States could not stay out of the conflict forever. Germany had declared all waters around the British Isles a war zone. On May 7, 1915, a German submarine sank the British passenger line *Lusitania* off the coast of Ireland, and 128 of the 1,198 persons killed were Americans. Despite a groundswell of anger in the United States, President Wilson insisted the United States would remain neutral. Many United States merchant ships were sunk in the following months, however, and the United States officially entered the war on April 6, 1917.

Initially after graduation from high school, Curly went to work for his father in the construction business for the summer. Marcel was busy building up his reputation and had also become the city's building inspector. That fall, Lambeau enrolled at the University of Wisconsin-Madison, but dropped out less than a month later because the freshman football program was canceled and he wasn't allowed to play with the varsity. Instead, he returned to Green Bay, played for the local team in the city league and went back to work for his father. A close friend of Lambeau since they were kids, diminutive Nate Abrams at 5 feet, 4 inches, organized the city football team and they were teammates that year. They only played a few games that fall, but their friendship would last a lifetime. Abrams, it turned out, would play an unusually helpful role for Lambeau and the Packers in the years ahead. Nate did not attend high school, as family financial needs required him at age 14 to work with his father in the cattle buying business.

Lambeau continued to work construction jobs for his father's company throughout the fall and winter of 1917 and into the summer of 1918. In the process, he built up his strength and muscle tone considerably. During the summer of that year, some of the citizens of Green Bay were encouraging Curly to attend Notre Dame in South Bend, Indiana that fall. One in particular was Dr. Henry Atkinson, a local physician who would turn up again and play a key role in Lambeau's life. Notre Dame was not yet the nationally recognized football powerhouse it would become in the short years ahead. "At the start of the twentieth century, Catholic colleges — the first in the United States was Georgetown, founded in 1789 — were few and small, rigid and spartan in discipline, and generally not up to the academic standards of most other non-Catholic schools. Isolated for the most part from the American mainstream, many Catholic institutions suffered from gnawing inferiority complexes and a dearth of first-rate students. Notre Dame was no exception to this stereotype, for in the last years of the nineteenth century no young man or boy would suffer a turndown at Notre Dame as long as he could find enough money to pay for his tuition and upkeep."[2]

Following the advice of others and using the money he earned working the past year, Lambeau enrolled at Notre Dame the fall of 1918. He was under no illusions, however, that he was there for the academics — football was his love and the main reason he decided on Notre Dame. While not recognized as a national college football power yet, the school had begun to build a winning reputation. A 147-36-14 record through 1917 gave the Irish a winning mark of 78 percent. When Lambeau showed up on campus that fall, it would be the legendary Knute Rockne's first year as head coach at Notre Dame. "In early March 1918, Knute Kenneth Rockne signed a one-year contract to become Notre Dame's football coach and athletic director at a salary of $5,000 a year. He was exactly thirty years old."[3]

Rockne would spend the next 13 years (1918-1930) as head coach at Notre Dame and build an unmatched college .897 winning percentage, with a 105-12-5 record. No coach past or present has been able to match that record in major competition. Rockne had five undefeated seasons, three national championships and six of his teams lost only one game. Much of his style of coaching (intense, sure-minded and master of his domain), his football formations and emphasis on the forward pass as an offensive strategy, would rub off and influence young Lambeau in later years when he would coach his own team. Even after he left Notre Dame his freshman year, Rockne continued to stay in touch with Lambeau and offered encouragement to the young Packer coach. He saw him win two NFL championships (1929 and 1930) before his untimely death in a plane crash in April 1931. Lambeau would also adopt Rockne's approach to selling the game. "Knute Rockne', said a Notre Dame alumnus, 'sold football to the men on the trolley, the elevator, the subway…the baker, the butcher, the pipe fitter who never went to college. He made it an American mania. He took it out of the thousand-dollar class and made it a million-dollar business.'"[4] Some of Rockne's novel motivational techniques may have rubbed off on Lambeau as well.

"A master of psychology, Rockne once wrote: 'A team in an ordinary frame of mind will do only ordinary things. In the proper emotional stage, a team will do extraordinary things. To reach this stage, a team must have a motive that has an extraordinary appeal to them.' The guileful Rockne was never at a loss when it came to motivation — his little boy, he once told the team, begged for a win before he died of pneumonia. In fact, the child was perfectly well. Rockne himself, when felled by phlebitis, was carried into the locker room to plead for a win and then, he pronounced, 'Let the blood clot move where it may.' The most legendary moment of all came when he exhorted his boys to 'win this one for the old Gipper.' Rockne used this in 1928, his poorest season, when Notre Dame was threatened by Army, the nation's number one team. At half time Rockne related the last words of George Gipp, the dazzling halfback who had died of a streptococcus infection eight years earlier. 'Some day, Rock, when the team's up against it; when things are wrong and the breaks are beating the boys — tell them to go in there with all they've got and win just one for the Gipper.' Army was defeated, 12 to 6."[5] It's not known that Lambeau ever used a death wish to motivate his Packers, but players from Packer teams during the 1920s, 30s and 40s say he gave inspirational talks at just the time they needed them.

Rockne got Notre Dame's head coaching job when the previous head coach, Jesse C. Harper, was forced to take over the family ranch. Rockne had been his assistant and had played for him for four years. "The Fighting Irish of 1918 had almost nothing to fight with or against. The war had taken scores of the best athletes and would not end until November of that year, and the schedule was curtailed to six games. But there were some impressive players on hand that would make a name for themselves in football: George Gipp, freshman guard Heartley 'Hunk' Anderson (Grantland Rice later called him 'the toughest man, pound for pound, I have ever known'), Clipper Smith, Eddie Anderson, Lambeau and Norm Barry."[6]

Notre Dame's first game that year against Case Tech, opened away from home for the first time, saw Lambeau, one of the heaviest men on the squad at 185 pounds, score the first touchdown of the Rockne era in a 26 to 6 win. Lambeau thought he would be playing halfback for Rockne. In fact, he had practiced that position in the weeks before their first game against Case because George Gipp was recovering from an injured ankle. There's a story related by Arch Ward of the *Chicago Tribune* that "on the train going to Cleveland for their opening game against Case, Curly was seated with a number of other freshmen when one of the team managers said, 'Hey, Rock wants to see you in his compartment.' So Lambeau walked into the compartment with trepidation, wondering what was going on, but Rockne put him at ease and told him to sit down. Rockne said, 'Son, you are going to be right halfback, but don't be surprised if you wind up as fullback sometime tomorrow in the game. Just something we might want to try out, you know if I have to call on you I know you can do that, that's all.'"[7] Lambeau did start the game against Case at halfback, but moved to fullback when Gipp came into the game in the first quarter.

The Irish finished the 1918 shortened season with a 3-1-2 record. One tie game was against a very good Great Lakes Naval team. One of the stars who played against Lambeau in that game was an end by the name of George Stanley Halas. It was the beginning of a competitive relationship between Halas and Lambeau that would last for more than 30 years. The Fighting Irish player roster listed Lambeau as a *"flamboyant one-year player for Rockne in shortened season. Excellent blocker and good short-yardage runner. In 1918, started at FB. Scored first TD of season in win over Case. Scored two TDs in slaughter of Wabash. Rushed for effective short yards in win over Purdue and in tie with Nebraska.*[8]

During that first semester on the Notre Dame campus, Lambeau lived at Sorin Hall and wrote letters regularly to his East High School sweetheart, Marguerite Van Kessel. A year younger than Curly, but in the same class in school, Marguerite was a rather thin, reserved young lady who was an excellent student and accomplished piano player. In one of his letters to Marguerite, he wrote he would try to carve out a half-hour every day to write her a letter. He signed it, *"Love, love, love, with love, Earl."* Another letter showed his concern of Marguerite's weight and had written he was worried about her being "pretty light." He wanted her to gain some weight, as he was afraid she would get sick. Concerned about her health, he wrote (his handwriting was very clear, almost feminine) hoping that "she got well" so they could go to midnight Mass together when he came home for Christmas.

He signed one of his letters, "Nice fat kiss" and drew a circle around it. In another, he wrote to Marguerite apologizing for his behavior on a visit home, *"Dearest little Marguerite, I want to tell you how sorry I am because of the way I treated you the last few days I was home. I've had plenty of time to think things over and have come to the conclusion that I was in the wrong and did not treat you the way I should. Nevertheless I hope you will forgive me.*[9]

Marguerite was working for Stiller Photo Supply at the time (they became well known for the early Packer pictures of that era) and many of Curly's letters were addressed to the Stiller Photo address. In one of his earliest letters that he wrote in September, Curly penned he was sitting at his desk at 7:00 in the evening in the dorm room, *"Dear Marguerite, words cannot explain how bad I want to be with you tonight. I never thought I would miss you so. What makes it worse is the scenery; there is a lake about 20 yards from my west window. It is so wonderful it makes me so lonesome. I went to High Mass this morning and felt so inspired."*[10]

Curly's letters seemed to indicate he was enamored with the Catholic church on campus, but his writing also suggested he did not attend Mass on a regular basis in Green Bay before coming to Notre Dame. He went to great detail to write Marguerite that as a member of the varsity he received special privileges not usually accorded to freshmen. For instance, he wrote that varsity players ate at separate tables in the dining room. He mentioned how impressed he was with the way Notre Dame "handled the athletes." He wrote how proud he was to wear the varsity blue and gold sweater around campus. He told her how much effort went into their football practices and that he was "hard as a brick." In reading his letters, however, one gets the impression he was somewhat lonely and missed the adulation he received in Green Bay. He often begged Marguerite to continue writing him on a daily basis. It seems she did write to him frequently and was looking forward to seeing him during the Christmas break.

Lambeau did get home during Notre Dame's Christmas break, but came down with a sore throat that turned out to be a serious case of infected tonsils. They became so inflamed the family doctor told him the infection would have to clear up somewhat before he could operate to remove them. It was nearly six weeks before the doctor could operate. By the time he was feeling better, Lambeau thought he had lost too much time in his studies to return to Notre Dame. In spite of the urging by Marguerite and Curly's parents to go back to school, he decided he would stay in Green Bay the winter of 1919.

In the meantime, a job opportunity came along that Lambeau could not turn down. Destiny had intervened. This job with this particular company would leave an everlasting imprint on the Green Bay Packers. As Arch Ward told the story, it started when Lambeau had a chance meeting with a management executive from a local firm. The Rival Dog Food Company of Chicago had recently bought the Indian Packing Company and moved it from Providence, Rhode Island to Green Bay. A man by the name of Frank Peck was part of their management team. Lambeau's boyhood buddy, Nate Abrams, now a cattle dealer who sold livestock to Indian Packing, introduced him to Peck. According to Ward, Lambeau and Peck ran into each other on the street in Green Bay one day in the winter of 1919. Since Peck had often heard and read about him in the *Press-Gazette*, their short meeting spawned a lunch invitation. During lunch, Peck supposedly offered Lambeau a position as traffic manager with the company at the unheard salary of $250 a month, twice the average for the time. Lambeau would recall later, "The Indian Packing Company offered me a job at $250 a month and I thought that was all the money in the world."

Spring blossomed into summer with Lambeau working at the Indian Packing Company in charge of their receiving department. Ruth Van Kessel, Marguerite's older sister, also worked for the same company. Since the Van Kessel's were neighbors, Curly walked a few blocks to their house to ride to work with Ruth in the morning. While conducting research for his four-volume *History of the Packers*, Larry Names recalls Marguerite telling him that Curly would often come over early in the morning and throw pebbles up at her second story bedroom window. She would open the window and talk to him until it was time for him to go to work.

Summer dates quickly turned to marriage plans by fall.

Destiny was about to have her way once more with Curly, this time through a meeting with a cantankerous, cigar-chomping sports zealot by the name of George Whitney Calhoun.

Late that summer Calhoun, then sports editor of the Green Bay *Press-Gazette,* and Lambeau had a discussion about forming a city football team. The story of their 'historic' meeting has been repeated thousands of times as it in some way pinpoints the unofficial birth (or at least the idea) of the Packers. Some of the anecdotes relate to their discussion while standing on a Green Bay street corner, while other accounts say the two got into the subject of putting together a local team over a beer in a local tavern. Lambeau would be quoted as saying, "I met Calhoun on the street one day in August and, after talking it over, we decided to organize a football team and ask the packing company to sponsor it." In either case, it wasn't that novel of an idea because Green Bay had its own city football team going back to 1896. They played at least one game each year, except 1916, through the 1918 season. In fact, Lambeau had played on the 1917 team with his friend and the coach, Nate Abrams. Nevertheless, Curly was itching to get back on a football field. He agreed with Calhoun, who had been writing about Lambeau's high school football exploits for years that they should try to get a team together for the 1919 season. As they talked, a simple yet effective plan emerged. Lambeau would get the players. Calhoun would ensure the team got proper coverage in the sports pages of the *Press-Gazette.*

George Calhoun, eight years older than Lambeau and close to 30 years old at the time, had already begun to build a local reputation for himself as a rather unique character. Once married and now divorced, the heavy, pear-shaped Calhoun often came across as being somewhat gruff and crude. Lacing his conversations with frequent profanity, Calhoun usually had a John Riskin cigar in his mouth (though seldom lit). He often ate his favorite, strong-smelling Limburger cheese sandwiches at his desk at the *Press-Gazette.* He took his dog, Patsy Tootsie, a little Boston terrier, with him wherever he went — even at his feet at work and at the bar of his favorite pub. More than once, he got into a shoving match with someone at the bar when they made a wisecrack about his dog sitting there next to him. Calhoun spent a fair amount of time in the local pubs, particularly Shamus O'Brien's bar on Main Street. He could put away his favorite drink, beer, in legendary proportions and speed.

John Torinus, who worked for a time at the *Press-Gazette's* sports desk, told how he learned Calhoun's method of drinking large amounts of beer in a short period of time. "He was the all-time champion," Torinus would say. "He taught me early on how to drink a bottle of beer without swallowing. You merely tip your head back and open your throat and let the beer guzzle down."[11] Calhoun's sports writing style was also rather unique. Perhaps not too different from the journalistic style at the time, his writing still appeared to be amateurish, more suited for a high school or college newspaper. More often than not, it lacked objectivity, smacking of opinion rather than fact and laced with trite phrases. A few years after the Packers joined the NFL, he would send out his "press releases" on the Packers to newspapers around the country. He always traveled with the Packers to away games and was somewhat of a joke to the more sophisticated sportswriters from the larger newspapers in Chicago and New York. By 1928, Calhoun was replaced as the *Press-Gazette* sports editor and assigned to a less demanding job — sort through the AP and UPI wire service releases and forward them to other editors.

Going by the nickname of "Cal" (he often simply used "Cal" as a byline on his articles in the *Press-Gazette*), Calhoun, a Green Bay native of wealthy parents, had been somewhat of an athlete himself. He played football, hockey and lacrosse while attending the University of Buffalo. But a sports career was not in the offing, cut short by a severe case of juvenile arthritis. In his later years, his hands became terribly gnarled from the arthritis. Though he could no longer play the game he so loved, Cal knew he could write about it. Some would say that caused Lambeau to become Calhoun's alter ego. Through Lambeau, Calhoun could actually build himself and the Packers to "larger than life" status. It was history in the making, and Calhoun was part of it all. It would become a rare combination: Lambeau, a gifted athlete, with his own influential publicist, the eccentric Calhoun.

Soon after their conversation about starting up a city football team, Calhoun ran an ad in the sports section of the *Press-Gazette* stating anyone interested in playing on a city team should meet in the newspaper office on the evening of August 11. In the meantime, Lambeau was busy contacting young men he knew from high school or college, encouraging them to meet that evening. The August 11 date has often been identified by journalists through the years as the official start of the Packers. For instance, Chuck Johnson, a sportswriter for the *Milwaukee Journal* in the 1960s, stated in his 1961 book on the history of the Packers, "On the night of August 11, 1919, a football team was formed." However, Larry Names, in his published history of the Packers, felt the August 11 meeting was basically for Curly and Calhoun to see how many would show up to join a team and that another meeting three days later at the *Press-Gazette* was the more appropriate date of forming the Packers.

In either case, sometime between the two meetings, Lambeau went to his boss, Frank Peck of Indian Packing, and asked if the company would sponsor a city team and help buy football uniforms, equipment and balls. Curly hair, dimples and plenty of charm. Lambeau had it all going. He exuded confidence in how well the team would do and how that would translate into favorable publicity for the company. Peck responded with $500 and the use of a vacant field the company owned next to the plant where Lambeau's team could hold practice. At the second meeting of the interested players, Lambeau was elected captain of the new team, primarily with the urging and backing of his old friend, Nate Abrams, who coached the city team in previous years.

The next day the *Press-Gazette* reported on the meeting in an article with the headline: **"Indian Packing Corporation Squad Meets; First Game Sunday, September 14."** The article noted that Lambeau was elected captain of the 25-man team and that George Calhoun would manage the team (as he had in previous years when Green Bay had a city team). Further into the article the team was referred to as the "Packers." This was the first time the "Packer" nickname appeared in print. Calhoun would call this team by several different names in his newspaper articles over the next few years before "Packers" stuck for good. "Most of the time he referred to them as 'Big Bay Blues,' in the *Press-Gazette* because of the blue jerseys the team first wore. However, the team's association with the Indian Packing Company made it natural to call them the 'Packers.' Actually, Lambeau didn't like 'Big Bay Blues' and even tried to get rid of the 'Packers' nickname."[12]

Busy as he was, assembling his city team, Lambeau was not one to walk away from opportunity. When Green Bay East High School lost their coach, Joe Hoeffel, who was drafted into the Army, Lambeau was asked to replace him. He did so with pride. Lambeau would look back on the three years he coached East High

School (1919-1921) at the same time he was leading the Packers: "We beat West 43 to 6 in 1920 with passing — Jim Crowley (later to become one of Notre Dame's legendary Four Horsemen) was a great passer. I remember the West fans didn't like it. They said, 'Run the ball, that's not football.'" To help him with the Packers, Lambeau asked Bill Ryan, a teacher at West High School to be the team's sideline coach and drill instructor at practices.

August 16, 1919. Culminating a year of courtship, on the first Saturday following the team organization meeting, Curly and Marguerite were married at St. Francis Cathedral. An unconventional, whirlwind honeymoon followed as the new couple traveled around the state. Marguerite recalled that Curly spent most of his time setting up game dates with teams from Wisconsin and Michigan for the upcoming season. But she was quick to add that she didn't mind — she was too much in love with him to be upset. Marguerite would be quoted numerous times through the succeeding years that she and Curly had a happy marriage, and she loved him until the day she died in 2001 at the age of 102. She would tell journalists she never fell out of love with him. Although not a particularly attractive girl (she was a mousy brunette and very thin, which made her facial features look peaked and gave her a rather pronounced nose), it was her character and temperament Lambeau found so attractive. She was even-tempered, optimistic to a fault, warm hearted, caring and deeply in love with the man — not the star athlete. He felt her genuine love, as he had never known from anyone. She was also extremely firm in her Catholic faith.

While traveling around on their honeymoon, Curly scheduled games with teams from Marinette, Menominee, New London, Ishpeming and Stambaugh in the Upper Peninsula of Michigan. He also got Racine and Sheboygan to agree to a game. Altogether, he secured eleven playing dates. Early on, Marguerite got used to not seeing much of Curly during the football season. In that first year, more often than not, right after work Lambeau would pick up a sandwich on the fly, skip supper and meet his team on the field for practice until dark. They would practice three days a week on the vacant field next to the Indian Packing Company.

The team's first season was a huge success. Calhoun had a field day sitting at his old typewriter, banging out glowing reports for the sports pages of the *Press-Gazette*. Lambeau was taking on star status once again. They won their first ten games by the unbelievable scores of 53-0, 61-0, 54-0, 87-0, 76-6, 33-0, 85-0, 53-0, 46-

0 and 17-0. Beloit was only the second team to score on them and handed them their only defeat. Even that loss was somewhat questionable. The battle, waged in Beloit, was somberly recounted by Calhoun in the *Press-Gazette* the following day. Trailing 6 to 0 with time running out, the Packers reached Beloit's three-yard line when Lambeau slanted off-tackle into the end zone. Beloit's hometown referee, Baldy Zabel, ruled the Packers were offside and penalized the team, moving them back to the eight-yard line. On the next play, Lambeau circled the left end and crossed the goal line. Again, an offside penalty was called and the Packers were pushed back to the 13. A very irate Lambeau called a timeout and told his teammates, "On the next play, stand still until after the ball is centered. Don't even charge." The Packers followed his instructions and without a single blocker, Lambeau raced around the right end into the end zone. Predictably, Zabel blew his whistle again and yelled, "No touchdown." "Why not?" asked Lambeau. "You were in motion," the referee said, penalizing the Packers back to the 18-yard line.

But by any measure, that inaugural season was a success. In full command of the proceedings, Lambeau did most of the running and throwing as well as designing the plays and implementing the on-field strategy. The team outscored their opponents over the entire season by a staggering 565 points to 12. Lambeau also played on defense as every player did in those days. There was no such thing as an offensive and defensive team. Just football. Hard-nosed, in the mud, in-your-face football for the entire game.

In his book on the Packers, Arch Ward pointed to the October game that year at Ishpeming, Michigan as one of the ten most important battles in Lambeau's reign. "For five years, no team had been able to beat the Michiganders on their home grounds, and they were acknowledged champions of the Wolverine state. They were big and tough."[13] After just three running plays, the Packers found out how big and tough. On the first play, a Packer back went out with broken ribs. On the next run, their tackle left the game with a cracked collarbone. On the following running play another tackle broke his ankle. For fear of running out of players since Lambeau only had 17 remaining of the 20 he brought, he switched from running the ball and called only pass plays or quick punts from that point in the game. With Lambeau doing most of the passing, the result of the new strategy against the enormous line was a 33 to 0 win for the Packers. The Stubben Ishpeming team continued to play with a seven-man line and dared the Packers to run. From that point on, passing became a Packer trademark. Clearly, it separated them from their run-oriented and plodding, grind-it-out opponents.

The team played their home games at Hagemeister Park, a glorified vacant lot near East High School that they marked off with chalk dust or lime for the game. Some of the fans stood behind ropes that were stretched around the field, while others would drive their Model T Fords to about ten yards behind the ropes and sit on the hoods or fenders. Most spectators to the first games at Hagemeister either walked eight to ten blocks or arrived on the Walnut Street trolley. Most fans preferred to get out and follow the play up and down the field. Because they moved with the play on the field, they always had a "50-yard line" location. Teams did not huddle then, or the fans might have been part of that as well. When the first half ended, the teams grabbed blankets and went to opposite end zones where they relaxed and discussed tactics for the second half. The crowd would form a ring around the players, a practice encouraged because it provided a windbreak. Since there were no dressing rooms or restrooms, more often than not Lambeau and the other players suited up at home. No tickets. No admission fee. Instead, Calhoun was in charge of passing a "hat" around for fan donations. On a good day, he'd walk among those watching the game and collect $200. At the end of the season, the players divided up the gate profits. That was all the money they took in minus all expenses (including medical bills). Each player got a grand total of $16.75. This amounted to about three days pay from a regular job.

Before the team broke up for the season, most of the players told Curly they would be back the next year. Since many of them came from around Green Bay or nearby towns, the team was building on the old neighborhood. Young men displaying hometown pride and a genuine desire to continue playing the game they had enjoyed so much in high school or college. Following Lambeau's spirited and confident leadership to unprecedented town club success, they were also building another kind of team pride.

During the off-season, Lambeau continued to work at the packing company, but under new bosses. The Indian Packing Corporation sold out to the Acme Packing Company. The 1921 Packer team proudly wore blue jerseys with white lettering across the chest that read "Acme Packers." A snapshot for the ages, this picture is most associated with the team when they became a member of the organized professional football league that season. But the 1920 team would wear the same blue and gold sweaters the Indian Packing team had given them. Sometime in early spring of that year, Marguerite announced she was pregnant and the baby would be due sometime in December. Secretly, Curly was hoping for a boy to follow in his footsteps.

As they got ready for the 1920 season, Lambeau, having added some new plays to his playbook, lined up a stronger and more difficult eleven game schedule with teams from Chicago, Kaukauna, Stambaugh, Marinette, DePere, Beloit, Milwaukee and Menominee. Their home field at Hagemeister Park now had wooden bleachers on one side of the field that could seat "a couple of hundred." Marcel Lambeau, with the help of American Legion volunteers, erected the wooden stands. The Packers opened a ticket office in the Legion building, which was just one block down the street from the *Press-Gazette.* A Legionnaire by the name of Spike Spachman became their ticket director. Jack Neville, another Legionnaire employed at the Kellogg-Citizens Bank, talked some of his fellow tellers into manning the ticket booths at the games on Sunday and charged an admission for the bleacher seats. The conquering heroes of the year before were now a much easier sell. Their first game drew the first recorded attendance at Green Bay of 1,200 fans to witness a 3-3 tie with the out-of-state Chicago Boosters in late September.

Community pride in their Packers was growing and escalated further during the 1920 season. Young Lambeau, now 22 years old, was an excellent spokesman for the team. Business meetings. Community gatherings. He came whether they invited him or he invited himself. Lambeau was passionate about the team and it rubbed off on those listening to him extoll the advantages the team would bring to Green Bay. He asked for their financial support and promised to put a winning team on the field in which Green Bay could take great pride. He was a natural born salesman. Over the next several years as the Packers were struggling financially, Lambeau must have reminded some of Professor Howard Hill, played by actor Robert Preston in the musical production, *Music Man,* as he sold the citizens of Green Bay and surrounding communities on the Packers.

With basically the same players as the previous year, the record of the 1920 team (9-1-1) was almost as good as the 1919 club against much stiffer competition. Again, their only loss was to

Beloit, 14 to 3. Opponents were in for a season of long afternoons as they were outscored by the wide margin of 227 to 24. Only two teams managed to score a touchdown. One of the new players to join the Packers in 1920 was Howard "Cub" Buck, a huge man for those times at 6 feet, 3 inches, and 250 pounds. He had played college ball at the University of Wisconsin and the previous season with a powerful Canton, Ohio team. He became the first player Lambeau would pay to play. Buck cost the team $75 a game, but he earned every penny since he was such a dominating factor on both offense and defense. Lambeau sought out Buck and sold him on becoming a Packer. It was a trait that Lambeau would hone to a fine art in drawing other outstanding athletes to play for the Packers in the years ahead.

At the end of the 1920 season, Calhoun found out about a new professional football league. The year before, a fellow named Ralph Hay who was the manager of the Canton Bulldogs, one of the oldest professional teams around, formed a professional football league. It was called the American Professional Football Association. It didn't work out, though, because Hay couldn't get any of the teams to follow the rules that he had set up. In August of 1920, he managed to get eleven professional football clubs together in Akron, Ohio. One of the men at that meeting was George Halas, representing the Decatur Staleys. Because Hay's office was too small, 14 men met in Hay's Hupmobile showroom on a hot August night while Halas and others sat on running boards, according to Halas' autobiography. In about two hours, the American Professional Football Association was created. Each of them had to come up with $100, and football's legendary Jim Thorpe was elected president of the group. This attempt to form a professional football league folded for a variety of reasons at the end of the 1920 season. So with Hay's direction, they met again in April of 1921 in Akron to reorganize and start all over again.

Calhoun found out about the new APFA meeting after the April session, but learned there was going to be another league meeting in Akron in August of 1921. Since he wanted to see Green Bay compete at a higher level, he urged Lambeau to attend and try to get a membership for their team in the league. Since he was also eager to test his Packers against stronger teams, Curly went to John Clair, his boss and one of the owners of the Acme Packing Company, to see if a company representative would go to the meeting and obtain a franchise in the company name for their team. Once again,

Lambeau's powers of persuasion came to bear. John Clair agreed to send his brother, Emmett, to the league meeting in Ohio in August.

The Packers were about to become a team in a legitimate professional football league. The Lambeau name was destined to become permanently etched in the annals of the game.

3

Trials of the Twenties

T he Roaring Twenties were known as the Golden Age of Sports. Larger than life stars and events awaited America's love of competition. Almost overnight, with the end of World War I, it seemed the country shifted from a straight-laced, conservative, mostly rural society to an urbanized one with a wide variety of excesses. Prohibition, notorious gangsters with star status, rampant political fraud, flappers, flagpole sitters, and a new music called jazz gained popularity.

As professional football was becoming organized as a league of its own, the Twenties were a prosperous, optimistic decade. New developments in the mass media — movie newsreels, photojournalism and radio — had created an appetite for instant celebrities. Movie stars like Rudolph Valentino, Gloria Swanson, Douglas Fairbanks, Tom Mix, Clara Bow and a wide-eyed, little Jackie Coogan. Heroes like Charles Lindbergh and his historic transatlantic flight in 1927 became objects of an adoring American public.

Various social trends were at work during the 1920s. Historians have characterized the decade as a time of frivolity, abundance and happy-go-lucky attitudes. Several years had passed since the end of World War I. People felt free-spirited and wanted to have fun. As a result, fashions became less formal. The feminine liberation was sprung on the nation as women dropped their corsets and took on a more masculine look, including flattened breasts and hips and bobbed hair covered with helmet-looking hats. For the first time in centuries, women's legs were seen.

With American appetites running wild, the country also developed a new and overwhelming passion for sports. New and larger stadiums replaced decrepit old wooden parks to house the increasing and adoring crowds. "A new opulence was being demanded to go with the "Golden Age of Sports." It was the emerging era of the "fan," a fitting short term for "fanatic," and from this new reaching out by the common people came the sports hero."[14]

The new breed of sports hero was splashed both in pictures and copy all over the daily newspapers in cities and towns around the nation. The fun-loving Babe Ruth hitting towering home runs at an unprecedented pace. Ruggedly handsome and muscular Jack Demspey, the most spectacular heavyweight since John L. Sullivan, fighting before huge crowds of 80,000 and unheard of million-dollar gates. "Bobby Jones, exquisite and elegant, taming golf courses as they'd never been mastered before, and making converts of ordinary people to a game that recently had been for the wealthy and elite. Big Bill Tilden, supremely arrogant, and Poker Face Helen Wills were making converts for tennis."[15]

In addition, baseball was the major professional team sport and extremely popular. The American and National leagues had been going strong since 1901 with the first World Series played in 1903. Large baseball stadiums were built around the turn of the century. Shibe Park in Philadelphia, the Polo Grounds and Yankee Stadium in New York, Comiskey Park and Cubs Park (later named Wrigley Field) in Chicago, Forbes Field in Pittsburgh, Ebbets Field in Brooklyn, and Griffith Stadium in Washington, D.C. were all built for baseball in the early 1900s.

Then there was the ugly stepsister — professional football. Hardly a popular sport, it lurked in the shadows of college football where fan excitement was huge. Large crowds and an enormous amount of newspaper sports pages and movie newsreels were devoted to the college game. Radio coverage would bring even more popularity. But not for pro football. The sport fought against critical abuse ever since it began in the early 1900s. Although there was a hard core of spirited fans and supporters in communities with clubs like Green Bay, the sport definitely was not regarded as fashionable. You couldn't even find pro football in the newspapers or radio stations of the larger cities in the 1920s. "The press looked at the game like wrestling," said New York Giants owner Wellington

Mara, whose family purchased the franchise for $500 in 1925. "Let's just say, from the stories passed down to me, we were looked at askance in the press.

Major league baseball and college football dominated. The organization that was the NCAA in those days wanted nothing to do with the pros. Several prominent college coaches, including Amos Alonzo Stagg and Fielding Yost, openly opposed playing football for money. They were joined by educators, bands of alumni, influential newspapermen and parents. Playing football for fun was quite acceptable; to take pay for it was contemptible, corruption of an adored sport. In fact, the first known headline in a newspaper ever to mention pro football said blithely, "Stagg Finds Method to End Menace of Pro Football."

Pro football was widely pictured as an unhealthy atmosphere, full of tramp athletes, gambling and fixed games. The attacks continued through the formative years and beyond. The criticism kept the crowds thin and many of the college players were reluctant to step into the pros. Professionalism in sports means play for pay, but it isn't likely money was the motivating force behind the decision of those early players who did join professional football. More often, it was simply that they couldn't get their fill of football in college or high school."[16]

It was with this backdrop that Emmett Clair, an executive with Acme Packing, boarded the train at the station in Green Bay. It was a hot Wednesday afternoon on August 24, 1920, and he was headed for a weekend meeting at the Hotel LaSalle in Chicago with the sole purpose of gaining a franchise in the recently reorganized American Professional Football Association (APFA).

"Prior to his departure, Chris O'Brien of the Chicago Cardinals and Ralph Hay of the Canton Bulldogs had agreed to sponsor the Green Bay delegate at the conference. They were also backing men from Minneapolis and Evansville, Indiana. The APFA already had 15 teams, and there was no guarantee that any of the newcomers would be accepted, especially Green Bay because it was the smallest town with the smallest surrounding population from which to draw fans. This was the argument against the Packers, but O'Brien and Hay pointed out the simple fact that of the 15 teams already in the league, nine of them were located east of the Ohio-Indiana line and six of those were in Ohio. Adding Evansville and Minneapolis would make the composition nine east and eight west, which was still inequitable, and adding Green Bay would balance it at nine and nine."[17]

After several hours of discussion, Minneapolis and Green Bay were granted franchises. "On Saturday evening, August 27, 1921, John and Emmett Clair of the Acme Packing Company were granted a franchise in the APFA for the sum of $50. Emmett Clair paid the fee and immediately called his brother in Green Bay with the news. John drove over to Lambeau's house to give him the report. They now had a team in the APFA. The next day Emmett was on his way home and Calhoun had a lead story for the *Press-Gazette*.[18] Thus, it was that Green Bay would become the site of one of the most incredible stories in professional sports history.

While most of the nation was liberating itself, the Roaring Twenties didn't roar too loudly in conservative Green Bay. Generally cautious, city businessmen never went for heavy expansion or new ideas, being satisfied with steady rather than spectacular progress. By the early 1920s Green Bay, with a population of just over 30,000, had become the world's leading producer of toilet tissue, milk and cheese. While the rest of the nation was "dry," "northeastern Wisconsin never took kindly to the advent of the Prohibition in 1920; in fact, Green Bay and the surrounding towns virtually seceded from the Union as far as enforcement went. Saloons simply converted to "soft drink parlors" and went right on dispensing "spiked" beer and bootleg liquor to known customers. Speakeasies and cabarets flourished all over the county, despite periodic raids by federal and state "dry" agents. The latter got no cooperation from local authorities; impending raids were usually tipped off in plenty of time for speakeasy operators to close down before raiders arrived. A surprise swoop in 1928 that netted nearly 100 violators so enraged the Green Bay city council that it passed a resolution condemning such "unwarranted" interference with local business. The resolution was soon rescinded, but not before the city received national notoriety."[19]

Like the rest of the nation, the citizens of Green Bay were in love with the automobile, and they were beginning to roll off the assembly line at a record pace. "By 1920 there probably weren't more than 2,000 motor vehicles in Brown County, but five years later every "average" family had one. By the end of the decade, 26,000 cars a year were coming into the port of Green Bay to be driven on rough dirt and gravel roads in the area. The development of the closed car was a significant factor in the growth of the motor sales industry in northern Wisconsin. Prior to 1922, almost all models were open cars that had to be stored on blocks during the long, cruel winters of Green Bay, but the "hard top" could be driven comfortably in any season. A bewildering array of models competed for attention.

"The standard Ford, Cadillac, Chevrolet, Buick, Dodge and Plymouth were in the competition, as well as the more recently remembered Packard, Studebaker and Nash. Now long forgotten were such names as Maxwell, Overland, Stutz, Marmon, Franklin, Mercer, Cord, Reo, Dort, Durant, Pierce-Arrow, Moon and Kissell, to name a few. Prices ranged from $680 for a Chevy coupe and $880 for a Maxwell sedan to $4,600 for the prestigious Caddy and Packard. Most were in the $1,100 to $1,500 bracket, seemingly give-aways by today's prices, but far from cheap in an era when $35 a week was a good wage."[20]

Lambeau was not yet among those with an automobile in 1920, but what he and Marguerite did have later that year was a son, Donald, born on a cold and snowy December morning at Green Bay's St. Mary's Hospital. He would be their only child and one that Curly would never get particularly close to early in his life. They eventually became totally disconnected by the time Curly was in his 40s and Donald in his 20s.

Still employed at Acme Packing as manager in their shipping department, Lambeau, now armed with a franchise in a legitimate pro football league, began preparation for the 1921 season. However, the APFA would suffer through a rocky first year. In April 1921, there was another meeting, this one at the Cortland Hotel in Canton. The APFA underwent a radical reorganization. Joe F. Carr of Columbus was named president with an annual salary of $1,000. While there would be 21 teams in the league that year, some would not even make it to the end of the season before going broke. In fact, there would be 49 different teams competing in the pro football league at one time or another during the Roaring Twenties. Small and mid-sized towns like Frankford, Akron, Canton, Rock Island, Dayton, Pottsville, Hammond, Columbus, Muncie, Louisville, Racine, Toledo and Duluth made up the league before larger cities such as Chicago, Cleveland, Milwaukee, New York, Minneapolis and Detroit became a part of the league during the 1920s.

Since he was still coaching the East High School football team, Lambeau asked Joe Hoeffel to coach the Packers while he played and held the title of captain of the team. While Lambeau has historically been given credit for coaching and playing for the Packers that year, Cliff Christl, a sports journalist for the *Milwaukee Journal-Sentinel*, found the inaccuracies and reported them in his paper in 2001. Larry Names also made reference to the inaccuracy in his book on the history of the Packers.

"Given the fact that Hoeffel served as coach in 1921, Christl pointed out the inaccuracies that exist in Lambeau's official NFL coaching record and in the tributes extended to him at the Pro Football and Packers' halls of fame. Lambeau is credited with 33 years of service as a head coach in the NFL — 29 with the Packers, two with the Chicago Cardinals and two with the Washington Redskins — tying him with Don Shula for the second-longest tenure in NFL history. George Halas holds the record with 40 years. Lambeau also ranks fourth in career victories. He has been credited with an overall record of 226-132-22, which gave him 33 more victories than Chuck Noll, who is in fifth place. Included in Lambeau's record was a 3-2-1 mark compiled in 1921. Some of the most convincing evidence Christl found was on the masthead of five separate issues of 'The Dope Sheet,' subtitled 'Official Program and Publication, Acme-Packers Football Team.' Editions published on October 9, 16, 23 and 30, and November 6, 1921, all listed Hoeffel as the team's coach and Lambeau as its captain. The *Press-Gazette* first announced that Hoeffel would be joining the Packers on August 11. The story noted that he would 'assist Captain Lambeau in coaching the team.' Almost a month later, but still 15 days before the Packers' first game, a *Press-Gazette* headline read: 'Joe Hoeffel Will Coach Packer Team.'"[21]

In subsequent *Press-Gazette* articles, Christl discovered how authority was divided between the two men. The stories left no doubt that Hoeffel handled the coaching duties, while Lambeau was team captain. Hoeffel had been a football star in his own right. He played on the University of Wisconsin's unbeaten football team of 1912 and was selected Second Team All-American. Green Bay would hold a special banquet to honor the former East High School football star that year. After graduating from Wisconsin, Hoeffel was an assistant coach at the University of Nebraska. In 1916, while working in his family business, he had helped coach the East High School team when Lambeau had been his star player.

While Hoeffel undoubtedly served as the Packer coach the first year they were in the APFA, coaching football was not the same in those days. "The rules dictated that the captain run the team during games by limiting a coach's involvement. The official rule book used in 1921 by what was then the American Professional Football Association read: 'There shall be no coaching…by any other person not participating in the game.' Another section under the same category read: 'No person shall be allowed to walk up and down on either side of the field.' Both rules remained in effect through 1939. In 1940, the latter of the two rules was amended to allow coaches to move along the sideline. It wasn't until 1944 that coaches were permitted to communicate with their players."[22]

How did the Packer history get distorted showing Lambeau as coach that first year? Probably because George Calhoun reported it that way and it carried down through the years. Since pro football kept few records on the game until 1932, Calhoun's word became gospel when it came to the Packers and Lambeau. As sports editor of the *Press-Gazette,* Calhoun often exaggerated or embellished the facts to glamorize the team or Lambeau's accomplishments and involvement. From 1930 through 1946, Calhoun sent out his own publicity to newspapers throughout the Midwest. He would consistently accentuate the positive and eliminate the negative. However, through the following years, neither Calhoun nor Lambeau sought to correct the facts of who coached the Packers in 1921.

Regardless of who coached the team, they were officially the Acme Packers as their new uniform jerseys proudly displayed in huge letters across their chest during the 1921 season. While Lambeau preferred the Notre Dame colors of blue and gold for the Packers, in those days it was difficult to tell one team from another because uniforms were often so similar. Teams too often resembled a tough looking rag-tag group. On many teams, the wool jerseys were faded and did not always have player numbers. The pants were a coarse tan canvas with strange looking high hips and backs for added protection. When it rained, Lambeau's crude, clumsy looking uniform would double in weight. Helmets, which were optional for years, were made of flimsy leather that often could be folded and shoved into their lower back pockets and frequently came apart during a game. Lambeau's players were expected to supply most of their own protective equipment. They had to come up with their own shoes, shoulder pads, elbow pads and other pieces if they wanted the added protection. A few of the hearty "he-men" disregarded the added gear and suffered broken bones as a result.

The Packers would play their home games at Hagemeister Park again this year with 1,000 added bleachers built by Curly's father. Over the next ten years, Marcel Lambeau would continue to add seats for the Packer games. As fast as he could build them, Curly and his team would fill them. A portable canvas fence was also placed around the entire field so everyone had to pay 50 cents to get in to see the game.

Lambeau and his players would dress at home and ride to the park carrying their cleated shoes or trotted over in stocking feet. Later that season, the team would dress in an armory building next to the field. Kids scampered across the field during the play and sometimes fans would dodge under the canvas fence and stand close to the scrimmage line. "The Packers even had their own band, known as the 'Lumberjack Band.' The first Packer band was the result of a casual conversation at George DeLair's restaurant on Washington Street in downtown Green Bay. DeLair and some of his cohorts rounded up a number of musicians to play during the Packer games. Many members of that original group played for the Green Bay City Band, and in 1923 the band actually took over playing for the Packer games in Green Bay and Milwaukee traveling to Milwaukee by truck and sitting on two-by-four seats for the several hour trip each way."[23]

Since there were no locker rooms, between the halves of the game the teams would hold their meetings in the open air at opposite ends of the field with Lambeau and the Packers surrounded by a dozen volunteer coaches, in addition to kibitzers and eavesdroppers. During time-outs, a devoted young lad would rush in and out with a big water bucket and a long-handled dipper.

Scoring was low in the 1920s. The ball was fatter and harder to pass, looking more like a basketball than the football we know today. All passes had to be thrown from at least five yards behind the line of scrimmage. A team that threw an incompletion in the end zone *lost possession of the ball.* Punting was more popular than passing. Few teams passed the fat ball more than a couple of times a game. Brute strength and precise punting determined field position. Lambeau was one of the few to develop the pass as a key part of his offensive strategy. He often told reporters years later that he once passed 45 times and completed 37 in a game in 1920 based on numbers he said were kept by a teammate.

"Forward passing had been permitted for 14 years, and most of the original restrictions had been removed. But the passer still had to throw from at least five yards behind the line of scrimmage, which greatly reduced the possibility of deception. In addition, if a pass fell incomplete in the end zone, it was a touchback and the defenders were given the ball on their 20-yard line."[24] Most teams averaged fewer than six passes a game, while Lambeau would average better than 17 a game through the 1920s (bear in mind, this is based on George Calhoun's Packer statistics kept through the years before the NFL official statistics came into existence in 1933).

Lambeau would call plays on the field with no help from the sidelines. Players from all the teams usually played 60 minutes, both on offense and defense. There were no specialists. If you wanted to play, you went both ways. Penalties were severe, 25 yards for clipping and sometimes longer for more serious infractions. There were no hash marks; when a player was tackled near the sideline or went out of bounds, the next play began at that spot.

Most teams used the single wing formation devised by Glenn S. (Pop) Warner in 1906 while he was coaching the Carlisle Indian School team. Lambeau used a similar formation known as the Notre Dame single wing shift he picked up from coach Knute Rockne when he played the one season with the Irish. Rockne's team lined up in a conventional T and then, on signal, shifted quickly into a trapezoid, with a halfback behind center and the other halfback outside his end. The line was balanced. The rules said that all players had to hold their new position for a full second before the ball was snapped. This formation, with minor modifications, was the Packers' formation for most of the nearly 30 years Lambeau coached the Packers. While successful for over 20 of those years, his hesitancy and unwillingness to change in the 1940s was one of the reasons for the Packers decline that decade.

When Lambeau assembled his 25-member team in early September of 1921, there were twelve players that had not played with the Packers the year before. His ability to replace nearly half of the players from the previous year while upgrading the talent would become another Lambeau trademark in succeeding years. He was never hesitant to drop a player for someone he thought would make his team better. With rare exceptions, Lambeau didn't get sentimental over his players. For instance, by 1925 he had an 18-man squad and only two, the massive lineman Cub Buck and himself, were on the team in 1921.

The 1921 season began with four non-league games that Lambeau had scheduled against club teams. All were lopsided with

Green Bay outscoring them by a 109-0 count. The regular season
against APFA teams proved more difficult for the Packers. They
finished the season with a modest 3-2-1 league record, good for
seventh place in the 21-team league. Victories came harder against
much better teams than the club teams they demolished the previous two years. Still, fan support for the team was growing at a rapid
pace. The first four league games were at home, starting in late
October. Nearly 6,000 turned out to see their new professionals in
action for each of the first two games, a 7 to 6 win over the
Minneapolis Marines and a 13 to 3 loss to the Rock Island
Independents. In the home game against the Minneapolis squad,
which was made up of ex-collegians and former servicemen from
World War I, the Packers trailed 6 to 0 with five minutes left. The
Packers recovered a fumbled punt by the Marines on the
Minneapolis 35 yard line. Lambeau's pass to halfback Buff
Wagner took the ball to the 14 where Lambeau and others in sev-
eral plays ran the ball over to score and tie the game. Of course,
Lambeau fittingly kicked the winning extra point in the Packers
first official APFA game.

When the team played their first road game in late November
against the Chicago Cardinals, Calhoun encouraged his readers to
attend the game at Comiskey Park in Chicago. Budding Packer
fanaticism took over. Approximately 400 Green Bay townsfolk
paid about $10 apiece to take the train for an overnight trip to
Chicago. "It was the first time a Packer team played in Chicago, so
this game was wired back to Green Bay. Western Union had a telegraph wire to Turner Hall, a huge athletic facility where basketball
and indoor baseball were being played in the winter. Hundreds of
true-blue Packer fans turned out to hear the play-by-play descrip-
tion of the game read to them by former player, Jimmy Coffeen."[25]
The game ended in a 3 to 3 tie, but the tradition of Green Bay fans
traveling by train to watch their team play Chicago teams was
begun and would not end for nearly 60 years. In fact, Calhoun and
the fans did it all over again the following Sunday when the Packers
traveled by train to Chicago to Cubs Park (later renamed Wrigley
Field) to meet George Halas' Chicago Staleys, soon to become the
Bears.

The Bears trace their roots to 1920, when they were established
as the Decatur Staleys and became charter members of the APFA.
The team moved to Chicago in 1921 and adopted the nickname
"Bears" the following year. The Chicago Bears and Green Bay

Packers would become without question the two most storied franchises in pro football. George Halas, player, co-owner, coach, promoter and "Papa Bear" of the Chicago Bears was called the nursemaid of professional football through its formative years. They say he kept the game alive, sometimes it seemed, by the sheer force of his will. "People think I invented the game of football," he once told an audience. "And I did!"

After his discharge from the Navy in March 1919, Halas joined the New York Yankees in the spring as a speedy, but light-hitting outfielder. Fortunately for professional football, he hurt his leg and his baseball days were over. He would play with another semi-pro football team that fall before going to work for the Staley Company in December of that year

In 1920, very much like Lambeau, Halas persuaded the A. E. Staley Manufacturing Company of Decatur, Illinois, a maker of corn products, to sponsor a semi-professional football team. Joining the APFA, the Staleys finished the season at 10-1-2. But the Staley Company had fallen on hard financial times. After a year, Mr. Staley suggested that Halas take the team to Chicago where they could get larger crowds. Later, Staley decided he could no longer underwrite a football team, so after receiving $5,000 to retain the Staley name for one more season, Halas moved his club to Chicago. Most of the team moved north with Halas and Sternaman to field the Chicago Staleys. Chicago Cubs owner William Veeck agreed to lease Cubs Park to the Staleys for 15 percent of the gross gate receipts.[26]

This was the franchise that became the Chicago Bears in 1922. Halas rented Wrigley Field and acted himself as right end, captain, coach, press agent, ticket seller, training-grounds keeper and all-around handyman. Halas was 26 years old (three years older than Lambeau) when he and a teammate and friend, Edward C. (Dutch) Sternaman, took ownership of the team for the 1921 season, moving it from Decatur, a small town about 125 miles southwest of Chicago.

"Halas and Sternaman, as well as most of the players on the Chicago Staleys, were living at that time in the Blackwood Hotel. It was an inexpensive, apartment-type hotel that accommodated both transient and permanent residents and had the distinct advantage of being within walking distance of Cubs Park. Its versatility was a virtue too, since Halas and Sternaman did not know at the time whether they would be permanent or transient guests.

Actually, neither of them expected to turn a profit at the start of their venture, and both had other jobs on the side, Halas as a car salesman and Sternaman in a gas station."[27]   Listed at 6 feet tall and 182 pounds, Halas previously played end at the University of Illinois and with the semi-pro Navy team, Great Lakes Training Station. The Great Lakes team hit its peak in the 1919 Rose Bowl with a 17 to 0 triumph over the powerful Mare Island Marines of California. Halas scored a touchdown in the victory.

It was with this background that Curly Lambeau's Green Bay Packers and George Halas' Chicago Bears would meet for the last APFA game of the 1921 season in Cubs Park. More than 300 Packer fans and the 22-piece Lumberjack Band traveled by train to Chicago. They left on the midnight train and arrived in Chicago's Loop early Sunday morning. George Calhoun would report to his *Press-Gazette* readers the day after the game, "Staid old Chicago got a new thrill on Sunday and the college authorities who claim that 'There ain't no such thing as spirit in professional football' stood back and gasped as the rooters from Green Bay, Wisconsin, took the town by storm Sunday morning and held full sway until the last car of the special excursion pulled out from the North Western about three bells Monday morning." It must have been a wild trip.

The Lumberjack Band, with their members dressed like Wisconsin lumberjacks — red and black plaid flannel shirts, Mackinaw coats, red hunting caps and rubber boots — played their instruments loud and clear into the early morning hours while they tramped through Chicago's misty streets to the Stratford Hotel. There they celebrated with several musical pieces including "*On Wisconsin*" before marching through other hotel lobbies on the way to the game. The Chicago police finally ended their musical spree, arresting them for "not having a parade permit." Ernie Stiller, one of those band members, recounted the experience to the *Press-Gazette* years later: "'I will never forget it. The ride to Chicago was a nightmare. Then came the parade from the station and the run-in with the police, which was soon smoothed over. We marched into several of the Loop hotels and spread the Green Bay football gospel all around.' Ed Smith, dean of Chicago sportswriters, was quoted as saying, 'Never in my experience have I witnessed a better display of spirit. I take my hat off to Green Bay. It was splendid.'

"Those back in Green Bay who could not make the trip again

got a play-by-play account via telegraph at Turner Hall. Within seconds after each play, a local announcer read a message off the wire, informing a packed house how much yardage had been gained on the previous play and the position of the ball."[28] Lambeau's Packers were thoroughly outclassed in the game and lost 20 to 0, giving the Bears first place in the league. To add insult to injury, the Bears' John "Tarzan" Taylor blatantly threw a cheap shot at the Packers' best player, Howard "Cub" Buck. The rivalry had begun.

It was about this time in the 1921 season that a bizarre situation took place that would cost the Packers their franchise. Exactly when it happened and how the league's president, Joe Carr, found out about a Packer infraction is muddled in the obscure facts available. The league had a standing rule that the pro teams could not use a college player before his class graduated. Most of the teams, however, used college players under fictitious names. There was an unwritten code that none of the teams would report the information to the league office. The Packers were victimized by the breaking of that code. It added spice to the budding Bear-Packer rivalry, as well as the animosity between Lambeau and Halas that would create grudge matches between their two teams for years.

It is clear Lambeau used three Notre Dame players, including Heartley "Hunk" Anderson, Lambeau's teammate from the 1916 season with the Fighting Irish, in a game late in the season. Doing so, he violated the league rule on using college players still in school. It is also a fact the *Chicago Tribune* reported the violation. Exactly which game produced the violation and who turned them in remains unclear. Was it the *Tribune's* writers who picked up on the Notre Dame players? Or did the opposing team recognize the non-roster players? Some accounts report it was a non-league game against a Racine club team, while other anecdotes say the illegal players were used in that last league game of the season in Chicago.

It seems most logical to use Larry Names' theory from his research for his book on the history of the Packers: "Lambeau used college players all right, but it was in Green Bay's game against the Decatur Staleys. George Halas spotted Lambeau's collegiate ringers, and Halas told the Chicago newspapers about it. Why would a Chicago sportswriter be covering a game that didn't have a Chicago team in it? Why would a Chicago sportswriter care about a game between two small town teams such as Green Bay and Racine? Why would the NFL care about the Packers using college players in a non-league game, especially since the circuit's rules didn't forbid such use of college players? One of the players used by Lambeau was Notre Dame's Heartley "Hunk" Anderson, a former teammate of Lambeau's and a native of the Upper Peninsula of Michigan. George Halas coveted Anderson's services, and if Green Bay was in the league, Anderson would more than likely sign with Green Bay to play in 1922. Therefore, Green Bay had to be removed from the NFL. Halas blew the whistle to the Chicago press, and the NFL gave in to their pressure to get rid of Green Bay from the loop."[29]

In any case, at the league meeting in December, the Packers were found in rule violation, and the franchise for Acme Packing was revoked on January 22, 1922. Apparently, there were a number of club owners, Halas included, who wanted the small, backwoods Green Bay out of the league, and the rule violation gave them the opportunity. The *Press-Gazette* reported that Emmett Clair attended the meeting in January and turned back the franchise with no argument for keeping it or requesting a reprieve. With urging of some Green Bay businessmen, Lambeau immediately applied for the franchise, now in his own name as representative of the Green Bay football club. Joe Carr said Lambeau's request would be considered and an answer given within 60 days. It took longer for an answer, in fact nearly five months, long enough for Halas to sign his coveted Notre Dame star, Hunk Anderson, to his Bear team and keep him from signing with Green Bay.

The eventual answer from the APFA (now the National Football League with a name change the summer of 1922) was not an approval of Lambeau's request for a franchise, but a notice of a league meeting June 24 and 25 in Cleveland. He was required to meet with league officials in person to make his pitch and to be prepared to pay the $1,500 re-entry league fee. A friend of Lambeau, Don Murphy, offered to help with the needed cash. That summer, Lambeau was in a minstrel show in Green Bay put on by the Green Bay Elks Club. One of the members of the minstrel show was Murphy, son of a wealthy Green Bay lumberman, along with his brother Brick, an investor in the Acme Packing Company. Most accounts on this situation report that Murphy sold his car, a cream-colored Marmon roadster, and gave Lambeau the cash. Lambeau attended the league meeting, made his appeal, received backing from some of the other owners who saw Green Bay as an asset to the league, paid the fee and was granted the franchise. It became official at the signing of the NFL franchise document on August 22, 1922, made to the "Green Bay Football Club, E. L. Lambeau of Green Bay, Wisconsin." Curly now owned the Packers.

With the pro league paired down to 18 teams from the 21 the year before, Lambeau began to prepare for the 1922 season by signing players from Wisconsin, Notre Dame, Marquette and Indiana. He signed quarterback Charley Mathys of Indiana, a former Green Bay West great, plus center Jug Earp from Monmouth, and guard Whitey Woodin of Marquette. All three would have a major impact on the team's success over the next decade. Lambeau, with his high school coaching behind him, now devoted his coaching exclusively to the Packers. He designed new plays and instituted daily team practice that fall, both unusual moves for NFL teams in those days.

Mathys, at 5 feet, 8 inches, became Lambeau's favorite receiver. He said when he played with another NFL team before the Packers they would only practice on Saturdays or Sunday mornings before the game. Mathys, who would play for Green Bay for five years, said of Lambeau's practices, "There was no standing around at practice. Everybody worked and worked hard — he was a driver. He meant business and everybody knew it and toed the mark." Lambeau's militant leadership was an extension of his own dedication to the game as a player. "Curly was rough and rugged," Mathys recalled. "He was a very good passer and a good hard runner, too. Curly was about 190 to 195 pounds; he had the weight and the determination."

1922 was not a year of distinction on the playing field for the Packers. They stumbled to a record of four wins, three losses and three ties, which placed them in eighth place finish in the 18-team league. But bigger problems loomed off the field. A stroke of bad weather and a lack of cash almost finished the team for good. Heavy rain resulted in a low turnout for a home game in November with the Columbus Panhandlers. To pay their guarantee to Columbus, the Packers went into heavy debt. Later that month, on Thanksgiving morning, Andrew B. Turnbull made his way from his home on East Mason Street to his office at the Green Bay *Press-Gazette*. As business manager of the newspaper, there were several tasks he wanted to take care of, even though it was a holiday. It was a miserable day. Threatening clouds darkened the sky, and the streets were slick with puddles from the heavy rain that had drenched the city the day before. When he got to the *Press-Gazette,*

Turnbull found Calhoun meeting with Lambeau trying to decide whether to play the scheduled exhibition game with the Duluth Eskimos. The game had been arranged with the hope of rescuing the Packers from financial disaster. Turnbull, an enthusiastic fan of the team, but a tough-minded businessman, understood the importance of the game. If the Packers did not play that day and pay Duluth its guaranteed fee, he reasoned the league might dump Green Bay. Turnbull strongly suggested the Packers play the game and work out the financial side later. Legend has it that Turnbull promised Calhoun and Lambeau that he would see to it personally the team would not go bankrupt.

Amidst a steady downpour and surrounded by empty seats, the Packers won the meaningless exhibition game, 10 to 0. The Packers had to pay the Duluth team the league required guarantee of $2,200, sinking them still deeper into debt. Enter, once again, Lambeau's old friend, Nate Abrams. By now, Abrams had become successful in the cattle business, heard about the team's financial problems and loaned Curly $3,000. It helped, but didn't solve the problem. The club was still broke at the end of the season. Turnbull knew if something wasn't done quickly to heal the team's finances, the Packers would fold. In December, he called a few of his Green Bay business buddies and asked them to meet him and Lambeau at the Beaumont Hotel's Attic Room to see if they could come up with a plan to keep the team solvent. Known to his friends and employees simply as 'A.B.,' Turnbull would become a key supporter to the Packers for years.

With a love for newspaper work, Turnbull had worked for the *Detroit News* and *Duluth News Tribune* before joining the *Press-Gazette* in 1915. The *Press-Gazette*, formed by a merger between two rival papers, came into existence at a time when Green Bay was one of Wisconsin's fastest-growing cities. In 1915, the *Green Bay Free Press* was founded by local attorney Victor Minahan, and the *Free Press* and the *Gazette* became intense competitors. The resulting war for readers pushed both papers to near collapse, so Minahan, editor John Kline and treasurer Turnbull created a syndicate that merged them. The *Green Bay Press-Gazette* hit the streets for the first time on June 29, 1915, a Tuesday afternoon.

Attending that meeting and several more over the next several months were Turnbull, Dr. W. W. Kelly, a well known doctor who once served as president of the Green Bay school board, president of the Wisconsin State Board of Health and regent of the University of Wisconsin; Jerry Clifford, a well known lawyer who was extremely active in Democratic affairs in Wisconsin all through the Roosevelt administration; and Lee Joannes, whose family operated one of the largest wholesale groceries in the state.

Along with Lambeau, they were called the "Hungry Five," a nickname given to them by Oliver Kuechle, a sportswriter for the *Milwaukee Journal,* after a popular radio program of the late Twenties. Kuechle would say later, "If it is true that there would be no Green Bay Packers today except for Lambeau and his idea of a home town football team, it is also true that there would be no Green Bay Packers today except for the 'Hungry Five.' They were the men who formed the corporation that saved the Packers in 1923. They were the counselors in moments of crisis later. They were the men who dominated the executive committee and who unobtrusively filled the most important corporate offices. (Turnbull was club president from 1923 through 1927. Dr. Kelly was president in 1929 and team physician until 1945. Joannes was president from 1930 through 1946. Clifford was legal counsel through most of these years.) They were Lambeau's close friends. 'The greatest coach in the game,' they said of him."[30]

In the spring of 1923, the "Hungry Five" called a town meeting at Green Bay's Elks Club where a capacity crowd of 400 heard inspirational speeches given by Turnbull and Lambeau. They exhorted. They pleaded. They extolled the many reasons Green Bay businessmen should back this professional football team that was putting their city on the national map. With the crowd worked up and properly motivated, pledges were taken for a share of stock at five dollars. For five shares, they were guaranteed a box at all Packer home games that fall. Fifty leading businessmen of the community put up $100 apiece, in case the team lost money. "On August 14, 1923, new articles of incorporation (Green Bay Packers, Inc.) were drawn up. A total of 1,000 shares of stock were issued. A fifteen-man board of directors and a five-man executive committee were set up. Earnings, if any, were to go to the Sullivan post of the American Legion in Green Bay. The corporation was to be operated without cost to the stockholders. Further, officers and directors were to serve with no salary or recompense, and each was to buy six season tickets to home games."[31] There would be no such thing as an "owner." It was to be a non-profit corporation and still ranks as the only publicly owned franchise in major league sports.

It would become the most unique setup for any professional

team in any sport at any time and one of the most amazing sports stories the nation has ever witnessed. The Green Bay Packers, led on the field by Lambeau, but owned by the citizens of Green Bay and surrounding communities, would nurse the team through one financial disaster after another for generations to come to create one of the most popular and successful franchises in any professional sport. With solid financial backing, Lambeau set out to build a championship football team. He located and recruited quality players primarily from the Midwest through the balance of the 1920s with Wisconsin, Marquette, Minnesota and Notre Dame providing most of his cast. Verne Lewellen, an outstanding athlete from Nebraska, Lavvie Dilweg and Joe "Red" Dunn, both from Marquette, Claude Perry from Alabama and Bo Molenda from Michigan were sought out and signed to Packer contracts by Lambeau. He made a science out of scouting and analyzing talent, in addition to persuasively selling a good athlete on coming to small town Green Bay to play football.

Structuring the team with the talent needed to win in the NFL became Lambeau's forte, and win they did. From 1923 through 1928, the Packers won 43, lost 20 and tied 8, one of the best winning percentages established by any NFL team during that six-year period. For two years, starting in 1923, the team played their home games before crowds nearing 4,000 in an old wooden baseball stadium at the end of Main Street. Hagemeister Park was dug up to make way for a new East High School. Two years later, they moved their home games to the new City Stadium built specifically for the Packers right next to East High School by Marcel Lambeau's construction firm. The new stadium would seat 3,000 initially and grow to hold 13,000 before the end of the 1920s.

City Stadium was barely completed in time for the 1925 opening, but was an immediate success; the Bear game that year drew a record crowd of 5,389. It was a typical small town park of its day, with wooden fences and stands on both sides between the 30-yard lines. Seating capacity was gradually increased until it seated 15,000 by 1934, with the end zones still uncovered. After filling in around the end zones, the ultimate capacity of 25,000 was reached. City Stadium became the first playing arena constructed for use by a professional football team. One unique feature of the stadium, however, was the fact that it didn't have any restrooms before the mid-1930s. Women just had to wait and go elsewhere while the men relieved themselves underneath the stands. "The ladies also faced other hazards at the old stadium. The footrests under the seats consisted of one 2x12 plank, and the rest of the footing was open to the ground. On frequent occasions, women dropped their handbags or even items of apparel down through these openings. The Packers would station security guards under the stands to retrieve any such items and take them to the lost and found counter where they could be repossessed."[32]

The rivalry between Lambeau and Halas continued to gain momentum through the 1920s. Winning became an obsession for these two immensely competitive and intense coaches. Their animosity toward one another filtered down to their players every time they met. Lambeau and Halas locked in more duels than any other combination of coaches in football. Yet never once during his tenure at Green Bay, the Chicago Cardinals or the Washington Redskins did Lambeau ever shake hands with the Bear boss before or after a game. On game day, they didn't even speak. Lambeau explained, "Shake hands? That would have been a lie. If I lost, I wanted to punch Halas in the nose. If he lost, Halas wanted to punch me."

The Bears continued to dominate play between the two. By 1928, the Packers and Bears had met 14 times with Lambeau winning only two. Marguerite would say later that Lambeau was impossible to be around the week of the Bears' game. He was tense, irritable and focused on nothing but beating his archrival, George Halas. She would recall how on the night before the game he couldn't sleep. He would lay in bed with a pencil and draw up last minute plays. Calhoun would add fuel to the fire with his articles in the *Press-Gazette* the week preceding each game. In Calhoun's mind, each game was a grudge match. That's the way he built it up, and the fans loved it.

Before 1925, pro football was viewed as a third-rate program compared to the much more popular college game. Crowds of 70,000 commonly attended the major college games, which were played on well-kept fields on a Saturday afternoon. In contrast, an average of 5,000 showed up for a pro game on Sunday, played in old ballparks and rough fields. Most sportswriters (outside of Calhoun and the *Press-Gazette*) paid little attention to pro football.

1925 ushered in radical change and pro football would never be the same. It would be the year journalists called the turning point; the year pro football found its savior in a ghost — a "Galloping Ghost" named Harold "Red" Grange. He had been a running star at the University of Illinois, came to the pro game and immediately transformed its image, putting pro football on the sports pages above the fold. Single-handedly, Grange legitimized the professional game when, on November 21, 1925, after his last game against Ohio State, he announced his intention to play professionally.

The shrewd George Halas worked out a contract with Grange's manager, Charles C. Pyle, for Grange to play with his Bears as soon as his college schedule was complete. It would guarantee Grange at least $100,000 to play with the Bears. Grange became the most publicized football player in the Golden Age of American Sports. Even though in the grainy black and white photos of the time, Grange looked like an old man, his broken-field running and ability to dodge, weave, twist, glide, and change pace left his would-be tacklers far behind. "Grange runs as Dempsey moves, with almost no effort, as a shadow flits and drifts and darts," wrote well-known sportswriter Grantland Rice. Americans were entranced and flocked to buy radios so as not to miss their hero's latest Saturday-afternoon exploits.

"Grange's official debut as a professional came on Thanksgiving Day against the Chicago Cardinals. Iving Vaughan wrote in the *Chicago Tribune*: "The whole town rose up on its hind legs and shouted, 'We must have tickets!' When the tickets did go on sale, the crush for them became so great that mounted and foot patrol officers were called to restore order. Grange's overwhelming popularity drew 36,000 fans (at the time, the biggest crowd ever to attend a pro game) to his debut at Wrigley Field. After the 1925 season, Grange and the Bears set out on two brutal tours. They traveled more than 10,000 miles and played seventeen games, from the opener in St. Louis on December 2, 1925 to the finale in Seattle on January 31, 1926. Hordes of people came out to see the great Grange in Boston, Jacksonville and New Orleans. Unbelievably, 75,000 people filled the Los Angeles Coliseum to watch Red play. Coral Gables, Florida, built a 25,000-seat stadium in only two days to showcase Grange."[33] Before it was over, 400,000 fans had seen him and the Bears play. Pro football had arrived.

So had the Packers, who improved on the field and financially off the field through 1928. Lambeau continued to function in the dual role of coach and player through the 1927 season. He played very little in 1928 and stopped entirely after the 1929 season. While official NFL statistics were not kept until 1933, Calhoun kept his own set of statistics that would become valuable in later years. "He cut out the box scores and statistics of every game played in the NFL and pasted them in notebooks which he kept up to date every week. In the 1950s, a writer by the name of Roger Treat got the idea of compiling an encyclopedia of pro football, and Calhoun's files of all the NFL's games became one of Treat's main sources of information."[34]

Data from that source confirms Lambeau's major contributions to the team in the 1920s. He led the Packers in rushing yards and passing attempts and completions every year through the 1924 season. While his running attempts diminished, Lambeau still led the team in passing through the 1926 schedule and continued to be a major contributor on offense until 1928. Throughout his active Packer playing career, Lambeau averaged more than three yards per carry and completed nearly 40 percent of his passes while the team posted a 52-26-13 record from 1921 through 1928, second only during this period to the Bear's George Halas.

The Packers came on strong toward the end of the 1928 season with two wins against the Bears and New York, sandwiched around a heartbreaking loss on Thanksgiving Day to the second place Frankford Yellow Jackets, 2 to 0, and a 7 to 7 tie to the league-leading Providence Steam Rollers.

When the Packers met the Bears in the last game of the season, they had been traveling by train for nearly a month. The Packers departed Green Bay on November 15 for five consecutive road games against the New York Giants, Pottsville Maroons, Frankford Yellow Jackets, Providence Steam Rollers, and the Bears. They spent the early part of the week prior to the Bears' game practicing in Atlantic City, New Jersey. The Packers arrived in Chicago two days before their final game on December 9 and beat the Bears, 6 to 0. The prior month when the Packers had played the Giants in New York on November 18, the New York press bad-mouthed the team. 'Hayseeds' and 'local-yokels' from the north woods of Wisconsin they called the Packers. Tiny Green Bay was just a small team against the big city Giants. Lambeau made sure his players knew what the New York players were saying about them. The Packers won, and the New York press would begin to change their view of the Packers over the next few years. Green Bay's devoted Packer fans and the Lumberjack Band continued to make the train trips to Chicago for the Bear games. Between the train and automobile, 2,500 saw the Packers beat the Bears at Wrigley Field in 1928.

"Green Bay *Press-Gazette's* sports editor, Arthur W. Bystrom, who had replaced Calhoun, had nothing but praise for the Packer's fans. He proudly wrote of the devoted fans that boarded the Chicago, Milwaukee, Pacific and Northwestern railroads to travel to the game in Chicago, while as many as 900 Green Bay enthusiasts had driven to Wrigley Field."[35] The Packers were becoming so popular, special trains out of Green Bay would carry more than one thousand fans to Chicago by the end of the 1920s and continue to provide service into the 1960s.

When the 1928 season closed showing the Green Bay Packers, Inc. on solid financial footing, Lambeau would bring in a group of new, more talented athletes to the team. They would now be poised to become NFL champions an unprecedented three years in a row, putting the Packers and Curly Lambeau in the national spotlight. Afterward, neither the team's reputation nor Lambeau would ever be the same.

4

Fame

The next three years would blanket Lambeau, his Packers and the "little city by the bay" in glory, honor and reputation far beyond their wildest dreams. Between 1929 and 1931, Lambeau would lead his band of overachievers to three consecutive NFL championships. The NFL playoffs of today had yet to be instituted. The champion was determined by the team that finished with the best record in the twelve-team league. In the short nine-year history of the NFL, no team had won three championships in a row. The remarkable feat put Lambeau, the Packers and the city of Green Bay into the national spotlight. While the brand of NFL football and the competition was not what it is today, the Packers were still the best of the lot at the time.

They became the nation's sports story — the stuff of legends. Here were the little "backwoods" Packers led and coached by a hometown hero, directing the epitome of the underdog against teams from New York, Chicago, Minneapolis, Brooklyn and other much larger cities. To the chagrin of the "more sophisticated" big cities, obscure and "uncultured" Green Bay would beat them again, again and again during this glorious three-year reign. It was the classic David vs. Goliath story week after week. Sportswriters from the nation's largest newspapers loved it. By the third championship, Lambeau and his Packers were hailed in national print and featured on movie shorts in theaters across the country.

Lambeau was featured in the *Saturday Evening Post* and *Life* magazines and became a "household word" in the sports world.

So dominant were Lambeau's Packers in 1929, they were unbeaten, finishing 12-0-1 for the season. It would be the only time in the proud history of the Packers they would go through an entire season undefeated, outscoring their opponents by the unbelievable margin of 198 to 22. Only three teams would score touchdowns against them. In addition, eight of the teams they played that year were shutout totally, including the detested Chicago Bears, 23 to 0 and 14 to 0.

The sweet success of the 1929 season for Lambeau would mark the beginning of a seductive triumphant period in his life that would forever leave its imprint on his personality and character. In the next two years, the Packers would achieve the NFL championship with a 10-3-1 record in 1930 and 12-2-0 in 1931. In that three-year span, the Packers won 34, lost 5 and tied 2, a record matched only in Packer history for a successive three-year period by Vince Lombardi and his 35-6-1 record for 1961, 1962 and 1963. If you add the 1932 season to Lambeau's successful run, the Packers' four-year record of 44-8-2 is the best four consecutive winning percentage in the proud history of the team. At one point, the Packers had won 22 games in a row spanning a three-year time frame.

By the end of 1931, Lambeau's charm extended far beyond hometown Green Bay. He became the darling in towns and cities across the entire nation. At that time, he even replaced Knute Rockne (who had perished in an airplane crash in early 1931) as football's coaching headliner. He was the chief attraction, with his picture and copy on sports pages of newspapers coast-to-coast. Now at age 32, Lambeau had matured to an even more athletically attractive man, with his dark wavy hair and captivating smile. Always well dressed (particularly for professional football players and coaches of the time), Lambeau came across strongly self-assured, almost brash, yet able to banter with the press, which they loved. Lambeau was selling again. Only this time, it wasn't just the Packers, but himself and he knew it.

Good players make good coaches better, and Lambeau added three excellent members to his 1929 team of already solid athletes — men who would make the Packers dominating champions. The three he came up with are well known in Packer lore: the flamboyant Johnny (Blood) McNally, Cal Hubbard, an incredible two-way athlete and "Iron Mike" Michalske, one of the finest linemen of his day. Together, they would make National Football League history. These three were added to a cast of proven veterans such as "Boob" Darling, a tall center at 6 feet, 3 inches; Lavvie Dilweg at 6 feet, 3 inches, an end from Marquette; "Red" Dunn, the gutsy quarterback; Jug Earp, the big tackle; Eddie Kotal, a small, but quick back; Verne Lewellen, a solid ball carrier and punter extraordinaire; Bo Molenda, a reliable runner; Claude Perry, a dependable tackle from Alabama; and Whitey Woodin, a short, but tough guard. Over half the players were from Midwest colleges. Most of the men on the team would stay with the Packers for the three championship years. While Earp and Hubbard were well into their 30s, the rest of the team were in their mid-20s.

Lambeau had now put together a well-balanced group of athletes who displayed all the necessary roughness, speed and tenacity to win in the NFL. Lambeau would provide the plays, strategy and motivation in addition to making all team travel arrangements, negotiating contracts, running practices and disciplining the players.

Prior to the start of the 1929 season, Dr. W. Weber Kelly was elected president of the Packer Board of Directors, replacing Ray Evrard who held the position for only one year. Lambeau appealed to Dr. Kelly and the rest of the Packer Board to do more to promote ticket sales for the 1929 season. They would have five home games, late September through late October, with the remaining eight games on the road. Dr. Kelly and the Board agreed to put forth an all-out effort to sell tickets for the home dates. Gerald Clifford, a prominent Democratic attorney in Wisconsin, was put in charge of a committee of Green Bay businessmen who would tour the state, selling the Packers' home schedule. (Both Dr. Kelly and Clifford would assume a much different role with Lambeau 20 years later.)

With the team prospering, City Stadium seating expanded. It could now hold more than 10,000 rabid fans. The playing field earned a reputation for being one of the best in professional football. It had a base of six inches of clay, another six inches of black dirt and was topped off by sod. Water was pumped into the field through tile drainage. The center was built up approximately twelve inches and rain could be drained off in about half an hour. Every spring the entire field was re-sodded.

Players were now selling tickets in their hometowns. Green Bay's businessmen were also running full-page ads in the *Press-*

Gazette encouraging people to back the team. For the most part, the ticket selling campaign was a success. They drew a record 39,000 for the five home games, including 13,000 for the Bear game. Lambeau would also help with the ticket selling process, but was limited for time. Since he had left Acme Packing Company, he relied on his salary from the Packers (probably around $2,500 a year) and his two jobs in the off-season (selling life insurance for Massachusetts Life and selling men's clothing at Steifels Clothing store in Green Bay). He had also set up an office that jointly served as the Packer headquarters and a place for him to handle insurance matters on the third floor of the Northern Building, located on the corner of Adams and Walnut Streets. In his rather sparse office consisting of a desk, chair and a brown leather armchair, Lambeau could look out of the one window and see the Green Bay court-house and post office across the street. That same courthouse would be the site of Lambeau's last official act as coach and vice president of the Packers 20 years later.

But for now, Lambeau was in charge, and since he had stopped playing he was coming into his own as a coach and organizer. He pleaded and cajoled; he paraded up and down the sideline, shouting encouragement and instructions; he cursed and gestured. He inspired his men and he drove them, at times ruthlessly. Heading into the 1929 season, the Packers were loaded, especially with the additions of Hubbard, McNally and Michalske. Hubbard, a 6-foot, 4-inch tackle, came from the New York Giants and later was a high-ly regarded baseball umpire. Michalske was a strong guard who had spent two seasons with the New York Yankees after starring at Penn State. And then there was McNally, a fabled character who adopted the name Johnny Blood from a movie character. Very much a character himself, Blood had been a four-sport letterman at St. John's University in Collegeville, Minnesota. He had also played freshman football at Notre Dame.

"Cal Hubbard, with rough looking facial features, but a big ready smile, was nicknamed 'The Enforcer,' and at a rock-hard 270 pounds, he was the biggest man playing pro football at the time. Russ Winnie, the radio voice of the Packers, used to say Cal weighed between 265 and 280 pounds, depending upon what he ate for breakfast. After one year with the Giants, Hubbard told the team, 'Trade me to the Packers or I quit.' He had decided he liked Green Bay after spending a week there the year before. 'We played the Packers in Green Bay one Sunday and had to play the Bears in

Chicago next so we stayed in Green Bay that week to practice,' he once commented. 'I kind of liked Green Bay.'"[36] He is the only person to be enshrined in both the Pro Football Hall of Fame and the Major League Baseball Hall of Fame.

George Halas said of Hubbard at one time, "There was never a better lineman." "The greatest football player who ever lived, lineman or back, college or pro," said his former coach, Bo McMillin, who was around long enough to see most of them. "A giant of a man who could outrun any back in the league for 30 yards," Steve Owen once said when he was coaching the New York Giants. Throughout most of his 31 years of coaching the Packers, Lambeau ran a tight ship. He was a tough disciplinarian that often rankled the players, even his stars. The outspoken Hubbard made no secret of the fact that he respected Lambeau, but didn't like him personally. The two had no fondness for one another. "They won't be able to find six men to bury the so and so," Hubbard once was quoted, but he was fair, too, admitting, "He was a hard driver, but he got the job done."

The outspoken Hubbard even questioned Lambeau's football knowledge during those early years. "'To be frank,' Hubbard would say, 'Curly really didn't know that much about football. After all, he just spent one year at Notre Dame, how much did he learn? Most of us knew more, because we spent more time learning during four years of college and then, for most of us, some professional experience, too. Hell, sometimes Curly would design a new play, draw it up on the blackboard and we just knew it wouldn't work the way he drew it. He'd have impossible blocking assignments, or the play would just take too long to develop. The defense would mess it up before it got going. We'd have to tell him that, and one of the veterans would go right up to the blackboard and change it around. Most of the time, Johnny Blood was the spokesman because he was always ready to speak up to Curly.'

"Johnny Blood would add, 'Not that I necessarily did the thinking. As Cal said, I was the spokesman. I'd go up and get the chalk, and then we'd all kind of talk about it, a group discussion, and we'd keep working on it until we got it right.' Mike Michalske had a somewhat similar perspective. He said much the same about the young Lambeau, but added qualifying remarks. 'I will say that Curly was willing to learn from us. He really learned football from his players, and after a few years I think he knew as much as any coach in the game. He just had to have that learning experience for a while.'"[37]

Michalske, a 6-foot guard, became available to Lambeau when the team he had played with during the past two seasons, the New York Yankees, folded.   Christened August at birth, Michalske became known as "Iron Mike" because not only did he play nearly 60 minutes every game, he also never was injured.   In high school and at Penn State, where he was an All-America pick in 1925, he played fullback, guard, end and tackle.   He first turned pro with the New York Yankees in the 1926 American Football League.   After the Yankees folded in 1928, with Lambeau's persuasion Michalske opted to become a free agent to join the Packers.   He became the premier guard in the NFL and was particularly good at rushing the passer of the opposing team.

"I just didn't get hurt, not until I injured my back in my last year of pro football," Michalske would say.   "I played both ways, of course, and 60 minutes of almost every game.   The players used to kid me by claiming that I must get paid by the minute."   As a line star of three of Green Bay's championship teams, Michalske may have been the first of the greats at rushing the passer among defensive linemen.   "We called it 'blitzing' in those days, too.   Our target was the man with the ball, especially the passer.   It may not have been exactly ethical, but it was legal in those days to rough the passer, even after he got rid of the ball.   We worked him over pretty good.   Hubbard and I used to do some stunting in the line to find an opening for a blitz break-through.   We figured the best time to stop them was before they got started."   Michalske would become a two-time All-Pro selection (1931 and 1935) and was inducted to the Pro Football Hall of Fame in 1964.

McNally, was one of the most colorful players in Packer history.   He would be Lambeau's constant headache off the field with his crazy shenanigans, but a delight on the field with his uncanny ability to run, catch and score touchdowns.   He played best when the Packers were behind.   When the Packers led, he often coasted and clowned.   He dropped easy passes and then caught impossible ones.   He broke training rules and curfews, missed trains, buses and bed checks and eluded teammates that were assigned to watch or guard him.   Despite his disdain for regular habits and hours, he was a star performer during the Packers' three consecutive championships.

Extremely popular with his teammates, at 6 feet, 185 pounds, Blood was unbelievably fast, a superb running back, and at that time, the finest receiver in the NFL.   He could throw passes and punt with the best. On defense, he was a ball hawk and a deadly tackler. His off-the-field antics, however, constantly drew attention away from his exceptional playing skills. One writer of the time referred to Blood as "a Peter Pan who would never shed his eternal youth."

Blood was a free spirit with a taste for booze, but not much success in handling it. After a game, he was known for buying the attention of all the women in a brothel and spending the night in conversation with them. But Johnny Blood was more than a flake. He was also a fleet, broken-field runner and probably the best pass receiver in pro football until Don Hutson arrived in Green Bay in 1935. It was Oliver Kuechle, sportswriter for the *Milwaukee Journal* at the time, who gave Blood the nickname "Vagabond Halfback." Kuechle had a real admiration for the Packer rogue and one time wrote, "John Blood is one of the grandest guys in all sports. All who ever played with him in football agree. Well read, exceptionally well read. Wild. Handsome. Unpredictable. As big-hearted as they come and as wasteful both of himself, with the wonderful physique nature gave him, and of his goods. And a great athlete. He could be one with the riff-raff in a waterfront bar one day, then recite Keats, Shelley or Shakespeare by the hour in different company the next. He could drop a pass thrown right in his hands and then get one that nobody else could, not even Hutson. He could hand over his last $100 to an acquaintance in need and pass an overdraft for $5 on a friend."

Blood was born and raised in the small town of New Richmond, Wisconsin. He was the only son of a wealthy and prominent family. A brilliant student, Blood said later: "My mother would teach me Shakespeare and my father taught me sports." He graduated from high school at the young age of 14. At 16, he attended a small teacher's college in Wisconsin for a few months before enrolling at nearby St. John's College where he lettered in football, basketball, baseball and track. He stayed for two years before enrolling at Notre Dame. He played football as a 19 year old freshman.

He might have finished his college education there except that on a late winter day, St. Patrick's Day to be exact, he "borrowed" a motorcycle and took off for Richmond, Virginia, with a young lady in a sidecar. As he later recalled: "I bought a motorcycle," he said later. "I was just learning to drive it fairly well, when I happened to attend a party in South Bend. There was a girl there and we got

to talking. I told her I had purchased a motorcycle and was planning a tour of the Eastern seaboard. She confided that she was married to a sailor who was due to sail from Norfolk, and she was anxious to wish him bon voyage. So we set out." He was found eventually, and returned home.

Blood would say later in a recorded interview, "That kind of
ended my career as a student. After it, I went to work for a newspaper in Minneapolis, and they put me in the printing end of it. It
didn't pay very much and I was quick to find out it was not my kind
of job. I'd also gotten one of my buddies from St. John's, Ralph
Hanson, a job there. Around that time, I'd heard that there was a
way to pick up some extra money by playing in a semi-pro city
league in the Minneapolis/St. Paul area. Ralph had played football
with me at St. John's so we thought we might be able to pick up a
little extra dough by playing football, something we both liked anyway. At the time, I was thinking that maybe one of those days I
might be going back to Notre Dame, in the unlikely event they'd
have me, but still it was a possibility. And if I did, I'd want to play
football there. I also knew we might play some games out of state
with that Minneapolis team. So I said to Ralph, 'I still have some
eligibility left and I don't want to lose it. So when we go out for
this team, let's use some fake names and we can protect our ama-
teur standing.' He agreed. I used to get around town on my own
motorcycle then, so we both hopped on it and headed out to where
this team practiced, some playground in back of a factory. On the
way there, we passed a movie theater on Hennepin Avenue and up
on the marquee I saw the name of the movie that was playing,
Blood and Sand with Rudolph Valentino. Ralph was behind me on
the motorcycle and I turned my head and shouted, 'That's it. I'll be
Blood and you be Sand.' And so we went to the practice, tried out,
and made the team, Johnny Blood and Ralph Sand. And, of course,
I kept it as a football name from that time on."[38]

He did go on to play pro football as Johnny Blood with several teams over the next few years — Milwaukee, Duluth and
Pottsville — before joining the Packers in 1929. While playing for
Pottsville, they went to Green Bay in 1928. During that game,
which was won by Pottsville, Blood scored three touchdowns running, passing and receiving with abandon. Lambeau was
impressed with Blood's performance. The next summer Blood
wrote to Lambeau and said he would like to play for the Packers.

Lambeau immediately replied by telegram, asking Blood to

come to Green Bay and talk about a contract. When they met in his office, Lambeau, having heard of Blood's drinking bouts, said he would give him $110 a game if Blood did not drink from Wednesday until after the game. Blood didn't even have to think about his answer. "Make it $100 a game and let me drink on Wednesday." Lambeau would respond, "You're so honest about it that I'll give you the $110 and still let you drink on Wednesday."

Blood would tell friend and author Ralph Hickok that Green Bay was his favorite city to play pro football. "Green Bay was definitely the place for me," said Blood "My destiny, maybe. I loved the place and, I have to say, the place, the people, loved me. If you play for the Packers, the people in Green Bay know you better than they know their own brothers. There were a lot of good times in Green Bay, it was a swell town in those days. We were kind of riding on top of the world, champs, well known. I have a lot of memories from up there." [39]

While Blood was instrumental in the Packers' championship years, his off-the-field antics are legendary. "The Packers were in Los Angeles one time for an exhibition, and Blood locked himself out when he left his key in his hotel room. It was after curfew when Blood returned from a night on the town and Lambeau was sitting in the lobby, but Blood remembered that he had left the window open. Blood's room was on the fifth floor. He climbed up the outside fire escape and entered a teammate's room that was on the sixth floor, but across an eight-foot court from Blood's room. Then, in a driving rainstorm, Blood leaped from one ledge and across the court to the other, climbed in the window of his own room and went to bed." [40]

At another time, the Packers were in New York and had just defeated the Giants in an important match. The Packers were staying on the eighteenth floor of the Lincoln Hotel. Blood and other teammates were having a party in their room when at 2:30 in the morning they ran out of ice. Blood looked out the window, saw an ice wagon making deliveries to Eighth Avenue bars, dashed out to the elevator, rode to the lobby, raced into the street, caught up to the ice wagon, bought a 140-pound block of ice and headed back to the hotel room. Through the lobby he went carrying the ice, up the elevator to the eighteenth floor where he staggered down the hall to his room and to the bathroom where he dropped the ice into the tub. The party continued until daylight.

John Torinus often told a story of one of Blood's exploits,

"Lambeau put Blood into a room with Michalske whenever they were on the road, thinking that the older and more staid Michalske could keep Blood in line. Even Mike, however, failed at that assignment. I happened to be present one Friday evening in the New Yorker Hotel when the Packers had come to the "Big Apple" to play the Giants on Sunday. Blood had been out beyond curfew hour and awoke Michalske upon returning to invite him to have a nightcap. Mike said he would, but complained that there was no ice. Blood said that was no problem; he could take care of that. He disappeared for about a half hour, and then reappeared, marching through the hotel lobby to the elevator carrying a cake of ice, complete with tongs. The next morning Blood was still in a state of inebriation, and Michalske suggested to him that he probably had the flu and would so inform Lambeau at practice. But Blood was not going to miss practice for a little thing like "bottle flu." That morning I was helping tag balls for the kickers who were practicing. Everyone stood around and watched as Blood tried to meet the ball with his foot during his turn. About the second try, he fell flat on his back, and Lambeau came storming over and fired him on the spot. He might have stayed fired, too, if Michalske and others on the team hadn't prevailed on Lambeau that evening to reinstate him. He went on to play a spectacular game against the Giants on Sunday."[41]

While an excellent performer for the Packers, he sometimes would pull crazy stunts that caught his teammates off guard. Red Dunn, the Packer quarterback during the championship years, once said, "I threw a long lateral to John on one play and he weaved some 50 yards down the field for a touchdown. About ten minutes later I called the same play and John, it seemed, could have gone all the way again. But he didn't. He just stood there an instant with a laugh and then threw the lateral back to me."

"Johnny Blood was the most fined man in pro football," Lambeau would often say. "But he never complained, whether it was for $25 or $200. He'd just say, 'I had it coming, Curly,' and pay.

"Before I signed him one year, I told him he'd have to promise not to take a drink all season. Finally, he agreed. I told him I'd pay him just $25 a week and keep the rest of his salary and give it to him at the end of the season. It worked fine. He didn't take a drink all season that I know of. Every day after practice, he'd take a couple of quarts of milk and go to the home of the editor of the *Press-*

Gazette. He had the best library in town. All afternoon, Blood would read books and sip milk.

"He had his best year. He was all-pro and we won the championship. At the end of the season, I congratulated him personally and gave him the rest of his money, a few thousand dollars that had accumulated. A couple of weeks later, I was in the Biltmore Hotel in Los Angeles and the phone rang. 'Curly,' the voice said, 'this is Blood. I'm busted.' I told him to come up to the room. He came in and I said, 'Johnny, I just gave you a few thousand two weeks ago. How could you have spent it so fast?' 'Curly,' he said, 'I've never had any money at Christmas before, so this time I bought everybody in the family, including my aunts, big presents. Now I'm a big man in the family, but I'm broke. Could you let me have ten?'"[42]

Lambeau did everything a coach could possibly do to control Blood except put him in a straightjacket. He gave him contracts in which Blood got no more than $25 a week and the balance at season's end. He fined him until Blood owed the Packers money. He had men on the team watch him. He often got so tired of Blood's antics he threatened to fire him.

While they had a somewhat adversarial relationship during the years Blood was with the Packers, Lambeau still let him call all the plays on the field. Lambeau would often comment on how he couldn't understand how such an irresponsible character off the field could be such a fine strategist on the field. During their time together, they formed a mutual respect until the end of Blood's career. Then it went sour. Blood would say in an interview, "I got along pretty well with Curly, for a while anyway. I was one of the only ones who did, most didn't like him at all. But for the first three or four years he put up with me and my antics. I think I was one of the few who could get the best of him; he had a hard time keeping up with me. Actually, in the long run, I guess I didn't get along so well because he finally fired me. On paper I was sold to the Pittsburgh team, but he really fired me. It came after several of us had been out one night — myself and a couple of other players. We were out all night as a matter of fact. Well, I went directly to practice in the morning, got all suited up. Lambeau was looking at me kind of funny as I remember. Anyway, I tried to punt the ball, missed it, and fell flat on my ass. Lambeau told me to get the hell off the field and after practice was over he told me he was getting rid of me. I came back to Green Bay a year later and Lambeau took me back, but we never got along very well after that."[43]

Blood would recall his playing days with Lambeau, "One thing about Curly was that his team always went first class. We traveled on the best trains, stayed at the best hotels. In Green Bay, we stayed at the Astor. Compared to what players get today, the money doesn't seem like much — the typical player got $75 to $100 a game. But, there weren't many guys our age earning that kind of money then. The YWCA was right across from the Astor, and we usually ate there. You could get a terrific meal for seventy-five cents."[44]

Ironically, they would be together again at the twilight of Lambeau's life. Blood would be inducted into the Pro Football Hall of Fame the same year as Lambeau in 1963, and held one last reunion.

The 1929 season was also one the Packers would finally get the upper hand against George Halas' Bears. They would whip the Bears once in Green Bay and twice in Chicago, and all three wins were shutouts, 23 to 0, 14 to 0 and 25 to 0. It was sweet revenge for Lambeau as the Bears had been beating Green Bay on a regular basis for eight years. The fierce competition between the Packers and Bears continued to escalate during the 1920s, 30s and into the 40s. George Musso, the Bears' Hall of Fame lineman, perhaps best summarized that fascinating relationship. "Halas and Lambeau were friends, like coaches would be friends," he said. "But when it comes to playing, hell, you're not friends. You're out to win. And you win any damn way you can."[45]

One of Lambeau's players would say, "The whole week before…oh, God! He hated 'em so bad, I think it always hurt us in the game, especially the first game of the season. We never played very well that first Bear game. Later in the season, we'd go down and have a good football game in Chicago. I think we'd get too high because Curly was so damn high. Before the game, he was wild. During the game, he was wild. He'd call for somebody to go into the ballgame who was no longer on the football team. He'd lose his cool when he was going to play Halas. I think Curly and Halas were such enemies, maybe I shouldn't say enemies, but they wanted to beat each other so damn badly, that Curly would just go wild before a Bears game.

"As demonstrative as Halas was, he had an equal in the fiery, flamboyant Lambeau, who was more than capable of matching the Bears' coach tirade for tirade on the sideline. 'And how he would rant and rave,' said John Biolo, a guard for the Packers in 1939 and longtime head of the Packer Alumni Association. 'During a game, nobody would want to talk to him. You'd stay as far away as you could on the bench.'"[46]

While the Bear-Packer rivalry continued to heat up, the train trips to Chicago for the games also continued through the years. As Packer victories became more prevalent, the number of people traveling by train and car to Comiskey Park against the Cardinals and Wrigley Field against the Bears would grow. As many as 4,000 Packer backers would show up for the Chicago games, always with the plaid-jacketed Lumberjack Band. The train ride to and from Chicago became an overly festive affair. An entire train car would be set up with a bar. Drinking would start with their departure in Green Bay and wouldn't stop until the train pulled into Chicago hours later.

About a third of the way through the 1929 season, the stock market crashed on October 29, ending a post-World War I period of prosperity that has been dubbed the Jazz Age and the Golden Age of Sports. The crash brought on the Great Depression. The prosperity of the 1920s proved top-heavy and thin, built mainly on stock speculation and wishes. Black Thursday brought ruin to the dream, the economy and President Herbert Hoover. Wall Street posted stock losses in the billions of dollars that day.

The ill winds of Wall Street blew rapidly across the dairy farms of Wisconsin, Pennsylvania steel mills, Kansas wheat fields, California fruit groves, Detroit auto factories, cattle ranches of Wyoming, neighborhood bakery shops, local diners, and nearly every corner of the nation. By early 1930, factories were closing. More than 1,300 banks closed by the end of the same year. Unemployment lists were growing. By 1932, twelve million Americans, one-fourth of the entire labor force, were out of work. The prices of wheat and cotton dropped drastically, and hundreds of thousands of desperate farmers glumly awaited foreclosure, the sheriff's sale and the loss of their land.

Like most other enterprises, professional football also suffered. At the end of the 1929 season, with the Depression's effect barely perceptible, the Pottsville Maroons, New York Yankees, Detroit Wolverines and Duluth Eskimos all called it quits. In 1930, the Boston Bulldogs, Buffalo Bisons and Dayton Triangle disbanded. The 1931 casualties were the Minneapolis Red Jackets and Newark Tornadoes. In 1932, the Providence Steam Rollers, the first-year

Cleveland Indians and the Frankford Yellow Jackets folded. The Yellow Jackets didn't even last to the end of the season, quitting on November 10.

By 1932, in the depth of the Depression, NFL membership fell to eight teams, the smallest in its history. Providence, who only four years before had won the championship, suspended operation for a year with the league's permission. But the Steam Rollers never played again in the NFL, and the franchise was forfeited to the league in 1933. In July, a four-man Boston syndicate composed of George Preston Marshall, Vincent Bendix, Jay O'Brien and M. Dorland Doyle, was granted a franchise known as the Braves. It wasn't a good time to start a team. By the end of the season, the Braves had lost $46,000, and Marshall was left as the sole owner of the team. Even the Chicago Bears were in financial difficulty, and the Packers would soon have their own financial hardship.

While the country was only beginning to understand the impact of the Wall Street crash, the Packers continued to win. A game against the heavily favored New York Giants in New York near the end of the 1930 season would provide a "defining moment" for Lambeau. The Giants had not lost a game thus far, but neither had the Packers. Nevertheless, the New York press and radio stations had belittled the Green Bay Packers all year, basically suggesting all along that little backwoods Green Bay was no match for the Giants of New York. Lambeau prepared by implementing a new defense against the Giants' effective passing game, made only one substitution the entire game and won going away 20 to 6. Watching in great delight, Lambeau stamped and leaped along the sidelines. "In order to stop New York's passing, Lambeau pulled big Cal Hubbard out of the line and let him roam around behind it, along with the fullback and the roving center, to spot and bump any receivers coming through and to plug up whatever holes might open. Cal gloried in the linebacker job, and he played it like a man in frenzy. When a crowd of blockers came roaring around end, as they often did in those power days, Cal would dump the whole herd of them into the lap of the ball carrier. Or he might single out the lonely ball carrier, collar him with one sweep of his paw, and then splash him on the sod.

"The details of this game were reported back to Green Bay, where half the town had packed into one smoke-filled room in Turner Hall to watch on a big green board called a Grid-Graph, a sort of reconstruction of the action on the field as it was given to the operator. Since there were few outdoor loudspeakers in that day, this was the only way a large crowd could be given the news. And when word came finally that the Packers had put the Giants down, the crowded room exploded with a roar."[47]

More than 25,000 were at the Polo Grounds that cold, wet and dreary afternoon to see the Packers move closer to championship with three games remaining on the schedule. Blood led his teammates in the celebration at a New York hotel that Sunday night that went into the early hours of the morning. Green Bay drank champagne while New York ate crow.

A few days later, some of the New York press would change their tune and compliment Lambeau and his Packers. One New York columnist, James Harrison, had this to say a few days after the Packers had defeated the Giants: *"Man and boy, these old eyes have been peering at football teams for more than a few years, but last Sunday we realized that all this time we 'ain't seen nothing.' What we fondly thought were the greatest football machines of our experience shriveled up and faded away in comparison with that matchless eleven which played at the Polo Grounds under the uneuphonius and uncollegiate name of the Green Bay Packers. Packers is right. They pack more of a kick than an Army mule. They pack as much explosive power as a can of TNT. There were folks in this world who believe that the New York Giants were the finest aggregation ever assembled on a gridiron, but if you have never seen the Green Bay Packers, to quote the song again, 'you ain't been nowhere and you ain't seen nothin.' To the naive chap who goes out to football games to see football — there are a few folks like that — the Packers' exhibition was a rare and delightful treat. Never have we seen football as good, never better ball-carrying, finer line play or more beautiful cooperation between the line and the back. These men knew how to play football. They were post-graduates in the school of the gridiron. Blocking, line charging, tackling, boxing the end, opening up holes, in all these fine points they were past masters. Strapping big fellows in their yellow jerseys, broad of shoulder and deep in chest, as sturdy and upstanding as young oaks, they had almost everything that a football team should have."*

With the Giants only losing one game, the Packers had to win their last game against the Bears at Wrigley Field in the final game of the season to gain the championship. Papa Bear and his boys never had a chance as Green Bay thoroughly dominated the Bears, 25 to 0. Completely overpowered, the Bears' one and only first down in the entire game came on a shifty 18-yard scamper by Red Grange. On nearly every other running attempt, Grange was stopped cold at the line. "It wasn't that the Bears didn't try," wrote *Chicago Tribune* sports scribe Wilfrid Smith. "They faced a team which had everything in a champion's repertoire."[48]

Lambeau had his first of six NFL championships and Green Bay began preparations for a Packer celebration before the whistle sounded the end of the game. The Monday evening *Press-Gazette* ran an eight column banner headline across the top of page one: **PACKERS WHIP BEARS — WIN NATIONAL TITLE.**

The team stayed at the Knickerbocker Hotel in Chicago Sunday night for a victory celebration party and then headed back to Green Bay by train the next afternoon. There would be another celebration on the train home. Johnny Blood described the hoopla in his interview with Richard Whittingham, "After a while, we began horsing around and I started throwing some wet napkins at Lavvie Dilweg. He was one of our ends, a big, tall, strong boy. He didn't like it a real lot and told me to stop. Of course, I didn't and he finally got up after me. Well, I took off down the aisle and he was chugging along trying to get his big hands on me. We'd been up near the front of the train, in the club car, and we just went racing through car after car, the people looking up wondering what the hell was going on. I kept razzing him all the way. And he kept coming. Well, when we got to the last car, he thought he had me, but I went out onto the rear platform. He kind of yelled in triumph as he came through the door. But I stepped up on the back railing and pulled myself up onto the roof of the train. I looked back down and you should have seen the look on his face. He just stared up in disbelief. Then I said, 'So long,' and ran on back up the train, on the roof, jumping from car to car as I went. Dilweg didn't follow me, of course. He had better sense than that. I went on past the club car, all the way to the engineer's cab. I surprised the hell out of him and the fireman when I climbed down from the roof, we were moving pretty fast at the time. I rode with them into town."[49]

"This story has been told many times, at least twice by John himself, that he went the entire length of the train, atop the cars, and finally dropped into the cab next to the engineer. But John admitted that it's not true. 'I went forward about seven or eight cars, just far enough to get past the Packers' car,' he said, 'and then I came down. I went forward, through the cars, all the way to the front. Then, when we stopped in Green Bay, I got out, ran up to the locomotive, climbed in next to the engineer, and let everybody think I'd made the whole trip on top of the train."'[50]

When the Packers pulled into Green Bay, they received an unprecedented welcome. Reportedly, 20,000 people bundled up in heavy coats and hats in the cold December night waiting for the team to arrive by special train. Flaming red flares lit up the tracks for miles leading to the Chicago & Northwestern train depot in Green Bay. Factory whistles blew, screeching sirens and car horns blared. People packed together, stumbling over each other trying to get close to the train and shouting at the top of their lungs to greet their heroes. Policemen had to push through the crowd to clear a path for the oncoming train. As Lambeau and the players looked out the train windows, they were shocked. They had expected a welcome home, but this mob scene was overwhelming. Thousands lined the streets, some were on top of roofs and boxcars, and in windows hoping to get a glimpse of the players. Paul Mazzoleni, a longtime Packer fan, who was then a teenager, remembers the wild celebration, "The chief of police allowed the bars to stay open all night," he said. "It was no holds barred. I remember being part of it. You couldn't get close to the railroad station. You were just part of the mob."

It took 15 minutes for the team to work their way through the crowd as they left the train and headed for a bus. Probably less than 1,000 of the 20,000 who turned out to greet the Packers actually saw the players. In the darkness there was a slight commotion in the sea of hats, and someone announced that the players were climbing into the bus. Their bright instruments identified the band coming through the crowd and the members of Battery B were also conspicuous. Each player got a round of applause as they became visible. Traffic was at a standstill for blocks in downtown Green Bay. Police and soldiers struggled to keep order. The players were eventually hustled into buses for a procession to City Hall where Lambeau was presented the key to the city and when asked to say a few words, he was so emotionally taken back it would be one of those rare times he could hardly speak. "It is pretty hard to say anything," said Lambeau. "This welcome is something that we didn't expect, and is a complete surprise. Speaking for the boys, I can say that they appreciate it and the only answer we can make is a championship again next year."

The next evening Green Bay threw a special banquet for the team at the Beaumont Hotel, complete with dinner, speeches and dancing. Andy Turnbull, now publisher of the *Press-Gazette*, presented each player with $220 from a $5,073 special fund that had been raised from Packer fans. The fund was started just weeks before and completed a few hours before the victory banquet. When Lambeau spoke to the more than 400 people in attendance that night, he had more to say than the night the team arrived in Green Bay. "I was given two of the greatest thrills of my life last night and tonight by the welcome tendered by Green Bay fans, and I know every other member of the team feels the same as I do," Lambeau beamed.

"When a city responds as it has done to our efforts, I'll say it certainly deserves a championship. It is going to take a lot of hard work, energy and the loyal support of all fans to give Green Bay another championship team next year. Other teams that won the championship always finished in the second division the following year, but we are going to do our best to break that precedent and if the fans are behind us we think we can do it."

Johnny Blood spoke on behalf of the players. "I'm in the greatest town in the world," he said, "and I'm glad to be here in Green Bay, the home of the perpetual fatted calf."[51]

Lambeau would have basically the same players for the 1930 season as he had the year before. The one significant addition that fall was young Arnold Herber, who had been a standout for Green Bay West High School before playing briefly for the University of Wisconsin and Regis College in Colorado. Herber would not be a major factor in the championship years of 1930 and 1931, but would go on to become a key performer for the Packers from 1933 through 1940. He would be inducted into the prestigious Pro Football Hall of Fame in Canton, Ohio in 1966.

Part Oneida Indian, the 20-year-old Herber had smaller hands and fingers that gave him a most unusual grip on the football. Instead of putting his entire hand around the end of the pigskin with his fingers on the laces and his thumb opposite, he cradled the ball in his palm with his fingers and thumb on the stitches. Instead of throwing, he actually heaved the ball. He was extremely accurate and could throw it a mile. He had a tough time, however, being accepted by some of the players. During his first season, some of the veterans were almost cruel in their treatment of the hometown rookie and nicknamed him "Dummy." Lambeau ordered this to stop. One veteran persisted within Lambeau's hearing and was immediately traded.

"Later nicknamed 'Flash,' Herber was known in high school primarily as a runner, but he grew to become the NFL's first great long passer. The ball was still rounder than the modern football, which came into the NFL in 1933."[52] Herber was proud of his ability to throw the football almost out of sight. Lambeau once said, "Herber is the best long passer ever." Another veteran coach, Clark Shaughnessy, later agreed: "Herber's touchdown passes can be as demoralizing as a Ruthian home run. He has the uncanny knack of arching a long pass so that the receiver simply races to the spot, makes the catch and speeds on without breaking stride."

During his first year with the Packers, Herber learned a passing lesson from a couple of veterans who played a costly practical joke on the young rookie. "One day in practice, Herber was firing his long throw, up to 80 yards on the fly, when two veterans, Mike Michalske and Johnny Blood, approached him. 'Rookie,' Michalske said, 'I'll bet you can't throw a football 100 yards.' Herber nodded. 'You're right, Mike,' he said. 'I guess 80 is about my limit.'

"'Mike means you can't throw the ball 100 yards, including the roll,' Blood said.

"Herber was interested now. 'You mean you'll give me the distance the ball bounces after it lands?' he asked.

"'That's right, kid,' Michalske said. 'We'll give you the roll. Johnny and I bet you $25 each that you can't throw the ball from one goal line to the other.'

"The bet was made.

"Herber hopped forward and threw, sidestepping to avoid crossing the goal line. The ball spiraled straight down the field, arching beautifully. It landed between the 20 and 15 and yard lines on the other end of the field, bounced backward and came to rest on the 25. Michalske and Blood collected $25 a piece after practice. Herber had learned a lesson. A long pass, properly thrown, describes a trajectory so that it lands nose forward and down, causing it to bounce back toward the thrower. Blood and Michalske, of course, knew this going in. Herber found out for $50, about a half of a game's salary for him then."[53]

In late September the Packers opened the 1930 season with a 14 to 0 win against the Chicago Cardinals in the recently enlarged City Stadium. Lambeau's father, Marcel, now chairman of the stadium grounds committee, had added another 2,000 grandstand seats. Marcel also had a special flagpole, painted blue, with a gold ball at the top, placed at a prominent spot inside the stadium. At that opening game, a flag proclaiming the Packers 1929 NFL champions was raised at a special ceremony.

Lambeau got the team off to a fast start, winning their first eight, running their consecutive win streak to 22 games spanning three seasons. Two of these eight wins were against the Chicago Bears. But the wins were not quite as satisfying because George Halas was no longer coaching the Bears. Constant bickering over the team's direction between Chicago Bears' co-owners George Halas and Dutch Sternaman had contributed to mediocre Bears' teams the past two years. For years it was said that Halas and Sternaman always took opposite sides in every minor argument at league meetings, but presented a united front whenever anything major was on the table. But, by 1929 their bickering had spread from league politics to how their own team was to be directed. The absence of a united front between its leaders split the team. The result was the worst year in the Bears' short history (4-9-2) underscored by a humiliating 40 to 6 loss to the cross-town Cardinals.

They resolved their differences by agreeing that neither would coach the team. In effect, they fired themselves, vowing to attend to their front-office knitting. Sternaman would sell his interest to Halas after the 1932 season and leave pro football for good. Halas would go on and on. For a new coach, the Bears tapped Ralph Jones, the head man at Lake Forest (Illinois) Academy and a leading proponent of the T-formation. While other pro teams lined up in the single wing, double wing or Notre Dame box like the Packers, the Bears under Jones continued to use their basic T, but with new refinements such as split ends and a man in motion in the backfield.

As the 1930 season dawned, a new legend emerged for the Bears — a bruising fullback and tackle out of the University of Minnesota named Bronko Nagurski. He stood 6 feet, 2 inches and carried 216 pounds. Running with his head down like a battering ram, he quickly became the league's top power runner. Such was his play that teammate Red Grange, who had the good fortune to face Nagurski only in practice, was led to comment, "When you hit him, it was like getting an electrical shock. If you hit him above the ankles, you were likely to get yourself killed." With Nagurski's muscle and Jones' strategic innovations leading the way, the Bears bounced back from a dismal 1929 season to finish 9-4-1 with five straight victories ending the campaign on a high note.

If football can be said to have a truly mythical figure, that figure is Bronko Nagurski. Coach Doc Spears of the University of Minnesota discovered him, so the story goes, when he asked directions of a boy plowing the fields at International Falls — without a horse. Nagurski responded by pointing the way — with the plow. Upon Nagurski's graduation in 1930, George Halas offered him $5,000 to play for the Chicago Bears. Halas recalled that he had never seen a more remarkable physical specimen.

Nagurski played seven years of the 60-minute game for the Bears, but turned to professional wrestling when Halas refused to raise his salary to $6,000. In 1943, at the age of 35, he was coaxed out of retirement to play tackle for Chicago. In the final game of the regular season, he took over at fullback, carrying the ball 17 times for 84 yards, scoring one touchdown and setting up two others. The Bears won over the Cardinals, 35 to 24, and Nagurski said, "That game gave me my greatest kick out of football." Grantland Rice, who observed that many coaches considered Nagurski the greatest player of all time, wrote, "He was a star end, a star tackle and a crushing fullback who could pass. I believe eleven Nagurskis could beat eleven Granges or eleven Thorpes." Nagurski and his Bears would have some epic battles with the Packers in the years ahead — battles that added handsomely to the illustrious Packer-Bear lore.

The Packers won enough games in 1930 to finish in first place again with a 10-3-1 record. Their popularity would continue to grow, particularly throughout Wisconsin. While the Green Bay *Press-Gazette* and the Milwaukee newspapers gave the team excellent coverage, radio would take Packer popularity to a new level. Home games were carried in live broadcasts by WHBY in Green Bay with Harold Shannon and Hall Lansing doing play-by-play announcing. It opened an entirely new promotion opportunity for the Packers that brought live action right into the living rooms of Wisconsinites.

Russ Winnie from WTMJ in Milwaukee began broadcasting Packer games back in 1929, but they were recreations that were handled in the station and were off a ticker tape with the play-by-play results. Winnie and WTMJ would broadcast the first road game when the Packers played the Bears in Chicago later that season. Also, in 1930, motion pictures of the first of two games at Wrigley Field were shown the next day at Green Bay's Fox Theater, located on Washington Street. After the Packers had clinched their second NFL championship in a row with a 6 to 6 tie against the

Portsmouth Spartans in mid-December, the team headed back to Green Bay to another celebration similar to the one they had the year before.

It was *déjà vu* for Lambeau and his players, with almost the same celebration schedule as the year before: thousands met the team at the Packers team train at the Chicago & Northwestern depot at 8:30 in the evening, paraded Lambeau and the team through the streets, held a reception open to the public at the Columbus Community Club auditorium, followed by dancing until midnight. A victory banquet and program were held at the Beaumont Hotel the following evening.

The parade, headed by a squadron of motorcycle police and the band, moved slowly through the streets, and crowds along the way shouted to the players in the buses. Lambeau's son, Donald, and other youngsters, some of them little more than knee-high, trudged along in the cold, gazing in rapt admiration at the heroes of the hour. Not one of them deserted along that line of march and an occasional salute from one of the players was reward enough for their efforts. Crepe paper in Packer colors decorated the Northwestern depot. The shrill tones of the steam whistle at the Fairmont Creamery company plant offered a victory salute as the parade passed by. The band preceded the players into the auditorium and played two numbers before the program opened.

Players sat in their dark overcoats on a stage in front of their adoring fans at the Community Club auditorium, while Marguerite and the players' wives sat in the first row of the balcony, directly across the stage. Amidst cheering and the popping of photographers' flash bulbs, Lambeau took center stage to speak to the audience. He was at his charming best. He expressed his appreciation and that of the team for the turnout of fans to welcome them home and said, "As long as you continue to show a spirit like this, we are going to try to have a winning team." In his introduction, Dr. Kelly said that Curly was entitled to the respect and admiration of all lovers of football in Green Bay, and that he was responsible for the fact that Green Bay had a football team capable of winning national championships. "Myself and the other cigar store coaches often abuse him," he said, "and we sometimes forget to praise him when he is most deserving of praise."

It was a rather interesting comment made by Dr. Kelly, the master of ceremonies that night. He and Lambeau had spent the previous year disagreeing about a number of issues when Kelly was

Packer president. Kelly stepped down from his president's role after just one year and was succeeded by Lee Joannes, a successful businessman in Green Bay much better suited for the president's position. Kelly stayed on the Packer board and for years was the team physician. Yet, he and Lambeau continued to be at odds and it was Kelly and a few other board members who much later wanted Lambeau fired.

For now, Lambeau was the center of adulation usually reserved for much higher dignitaries than a football coach. After all, this was Green Bay, and this was their hometown 'boy' who had brought them another professional football world championship. If there was anyone more esteemed in Wisconsin than young Lambeau at this time, they were certainly unknown to the media and general public. Intoxicating and overwhelming as it was, the entire process would repeat itself again the next year. No doubt, Lambeau's ego had to be inflated by his success and the excessive adulation pouring out from the people of Green Bay. It was the beginning of a growing ego that would get him into conflict with authority figures he would deal with in the years ahead.

Not all was rosy for Lambeau as he awaited the 1931 season. On April 1, the giant, tragic headlines were plastered in newspapers coast-to-coast. Knute Rockne was killed in a plane crash in Kansas. Lambeau had lost his mentor.

Rockne was Notre Dame's football coach, but he was much more: a celebrity whose face and voice were familiar to millions through magazines, newspapers and radio; a symbol and a beneficiary of the sports boom of the 1920s. Rockne had become synonymous with coaching. He raised the status of the profession and helped develop his team's nationwide following — millions of Irish and other Catholics, many of whom had never entered a college classroom.

Among Rockne's friends were such public figures as Will Rogers, Babe Ruth, Mayor Jimmy Walker of New York, Jack Dempsey, Bill Tilden, Bobby Jones and Red Grange. Lambeau considered himself among this list of Rockne's closest friends. Years after Lambeau had left Notre Dame, he and Rockne would stay in touch. Rock always urged Lambeau on: "Keep it up, boy, you're on to something big!" Rockne's death had a lasting affect on Lambeau, who later admitted to a friend, "Rock's death made me stop and think, life is short, you should live it to the hilt while you're here."

Lambeau continued to get favorable press from the Green Bay *Press-Gazette* even though George Calhoun was no longer sports editor. Calhoun, however, was still handling the reporting of road games and publicity for the Packers. "He originated the idea of writing a weekly newsletter about the Packers and mailing it to daily and weekly newspapers throughout the area. It was printed for free by an American Legionnaire at the Landsmann Printing Company, Fred Gronnert. Calhoun really came into his own notoriety when the Packers hit the big time and started traveling to major cities like Chicago, New York and Philadelphia. Calhoun could talk newspapermen's language, and in those days when professional football attracted little attention in prestigious papers like the New York *Times* or *Herald-Tribune,* he got more ink for the Packers than any other team in the league. Calhoun was always plugging Lambeau as a coaching genius wherever he went on tour."[54]

Young John Torinus worked with Calhoun at the *Press-Gazette* and had the opportunity to travel with Calhoun when the team made its annual swing through the East at Thanksgiving time playing the New York Giants, the Frankford Yellow Jackets on Thanksgiving and the Staten Island Stapletons the following Sunday. He would tell the story of one of their times together in his book, *Packer Legend*: "When Cal would arrive in New York City, he would order up cases of beer and a block of ice and fill up his bathtub with ice water and beer. He always brought along a daisy of Wisconsin cheddar cheese. Then he would get on the telephone to Art Daley and John Kieran of the New York *Times* and Red Smith at the New York *Herald-Tribune* and announce that the Packers were in town, the beer was in the tub, the cheese was on the dresser, so come on over. One evening after the Packers had lost a very tough game to the Giants, I was sitting in Cal's room helping him with a case of beer, which he had ordered up from the hotel commissary. We were only into our second bottle when he remarked he had better get a hold of 'the Belgian' because he knew how badly he was taking the afternoon's loss. He got on the phone to Lambeau and told him he had a case of beer in his room and invited him to come on down and help drown his sorrows. Lambeau did so, and my recollection is that Curly and I each drank about two or three bottles of beer and went to the case for another when we found it empty. Cal had finished off about 18 of those 24 bottles all by himself."[55]

Calhoun still had plenty to crow about in his Packers news releases in 1931. Few people were surprised to see the Packers win their third straight NFL championship. Lambeau had time-tested stars: Verne Lewellen, Johnny Blood, Red Dunn, Cal Hubbard, Mike Michalske and Lavvie Dilweg. To the returnees, Lambeau added veteran help in linemen Dick Stahlman and Rudy Comstock from the New York Giants and promising rookies Hank Bruder, Roger Grove and Milt Gantenbein. The Packers excelled both on offense and defense; their 291 points for the season were more than 100 better than any other NFL team, and the 87 points they allowed ranked as the league's second best. For the fourth year in a row, they intercepted as least 30 passes. They finished the season at 12-2-0 with an unprecedented third consecutive NFL championship.

By the end of 1931, Lambeau had definitely reached star status. His name was recognized not only in his home state of Wisconsin, but also around the entire nation by anyone who had even a slight interest in sports. Between Calhoun's publicity and his Packers' own accomplishments, Lambeau was being elevated to intoxicatingly lofty heights that enabled him to see far beyond Green Bay.

5

Tarnished Luster

Fame is fleeting. The glory and jubilation of three straight NFL championships soon faded into distant memory. Though it would be four years before Lambeau would achieve another title because of their record, the Packers should have been champions again in 1932. Ties did not count in the NFL standings in those days and although the Packers won more games (10-3-1) than any other team, they would finish in second place. The Bears finished first with seven wins, one loss and six ties. The Packers' string ended in 1932, but only because of the vagaries of the league's system of deciding championships by percentage.

Ties are rare today, but if they occur they are counted as half a win and half a loss. Today the Packers would have been champions. But 1932 was to be the last year Lambeau would even come close to the previous three years of success. The following year the team had their first losing season (5-7-1) since Green Bay joined the NFL. Dropping faster than the mercury in January, Lambeau's team was only one game above .500 the next year (7-6), before beginning to show promise with a solid 8-4 record in 1935. Making matters worse was the return of an old tormentor. George Halas was again the Bears' coach after a two-year absence to renew his bitter rivalry with Lambeau. The Bears were back on top again. Over the next four seasons, Halas' Bears dominated, winning six in a row from the Packers before Green Bay won both games in 1935.

There was a glimmer of hope, however, as Lambeau's gamble in signing Green Bay native Arnie Herber in 1930 was beginning to pay dividends. Herber came into his own in 1932 and continued to improve over the next nine years. He would eventually enter the Pro Football Hall of Fame. His teammates would tease the young, bushy-haired, part Indian his rookie season, calling him names, but were simply in awe of his passing skills later in his career. As a teenager in Green Bay, Herber sold programs to watch the Packers play. He eventually attended tiny Regis College in Denver, but he soon came home and worked as a handyman in the Packers' clubhouse. One day Lambeau, much to the amazement of the other players, decided to give Herber a tryout. Some of the players still saw Herber as the boy who ran errands at Packer camp. He was the butt of jokes and earned the nickname, "Dummy." The name stuck when Herber came back to the Packers from Regis College. One day, Lambeau solved that problem by giving Herber the wrong time for a practice session. Then, with Herber absent, Lambeau told the Packers: "Lay off the 'Dummy.' We're going to play football and this kid is going to win with us. I'll punch the nose of the first man who forgets that."

Herber was the NFL passing leader in 1932, 1934 and 1936. His career record shows 410 completions for 6,741 yards. While he was considered an outstanding passer in the 1930s, his statistics would not compare well to today's NFL quarterbacks. He completed about 45 percent of his passes and averaged about 120 passes a season, less than ten a game. Herber did win the league's first passing crown in 1932 and then added two more in the next four years. His passes accounted for 8,033 yards and almost 90 touchdowns. His best season came in 1936 when he completed 77 passes for 1,239 yards and eleven touchdowns.

Suddenly, Herber went from "Dummy" to "The Kid" and as respect and acceptance grew, his teammates called him "Flash." Nevertheless, he managed to get in Lambeau's doghouse. He continually fought a weight problem that irritated Lambeau. Then there was the "accident."

"On December 7, 1933, three days before the Packers met the Bears at Wrigley Field, he suffered serious injuries (in a car accident), but little damage to his reputation. Today, Herber, in all likelihood, would have been arrested by the police, slammed by the media, and perhaps suspended by the NFL. Herber was involved in the accident at 4:30 in the morning the Thursday before the game and was unable to play the following Sunday. He dislocated his right hip, injured his right forearm and sustained a four-inch laceration on the left side of his face when he drove into the rear of a truck near Green Bay. The *Press-Gazette* carried a story about the accident the day it occurred, but made no further mention of it before the game. Typical of the slanted coverage in the *Press-Gazette* in those days, there also was no mention in the story about whether Herber might have been driving under the influence of alcohol. The loss of Herber left the Packers with only 17 players for the Bears game. Thirteen of them played, including nine who went the full 60 minutes, as the Packers lost, 7 to 6."[56]

1932 saw Lambeau land another key player, one who would go on to greatness as a Packer and also be inducted into the Pro Football Hall of Fame. Hinkle was the name. Brute force was the game. Clarke Hinkle joined the Packers out of Bucknell College and played with them through 1941 when he went into the service. At 200 pounds, he was Green Bay's answer to the Bears' 238-pound Bronko Nagurski. Hinkle was not especially big at 5 feet, 11 inches, but he was one of the most bruising hitters either rushing or tackling in the 1930s. "When he hit you," Ken Strong, legendary New York Giants' back once said, "You knew you were hit. Bells rang and you felt it all the way down to your toes."

"No one in the whole league ever bruised me more than Hinkle did," said John Sisk, who played halfback for the Bears in the midst of Hinkle's career. "After we had played the Packers, I'd be black and blue down to my toenails," Sisk recalled. "All I'd want was peace and quiet. Hinkle had a lot of leg action. I broke my shoulder twice tackling Mister Hinkle." Actually, there was no part of football at which Hinkle did not excel. He blocked savagely, both on runs and in protecting the passer. He was the workhorse runner and the leading ground gainer of his day. He carried the ball 1,171 times in ten league seasons and gained 3,860 yards, which is still the Packers' fourth best career rushing total.

An All-American running back from Bucknell, where he led the nation scoring as a sophomore and led in touchdowns as a senior, Hinkle became a Packer in a roundabout way through Lambeau's persistence and eye for talent. Hinkle would recall the circumstance: "When I was a senior at Bucknell, we played Fordham in New York on a November afternoon. Before that game, I had received a letter from the New York Giants to be a guest the following day when they were playing the Green Bay

Packers. So after our game, I stayed over and with the Bucknell line coach, went to the Polo Grounds and watched the Packer-Giant game. I was more impressed with the Green Bay Packers than I was with the New York Giants, so during the second half we went over and sat on their bench. My line coach said, 'Maybe we can get more money from the Packers.' Of course, Curly Lambeau, who happened to be losing at the moment, wasn't about to be interested in a guy from a small college like me. So I never got to meet him that day. One thing I do remember about that game was that a fellow they had on their club by the name of Cal Hubbard impressed me. He stood about 6 feet, 5 inches and weighed about 250 pounds. I thought I might be better off playing on his side than playing against him. Later I was selected for the East-West game, and I had a pretty good day and got the award after the game. Well, lo and behold, it wasn't an hour after the game and we were back in our hotel; Jim McMurray, who was an All-American player from Pitt, was my roommate, and we were there having a little drink. There was a knock on the door and there was Curly Lambeau with a contract in his hands. He scouted those games every year and often picked up players from the East-West game. So I signed a contract, $125 a game."[57]

Like so many of the players Lambeau would scout, recruit and sign to a Packer contract in those years, Hinkle wanted to play in a smaller city with more of a college town spirit. "Coming from a small town in Ohio, Hinkle fit right into the village-type atmosphere of Green Bay. 'I thought Green Bay would be like a college town with a lot of college spirit, and it was. They took their football seriously in Green Bay. If we won a game we were in all the bars that night and never bought our own drinks. We had a ball! Lambeau would say, 'The lid's off; just don't get thrown in jail.' But if we lost a ball game we never left the hotel. People were mad. If we had to leave the hotel we would go down the alleys," Hinkle remembered.

"But the small town atmosphere was the convincer for Hinkle: 'I also liked the idea of playing in a small town. I figured with a small town like that, everybody knowing everybody, they would have pretty good spirit, like a college. And besides that, they'd been the NFL champions for three straight years. When I went to Green Bay, I found we were accepted right into the social life of the town and became part of the community. It was the first time I had ever had a chance to make any money. We were the children of the

Depression.'

"Hinkle played the linebacker on defense where his encounters with the Bears' Bronko Nagurski were nothing short of barbaric duels."[58] "Hinkle has the unique if painful distinction of being the only man ever to knock Nagurski out of a game. It happened as a result of one of their frequent bone-shattering collisions, and in that particular one the Bronk came out of it with a broken nose and a broken rib."[59] "Hinkle and Naguski both played fullback and linebacker, and they met head-on many times. Perhaps their most resounding contact occurred in a game at Green Bay. In those days, punting on third down with long yardage was not uncommon. The Packers had the ball on their 20, third down and 14 to go, and Hinkle went back in punt formation. Instead of kicking, though, Hinkle ran to his right and Nagurski moved up to meet him. Nagurski, in tackling or blocking, rarely left his feet. 'He just ran through the man and rooted him out with his huge forearms,' a teammate said. Nagurski did not wrap his arms around the runner, he merely blocked him with a shoulder or hip, with his forearms or body, depending on the situation. On this occasion, Hinkle neared the sideline. Nagurski tried to block him out of bounds, but instead Hinkle lowered his shoulder and smashed it into Nagurski's face. Hinkle ran into Nagurski and over him, stayed inbounds and reached midfield for a first down before he was brought down from behind. They didn't wear facemasks or guards in those days. Nagurski had to be helped from the field. He suffered a broken nose, bruised ribs, a fractured hip and a wrenched shoulder."[60] Hinkle recalled the hit, "I saw Nagurski coming over to really nail me to the cross, but I had the ball and knew what I was going to do. So, before I went out of bounds at the sideline, I cut back in on him and caught him square with my shoulder and head. He knocked me back pretty near five yards. I sat there for a few seconds, because it really shook me up. Then I looked over at old Bronk and his nose was all over his face and he was in a helluva shape. Nagurski had a broken nose and later they found he had a broken rib too. George Halas was really mad about it, and he said I played Bronk dirty. I don't know how he got that. I was carrying the ball. I couldn't be doing anything dirty."[61] After their playing days were over, Hinkle and Nagurski remained friends. Hinkle would say: "Nagurski was a great guy and we have become real good friends. He was my presenter when I was inducted into the Hall of Fame."

Hinkle's dedication to football and to the Packers was legendary. Lambeau could get him fired up before a game, but Hinkle was so emotional he would sometimes sit by his locker and weep after a loss. "I've never known a man who wanted to win like 'Hink' did," said a teammate. "Before a game he would get glassy-eyed, he'd be so fired up and eager to play. After the game, if we lost, he'd sit at his locker and cry like a baby. He didn't know how to lose."[62]

Although Hinkle would be one of Lambeau's toughest, most productive players for nearly ten years, the two were never close. Hinkle would say about Lambeau: "I never liked him. Didn't really respect him either, but he was paying me and I gave him a thousand percent every time I played football for him. There is one thing I do respect about Lambeau. Whenever we went out on the road, he'd make us wear suits, coats and ties. If we were in Green Bay, he wouldn't let us smoke in public because the people might think less of us. When we would leave Green Bay on the train, we had two Pullmans and a dining car. We'd stay in the finest hotels on the road, and he'd sign the check so we could eat at the hotel. He wanted us to get the proper food, and he was trying to project the image that we were educated people who happened to be playing sports."[63]

It was not only the players' appearance that was important to Lambeau. It was about this time in his life that his own physical appearance and how he dressed became almost an obsession. Now that his picture appeared in national magazines like the *Saturday Evening Post* and *Life*, as well as newspapers around the country, his clothing became extremely important. Known as the best-dressed coach in the NFL, Lambeau even took his dedication to dress to the sidelines during games. He often wore spiffy slacks, smart looking sport coats, shirts and ties as he marched up and down the sidelines, usually with a cigarette dangling from his lips. Some said it looked like he was acting out a character in a movie. He was constantly concerned how he looked on and off the field.

Packer players from that period would all say Lambeau was a great organizer, but they were less impressed with his ability to design plays. They were often quoted about his skills as a football strategist, and Hinkle had his own opinion: "Lambeau learned his football from the players who played for him. Back in the early years, when he had Cal Hubbard, Mike Michalske and Jug Earp and those guys up there, he would put a play up on the board and some of his blocking assignments were impossible. Of course, the players would pick the play apart and get him straightened out on it. Down through the years with this happening to him, he became a good football coach."[64]

Hinkle told the story in an interview about how Lambeau once designed a defense to stop Halas and the Bears with their T formation: "Lambeau went to the library one day in Green Bay to look for a defense in one of the old books on early football. You see, the T formation was actually one of the oldest in football history. Anyway, Lambeau found one from about 1890, a seven-spear defense, I think they called it. They lined up with seven linemen, then a fullback, like a linebacker, two halfbacks and a safety. We used it against the Bears that day in 1941. We beat the Bears, 16 to 14."[65]

Almost every Packer who played for Lambeau remembered how tight-fisted he was when it came to negotiating their salary at contract time. The Packers were always fighting a tight budget and for decades would experience financial problems. Lambeau's customary player contract in the 1930s averaged $125 a game, or about $1,700 a year. The star Packer performers commanded as much as $200 a game while some of the top headliners in the NFL would get between $300 and $500 a game.

While the Packers were narrowly missing a fourth consecutive NFL championship in 1932, the Green Bay Football Corporation put together a "Coach Lambeau Day" during the final home game of the season. Marguerite and Donald, now twelve years old, were on the field with Curly at halftime when he received gifts and congratulatory comments from city dignitaries, as well as retired Packer players. It would be the last time Marguerite and their son would be part of any official Packer celebration that involved Curly. Rumors and gossip about Curly's involvement with other women began to circulate in Green Bay. Problems began to surface in Lambeau's marriage and were magnified during a trip the Packers took to the West Coast and Hawaii for an exhibition tour after the 1932 reason.

The Hawaiian excursion had its origin when Johnny Blood had a conversation with Ernie Nevers, who had played pro ball for several years, but was now retired. "They had a few drinks together and Nevers mentioned that there was a lot of interest in Hawaii bringing over a professional team for post-season exhibition games. Nevers had been approached about it, but had decided against going. Blood filed the information away."[66]

At the end of the Packer season in 1932, Blood decided as long as he had nothing else going on, he might see if Hawaii would have any interest in having the Packers play some exhibition games. "He sent a telegram to the sports editor of a Honolulu newspaper, *The Honolulu Star Bulletin,* asking if anyone in Honolulu would be interested in bringing the Packers over for post-season play. Within four hours, a telegram came back, telling him to contact a man named Scotty Shuman. Blood wired Shuman, who asked how much money the Packers would want to play two games. Blood took the telegram to Lambeau. 'Here's something we can do after the season,' he told the coach. Lambeau decided he wanted $9,000 plus expenses for the trip. Blood promptly wired Shuman that the Packers would play the two games in Hawaii for $10,000 plus a cut of the gate receipts. Shuman agreed."[67]

The Packers also agreed. Lee Joannes accepted the invitation on behalf of the Packers. Four days after the end of the season, Lambeau and 17 of his players got on a train and headed for Los Angeles on December 13, 1932. They would travel by ship to Hawaii. The *Press-Gazette* couldn't afford to send any reporters along to cover the exhibition so Blood became the onsite "reporter" covering the highlights of the trip. In an interview with Ralph Hickok, Blood recalled how he almost missed the train out of Green Bay that December morning. Blood explained he had spent the night before with a stripper and was racing to the train station because they both had overslept. "As they were driving to the rail-road depot in her car, a policeman stopped him. By the time Blood explained who he was and where he was going, they couldn't make the train on time. The train had waited for a couple of minutes, but finally the conductor told Lambeau they couldn't wait any longer. Lambeau nodded. They would go to California without Blood. The train pulled out, but there was a car stopped on the tracks at the first intersection. Blood had put it there. The train had to stop for the temporary obstruction. Blood kissed his girlfriend goodbye and climbed aboard. 'I could see that Lambeau wasn't happy,' Blood told Hickok. 'But he didn't say anything. Nobody did. I was pretty popular because I had arranged the Hawaii trip.' Blood became even more popular when a friend of his got aboard at Tucson with several gallons of moonshine. 'From then on, we had a merry trip.' The trip to Hawaii was sponsored by the Matson Steamship Lines, which had a virtual monopoly on passenger and freight traffic to and from the island, in addition to owning the Royal Hawaiian Hotel in Honolulu."[68]

Lambeau, Blood and the rest of the Packers had the run of the ship during the five and a half days it took to get to Honolulu. Once the ship got outside the three-mile limit where drinking was permitted, the bar opened. As Blood would say later, "The Packers were pretty well known with those three championships. We had no trouble at all making acquaintances. We had a ball."[69]

While the games were to be an exhibition, Lambeau took them seriously. He had his team practice at the University of Hawaii playing field, and then had them transferred to Waikiki beach and ordered them to take a swim in the ocean. That was the first day they arrived. He then took them to a hotel and checked in. They practiced three more days before the game, and then played the University of Hawaii college team before a crowd of 13,000, beating them, 19 to 13. A few days later, the Packers beat another group of Honolulu all-stars, 32 to 0.

Just before the team made the return trip to California, Blood consumed a good deal of a popular and potent Hawaiian drink known then as Okolehao. (Mark Twain wrote about it, saying, "It turns a man's skin to white fish scales that are so tough a dog might bite him and he would not know it till he read about in the papers.") They had been out to sea for a few hours when some of the players noticed Blood was not with the rest of the team. After searching the deck and not finding him on that dark and windy night, Hinkle and a teammate happened to check the stern of the ship.

"Hinkle remembered: 'We turned white. We froze. Blood was outside the safety railing on the extreme stern end of the ship. He was hanging onto the flagpole. There he was, in the middle of that pitch-black night with the ship pitching and he was swinging around that flagpole. He didn't even know he was in any danger.' With the help of a couple of crewmen, Hinkle rescued Blood. 'If he'd have dropped off that stern,' Hinkle said later, 'nobody would have ever found him.'"[70]

The Packers took the luxury liner, *Maui,* back to the States, docking in San Francisco. The city's mayor, Angelo Rossi, greeted Curly and his Packers. Blood, who had too much to drink on the ship and suffering from a hangover, actually passed out in Rossi's office. Ah, but for Mr. Blood, this was only a slight delay in his ongoing party. When the team checked into their hotel, Blood put a hit on Lambeau for a cash advance because he wanted to make a side trip to Catalina before their next exhibition game. Lambeau refused and went up to his hotel room. Blood would tell Hickok: "I was mad. I had set up the Hawaiian tour. I even got him more money than he had asked for. He was really surprised when I gave him the check from Shuman because I hadn't told him about the deal I had arranged. I figured he ought to give me a cut, but he didn't. So I thought he at least owed me an advance.

"Blood thought about it for a while and called Lambeau on a house phone. Lambeau refused again. Blood thought about it some more, then went up and banged on Lambeau's door. 'For once I'm going to know exactly where you are,' Lambeau said. 'You're going to have to stay right here in this hotel because I'm not going to give you any money. I don't want you to call again and I don't want you to knock on this door again.' Lambeau's room was on the eighth floor. Blood found out from a chambermaid that there was an unoccupied room across an airshaft from Lambeau's, and he charmed her into letting him in. The airshaft was about twelve feet across. Blood opened the window and climbed out on the ledge in the drizzly weather. At that moment, Mike Michalske happened to look out of his window, a few floors below and saw Blood. Michalske opened his window. 'Is that you up there, Johnny Blood?' he called. 'It's me, Mike,' Blood replied. 'What are you doing?' Michalske asked. 'Curly wants me to discuss our strategy for the game, so I'm going to his room,' Blood answered, and leaped across the airshaft onto the ledge outside Lambeau's window. The window was unlocked. Blood opened it and climbed in. Lambeau awoke, startled out of his wits to see Blood standing beside his bed. He pointed to a pair of trousers draped over a chair. 'My wallet's in there,' Lambeau said. 'Take all the money you need. Just don't ever do anything like this to me again.' So, Blood enjoyed himself in Catalina after all. 'After 20 years,' he says, 'Lambeau laughed about it.' But he was not amused at the time."[71]

Ernie Nevers, a player who had been a star with the Chicago Cardinals, put together a team on the Pacific Coast that was called the Pacific Coast All-Star squad. They played the Packers before a crowd of 30,000. The Packers lost, 13 to 6. With the exhibition tour over, most of the players returned to their homes except Lambeau and Blood. Blood returned to Hawaii, and Lambeau remained in Los Angeles for another two weeks. There he visited with a number of Hollywood personalities he had met on his scouting trips to the West Coast in previous years. He also had several meetings with screenplay writers and movie directors. There was talk that Lambeau could become an advisor on some movies being filmed that had to do with football. There was also the rumor that Lambeau was seeing an actress, Myrna Kennedy. A movie studio had "loaned" her to the Packers during their stay in California, and she became their official tour guide. She sat on the Packers' bench during the game against the Pacific Coast All-Star team. Pictures of her sitting next to Lambeau appeared in the *Press-Gazette* and other newspapers across the country. The collective eyebrows of the conservative Green Bay populace began to rise. Marguerite was finding the situation somewhat embarrassing. It is believed that during this time Lambeau also met a young and vivacious blond, Susan Johnson, who had recently been a Miss California contestant. This relationship would eventually turn out to be more than casual.

1933 brought a new NFL season and several new rules geared not only to open up the game for more scoring but also reduce the number of tie games. Standing to benefit from these changes was Curly Lambeau. One rule change proposed and pushed by Lambeau to aid his passing attack made it legal to throw from anywhere behind the line of scrimmage instead of the mandatory but difficult to enforce distance of at least five yards back. Halas, Lambeau, Steve Owen and the league's other coaches quickly learned to use the less restrictive rule to create clever, razzle-dazzle offenses featuring forward passing as a major weapon. For the first time, professional football would have more wide-open fan appeal than the college game.

Less spectacular, but equally important in opening up the game, was the rule that moved the ball ten yards in from the sidelines on any play within five yards of the out-of-bounds line. No longer forced to waste a down just to bring the ball back to the center of the field, offenses could concentrate on the main order of business — getting the ball into the end zone. Another change in the playing rules brought the goalposts back to the goal lines where they had been stationed until 1927. The ten-yard difference brought a spectacular increase in the number of field goals tried and made. In addition, the NFL made two major decisions: to start keeping official individual and team statistics and to stage a championship game between the two best teams.

League owners, acting on a proposal by Bert Bell, founder-coach of the Philadelphia Eagles and later the NFL commissioner, had decided to set up two divisions with a championship playoff game between the division champions after the season. The 1933 Packers were part of the five-team Western Division with the Portsmouth Spartans, Chicago Bears, Chicago Cardinals and Cincinnati Reds. The Eastern Division included the New York Giants, Brooklyn Dodgers, Boston Redskins, Philadelphia Eagles and Pittsburgh Pirates.

As positive as the rule changes were, they didn't help Lambeau in 1933. Sadly, his team fell to 5-7-1, and Lambeau endured his first losing as their captain and coach. Things went south even before the season got underway. A fan, Willard J. Bent, drank too much and fell from the wooden stands at City Stadium in 1931 and was taken to a nearby hospital. He then sued the club for $25,000, which the club did not have at the time. Finally, in July 1933, he was awarded a judgment of $5,200. In the meantime, the company insuring the Packers, Southern Surety, went into bankruptcy. The Packers themselves then went into the friendly receivership of Frank Jonet, who later was treasurer of the corporation. They had debts totaling $12,300 and no cash reserves. A letter to the bankruptcy court from attorneys Gerald Clifford and LaVerne Dilweg, written on July 27, 1933, described the Packers as a non-profit charitable organization. The letter stated the Packers were a "charitable institution...for the purpose of furthering the interests of the city of Green Bay, advertising it and the community, and developing community spirit."

On August 15, 1933, the Green Bay Packers petitioned the circuit court to appoint a receiver for the corporation "in behalf of all creditors." Frank Jonet got the nod. The exhibition game tour to Hawaii and the West Coast was supposed to bring the club additional cash, but it did not bring enough because sponsors failed to make good on their financial guarantees. Lee Joannes loaned the club $6,000 to pay off its bills, became the chief creditor and would guide the Packers through receivership and eventual solvency. Joannes made his case for the club in an article that appeared in the *Press-Gazette: "The Green Bay Football Corporation is solvent and, if given a chance, will work out of its present situation. Unfortunately, the insurance company which has been carrying our public liability insurance for the last twelve years and which has always been rated as a high grade concern, like many other concerns during the last few years, got into serious difficulties, leaving us without any protection in defending the lawsuit which resulted in a judgment being obtained against us. The amount of this judgment was such that we will be unable to pay it at the present time, because of two very unprofitable years of operation, due not only to business conditions, but unfavorable weather, which is a big factor in this game. The Packer team, an institution in Green Bay, has brought more advertising to this city and for that matter to Wisconsin, than any other medium. In these days (sic) of stress and uncertainty, the club and the management need more than ever the support of all of the loyal fans of this community. In a few days, the season ticket selling campaign will be underway, and while we realize that many will have to stretch a point to buy tickets this year, we are hopeful that the sale will surpass that of last season. It seems certain that the club will be a strong contender for national championship honors, and there will be plenty of thrills and excitement for the fans this fall. Let us all get behind this marvelous club and assure the continuance of professional football in Green Bay."*

It was one more example of the dogged determination of several businessmen of Green Bay during that time. They often would do whatever it took to keep their team financially viable enough to compete in the NFL. While the Packers were experiencing their first losing season in 1933, to add insult to injury, Lambeau was also starting to receive some mild criticism from the *Press-Gazette*. Art Bystrom, its sports editor, and even George Calhoun were questioning his game strategy and were critical of his supporting a Packer home game in Milwaukee.

In October of that losing season, the Packers started a tradition when they played the New York Giants in Milwaukee's Borchert Field, a minor league baseball stadium. A crowd of 12,467 jammed into the old wooden ballpark to see the Packers lose 10 to 7. In spite of the good turnout, conditions were so bad at Borchert Field that Lambeau swore he would never return. The next summer in 1934, Oliver Kuechle, a sports reporter for the *Milwaukee Journal*, arranged a meeting between Packer officials and Ralph Ammon, the manager of the State Fair. As a result of that meeting, the Packers decided to play two games a year for the next three years at State Fair Park, which held more than 32,000 fans. The capacity of City Stadium was 22,370. The Packers continued to play a few games every year at Milwaukee State Fair Park into the 1950s. In 1939, league officials even forced the Packers to play the NFL championship game in Milwaukee. The Packers beat the Giants, 27 to 0, drawing 32,279 fans and brought in a record gate of more than $80,000. However, playing games in Milwaukee did not go over well with the Green Bay fans. They began to raise their objections and their howls of discontent were printed in the *Press-Gazette*. Lambeau was beginning to feel some heat for the first time.

After the 1933 season, Lambeau returned to the West Coast to scout college players who would be playing in bowl games. When he returned in January of 1934, he dropped a bombshell on Marguerite. He told her he had fallen in love with another woman, the young (age 25) and attractive model, Susan Johnson. He told Marguerite he wanted a divorce, leaving her devastated and heart-broken. She had heard the rumors of Curly's indiscretions and was well aware of the distance between them that had grown in recent years, but divorce was most difficult for her to comprehend. While not nearly as common as it is today, divorce was considered a stigma in that era. Besides, as a devout Catholic, divorce was unthinkable for Marguerite.

The teachings of the Catholic Church that Marguerite faithfully followed stated, "that marriage is indissolvable, even on account of adultery."[72] She was terribly disappointed in Curly. Their son, Donald, became extremely upset. He couldn't believe his parents would split. He became angry with his father who also had been his hero. How could he leave them for someone else? He felt abandoned by his own father and never really forgave him for leaving them. Donald's resentment would grow through the years. Though Curly made an attempt after the divorce to spend time with him, the animosity between them increased and their relationship would eventually totally disintegrate.

A note, handwritten in pencil, by Marguerite was found in her belongings after her death. It begins, *"You ask me what I think of the mess and my plans for the future."* She wrote it was a shock to learn of his love for another. The note described how her feelings were hurt and that she felt she had given him 15 years of the best time in her life. She asked that he provide financially for her and Donald. There were "no plans" on her part, she added. The scribbled note, having now grown yellow with age, left no doubt of her sadness, despondency and distress. There is no way to know if this letter was ever mailed — if it was a draft of a letter — or if Marguerite was just expressing her grief.[73] The divorce was granted in early 1934, after 15 years of marriage, on grounds of "cruel and inhumane treatment." Curly was 36 years old and Marguerite was 35. Marguerite would never marry again and nor did she speak negatively about Curly for the rest of her life. She would outlive Curly by nearly 35 years.

Lambeau's personal troubles were to extend beyond his home. When the news got out that Lambeau was divorcing his high school sweetheart for a Miss California type, his stock began to drop with the Green Bay locals. They didn't take kindly to an action they considered a betrayal — to Marguerite and to the community of Green Bay. It was the beginning of a small split between Lambeau and Green Bay citizens that would widen through the years ahead. Lambeau's celebrity status, while growing nationally, was beginning to tarnish locally. Lambeau would marry Susan Johnson later in the summer of 1935 and divide his time between the Los Angeles area and Green Bay. He rented an apartment for the two of them in DePere, a suburb of Green Bay, where they lived during the summer and throughout the Packer season.

The Packers' 1934 season was mediocre at 7-6, but the breakthrough for major improvement and a return to championship status would take place in the months just after the completion of the schedule. When the season was over, Lambeau, along with his new wife, headed to the West Coast again to scout the Rose Bowl game between Alabama and Stanford for potential Packer players. What he found there would have a dramatic impact on Lambeau lore and the Packers for the next ten years.

When he arrived in Pasadena, California, Lambeau was invited to attend an Alabama practice session by their coach, Frank Thomas, who was a former player for Notre Dame. Alabama had several days to work out before the game. One Alabama player stood out. Immediately. A lanky kid named Don Hutson, who had earned All-American honors. Lambeau knew Hutson would be a tremendous asset to the Packers' passing game. "I'd always dreamed of an end who could do the things Hutson did. And out at practice for the Rose Bowl in Pasadena that day, there he was," Lambeau said later. The 6 foot, 1 inch end was fast and could catch anything thrown reasonably close to him. When Hutson snared two touchdown passes in the Rose Bowl game on January 1, 1935 to help Alabama beat the previously unbeaten Stanford, 29 to 13, Lambeau knew he had to do anything he could to get this kid to Green Bay.

Since there was no college draft of players at that time, NFL teams could go after any graduating college player they wanted and the highest bidder usually won. Lambeau contacted Hutson a few days after the Rose Bowl game with a contract offer only to find out another team beat him to the punch. The owner of the Brooklyn Dodgers, John "Shipwreck" Kelly, had visited with Hutson on the Alabama campus before the Rose Bowl and made a contract offer. Kelly was a colorful character from a wealthy Kentucky family who had played pro ball before he became the owner of the Brooklyn team when he was still in his early 20s.

"An All-American halfback at the University of Kentucky who was dubbed in his college yearbook as 'the fastest man in the South' because he ran the hundred-yard dash in 9:8, 'Shipwreck' Kelly was equally adroit, he quickly proved, at moving through New York's cafe society. He was a fine football player. He led the NFL in pass receptions in 1933 in fact, but his name was found more often in the social columns than on the sports pages of the 1930s. His closest friends included people like Dan Topping, Jock Whitney and Bing Crosby. He dated Tallulah Bankhead and various Broadway starlets."[74]

Hutson told him he would sign if Kelly would match any offer made from another pro team. Several teams, including George Halas of the Bears (he dropped out at $75 a game), made offers, but when the bidding got too high, everyone dropped out except Lambeau and Kelly. The two kept bidding and matching each other's offer for Hutson, who would recall: "Finally it was just Curly and Shipwreck. Each time, Curly would make an offer, I'd wire Shipwreck and he would match it. Well, it finally got up to $300 a game, quite a bit of money in those days. When Curly gave me his offer of $300, I sent the wire to Shipwreck, but I didn't hear back from him. Curly kept calling me and after about a week went by I sent another wire to Shipwreck, and I didn't hear anything from him again. Finally, Curly sent me a contract and I just went ahead and signed it. The day I put it in the mail, Shipwreck showed up in Tuscaloosa. He said that he had been in Florida on vacation and that he had just gotten the wires forwarded to him. He wanted to match the $300 offer. I told him that I couldn't because I had already signed with Curly and had put the contract in the mail that morning because I hadn't heard from him. Shipwreck said, 'Don, I think you at least owe me a chance to meet it.' I said, 'Well, hell, I can't. As I told you, I already signed one and it's gone off.' 'Don't worry,' he said. 'Sign a contract with me, too, and let me worry about it.' Well, I felt I did owe it to him after our agreement.

So I signed one with Shipwreck, too. Later, both contracts were sent to Joe Carr, the NFL commissioner then, to decide which one was valid. The Green Bay contract got to him before Shipwreck's did so he ruled I should go to Green Bay. And it was probably the biggest break I ever got in football. Green Bay had a real good passer in Arnie Herber, and Lambeau was a very pass-oriented coach. He emphasized passing as well as running and it was obviously a real break for me to end up there."[75]

"Carr received two contracts in the mail, both signed by Don Hutson — one with the Green Bay Packers and the other with the Brooklyn Dodgers. Carr determined the contract received earlier would be honored. All incoming mail was stamped on arrival. Lambeau's had arrived at 8:30 in the morning and Kelly's at 8:47. 'It's lucky I sent my letter special delivery,' Lambeau said later. 'I had signed Hutson for $300 a game. I didn't believe in season contracts. One of the big selling points was that we had a good passer and Brooklyn didn't.' So Hutson belonged to the Packers — by 17 minutes."[76] Once Lambeau got Hutson to Green Bay for $300 a game, he did not want the other players to know how much he was paying the rookie, which was close to double what many of the veterans were getting. To keep Hutson's salary a secret, Lambeau set up an arrangement with two banks in Green Bay to each pay $150 so that word would not get out what Hutson was getting.

A soft-spoken man of a few words, Hutson, who was Arkansas' first Eagle Scout, would go on to an amazing career with the Packers. In spite of doubts whether someone with his slight and skinny build could survive the rough-tough world of pro football, "it wasn't long before Hutson's presence changed entire defensive strategies. In his second game as a member of the Packers, Hutson scored on an 83-yard pass from Arnie Herber against the Bears. He finished his career with an NFL-record of 99 touchdown receptions. When he retired in 1945 after eleven brilliant seasons, he led all receivers with 488 career catches. He was inducted into the Pro Football Hall of Fame in 1963, the same year as Lambeau.

"As a prime target for Herber and later Cecil Isbell, Hutson could outmaneuver and outrace virtually every defender in the league. Measures such as double coverage and triple-teaming were unheard of until Hutson entered the NFL."[77] He was a gift from the future, a premonition in helmet and cleats. To say Don Hutson was ahead of his time is well beyond understatement. Hutson, known as the man who forever changed the NFL, was professional football's first great receiver, a pass-catching pioneer who helped map the course the game would follow through the second half of the twentieth century.

"Hutson was almost three times as productive as any of his peers. No other player in football history can make that claim. To be sure, Hutson was helped by Lambeau's devotion to the pass and by the fact that a good many talented players left the NFL during World War II. However, his feats are still astonishing. And like all players in the days before free substitution, Hutson also played saftey on defense. In his final four seasons, he intercepted 23 passes. He also was the Packers' kicking specialist. In 1941, he was the NFL's most valuable player."[78] In his early years with the club, Hutson also played defensive end and played it well considering that he never weighed more than 178 pounds. But, as the Packer offense was built more and more around him, Lambeau decided not to risk him in the path of powerful pro blocking on the line and kept him in the defensive secondary.

"He was elusive and fast, the rare athlete who could find an extra gear and explode past helpless defensive backs. Hutson also could out-leap most defenders, and his big hands and long reach turned poorly thrown passes into highlight-film touchdowns. Packer fans marveled at the sight of Hutson pulling in long passes and loping gracefully into the end zone. Hutson became the centerpiece for Lambeau's innovative quick-strike offense from 1935 to 1945. Lambeau would tailor his offensive strategy and pass patterns to exploit the strong arm of Herber and Hutson's outstanding receiving ability. Over his eleven-year career, he led the league in receptions eight times and touchdown catches on nine occasions. His season receiving yardage totals consistently topped opposing team totals and most of that yardage was compiled while battling double- and triple-threat coverage, unheard of strategy at the time."[79]

While the players' equipment such as pads and helmets was much improved over what they used in the 1920s, Hutson would modify his for more speed and agility. He had his shoulder pads cut down so they were much smaller and less restrictive. In order to give him more speed and maneuverability, he did not wear hip pads. Later in the season when the Wisconsin weather turned bitter cold, Hutson would stuff *Saturday Evening Post* and *Colliers* magazines under his long underwear before games because he never did get used to the frigid Green Bay weather.

However, he did get used to Green Bay where he became an idol and a financially successful businessman. Since he was married when he came to Green Bay, Hutson was anxious to settle down. While still playing, he owned a bowling alley, a cocktail bar, and a finance business. Hutson also owned a Kaiser-Fraser automobile distributorship for 32 northern counties in Wisconsin at a time during the war when it was almost impossible to get any make of a car except a Kaiser-Fraser. The bowling establishment had 20 alleys, and a downstairs cocktail lounge with a huge bar shaped like a football. He had a big picture above the bar of Lambeau kneeling with a ball beyond the enemy goal posts. Lambeau and Hutson created a bond during and after his illustrious career that few others would experience. Hutson would say later: "I was fortunate in having a creative coach like Curly Lambeau, one who really saw the merits of the passing game at a time when just about no one else did. He was a stern coach and there was a big gap between Curly and the players. He didn't mingle with them. He was the coach and that was that. After I left football, we became very close friends. We both had homes in Palm Springs. He used to ask me to go to the league meetings with him and I would ordinarily, but in the beginning, he was the coach and I was just an end."[80] When Hutson retired in 1945, he was earning $15,000 a year. In 1994, Hutson returned to Green Bay to dedicate the Packers' new indoor facility that was named in his honor. He died in June of 1997 at age 84.

At a time when Lambeau's fortune seemed to be in reversal from his championship run in 1929, 1930 and 1931, the signing of Hutson in 1935 would become the touchstone for his success spanning the next ten years.

Before the 1935 season, Lambeau decided to give the team a new look and changed the colors of the Packers' uniforms for the first time since their inception. Switching from the traditional blue and gold, Lambeau designed a new uniform using green and gold. The jerseys were green with gold sleeves and numbers along with the gold pants and green stockings. They would use this combination for two years, before going back to the blue and gold look.

Lambeau also experimented with another innovation that summer when he took the entire team to a resort near Rhinelander in northern Wisconsin for a week of training prior to the start of the regular season. On the morning of August 24, 1935, 24 players and Curly's son, Donald, boarded a bus in Green Bay and headed for Rhinelander, 130 miles to the northwest. Hutson did not join the team until later in the week because he was playing in an all-star game in Chicago. The Packers spent a week at Pinewood Lodge, located on Lake Thompson, eight miles east of Rhinelander. They would practice for a week on the high school field, and then play four exhibition games in a span of eight days against semi-pro teams from other Wisconsin cities.

Lambeau had previously held pre-season workouts in Green Bay. By segregating the team in the north woods, he hoped to build team chemistry and get the players into shape in order to get the season off to a good start. Lambeau's first official training camp had few, but very specific rules: Players were expected to eat breakfast at 8:00 am, curfew was 11:00 pm, there was to be no smoking in uniform, there was to be no drinking of alcoholic beverages at any time, football pants were to be worn at every practice and all injuries, regardless of how trivial, were to be reported to the team physician.

"We didn't have cars," said Herm Schneidman, then a rookie blocking back. "We couldn't sneak out. The camp was out in the woods. Lambeau was pretty shrewd that way. We were up there and that was my first year. I didn't know anything, I was awfully nervous and didn't know whether I should be there or not. At night, I would watch the guys play cards and I would want to ask a question and wonder who would answer me. One night a teammate, Walt Kiesling, was on his way back to his room and I followed him and asked if I could ask him a question. I asked him how long do you have to play in this game before you get used to it and not get upset. He said it gets worse and worse every year. I think that's the year Curly was trying to make it worse." Schneidman would recall the Packers' practice sessions Lambeau would run later that year: "They were short. But, the one thing I noticed about Curly, especially at a Bear game or a game that was close at the half and we had made a few mistakes, he would come into the dressing room and he would be madder than hell. He just chewed everybody out and said, 'I'm damn sick and tired of this. I'm going to do something about it. Some of you played good and some played lousy, you either pick up the second half or I'm going to do something about it.' Then he would leave the room."

Schneidman would also reiterate other players' recollection of how Lambeau would develop plays: "He had a group of five or six guys that he would go over the plays with. Always there was Cal Hubbard and Mike Michalske. They would go over the game plan on Monday and Curly would say we would have to come up with some plays and defenses for the team that we were going to play. In the meantime, I think Mike Michalske or somebody in the room thought up most of the plays and Curly took most of the credit."

When the team got to Rhinelander, they were greeted by large banners welcoming them to the city. Hundreds of spectators also were on hand for their first workout. They practiced all week at the city's old high school field that had a large, grassy hill on one side where people would sit to watch the workouts. After single workouts on Saturday and Sunday, the Packers held two practices a day most of the week, then a final session the next Saturday morning. But it wasn't a particularly grueling camp. "He never worked anybody hard," said fullback Chester "Swede" Johnston before his death in 2002. "Some of these coaches make you run, run, run. Curly never did that."

The only time the squad "dissipated" was the night the players were guests at the State Theater for a movie, courtesy of Sam Miller, the owner. Otherwise, lights were out at 11:00 pm. Kriss Gilbertson, a reporter for the Rhinelander paper, *The Daily News*, at the time recalled the Packers' trip: "I remember that members of the newspaper staff could wander in and out of the locker rooms and chat with players at any time."

The players stayed in four cabins at the lodge with six to a cabin. A few with wives were allowed to stay in private rooms in the lodge since Lambeau wanted his new wife, Susan, to have company. "Swede" Johnston's wife, Janice, was one of the players' wives invited to Rhinelander. She recalled Lambeau's wife as very attractive and the players all gave her the eye. "I was up at camp with her and we became very friendly. She had long, blond hair that really got the guys' attention. She said that in Hollywood she had a certain way of doing her hair, but couldn't get anyone to do it right here. She would do my hair and I would do hers. Curly had a boat that he called 'Susie' when he was married to her. I remember she and I went out on the boat and we had a sandwich and sat there and talked."

Lambeau usually did not get too chummy with his players and preferred to keep a distance. Janice Johnston said, "He didn't mingle too close with the fellows. We all admired and looked up to him, or I should say most of them did. You either liked him or you didn't. Curly would smile at you with those dimples and there was just something about him. You couldn't help but like him if he was on your side, but I guess if he wasn't, he could make it kind of rough. He was always nice to us."

Confined to the resort whenever they weren't practicing, the players spent their free hours fishing and playing horseshoes, shuffleboard and cards. Some went swimming, but the weather was unseasonably cold for part of the week. Janice Johnston did some swimming that week and recalled: "I swam out to the raft and it started to snow! It was a fluke. It was blowing and Curly's son and I were out on the raft. I'll never forget it. It didn't last long, but it was just one of those freak things. After that we had nice weather. Donald was up there with his dad. I don't think they were real close based on things I heard. But he seemed to be around quite a bit in those days."

At the end of the week, Lambeau scheduled several exhibition games. The Packers beat four different teams from Merrill, Chippewa Falls, LaCrosse and Stevens Point by a combined score of 145-0. Johnny Blood was one of the players who played against the Packers during those exhibition games. In fact, he played for both Chippewa Falls and LaCrosse and made enough of an impression that Lambeau re-signed him. Blood had been sold to Pittsburgh before the 1934 season because Lambeau had grown tired of his off-field antics.

With the addition of Hutson and Blood, plus Lambeau's more disciplined approach, the 1935 season would be much more successful than the previous three years. With a record of 8-4, the Packers narrowly missed taking the Western Division championship when they finished second to the Detroit Lions (7-3-2). But the Herber-to-Hutson combination was just starting to warm up as the Packers went on a 10-year spree of dominating the NFL Western Division.

6

Image of Greatness

Over the next nine years, Lambeau would reach the pinnacle of his coaching career. His Packers would win 75 percent of all their regular NFL season games, win the Western Division championship four times, finish second five seasons and take three world championships. The record speaks for itself. 73 wins. 21 losses. 4 ties. No other NFL coach came close to matching Lambeau's success during this period.

From 1936 to 1944 Lambeau was at his coaching best. With more than 15 years of experience, he had matured into a seasoned pro football strategist, motivator and recruiter. He found the players he wanted, negotiated their contracts, set up exhibition games, handled team travel arrangements, and basically ran the Green Bay Packer organization. Lambeau was at an age (between 38 and 46 years old) where he was more focused and passionate about winning than at any time in his 30-plus years in coaching. Lambeau put the team through twice a day practices over the next several years. He cajoled, disciplined, fined, pushed and punished his teams into a pack of wild animals that literally tore through opposing teams. Lambeau did not win the hearts of his players, but they won football games. In winning, they gained a confidence few other NFL teams could match.

The Packers' championship clubs during the era of Don Hutson may have lacked the flamboyant color of the triple championships of 1929-31, but they had one thing the earlier kings didn't enjoy. They had Hutson. Not that the NFL champions of 1936, 1939 and 1944 were one-man teams. If anything, both the 1936 and 1939 clubs were probably better balanced and more powerful than their championship predecessors. Even without Hutson, they would have been powerhouses. With him, they were awesome. In Herber, Lambeau had a quarterback who could throw the football a mile, and in Hutson he had someone who could outrun everyone to get under and catch it. If Herber and Hutson weren't terrorizing opponents through the air, Clarke Hinkle was pillaging them on the ground. To protect a lead, the Packers also had a defense that allowed the fewest points in the NFL during this nine-year period. "When the Packers hit the glory road again in 1936, it was an almost entirely new cast of characters. The only holdovers from 1931 were Johnny Blood, Arnie Herber, Hank Bruder, Milt Gantenbein and Chester (Swede) Johnston. It was, however, an experienced club, solidly blended of veterans and promising rookies, of which Hutson represented the key to greatness."[81]

While Lambeau had his coaching critics through the years and some of his players were quoted carping about his discipline and the distance he kept between himself and them, he still led the Packers to a level of success no other pro team could match during this period. Coaching a professional football team is only for the strong-willed, highly disciplined, well-organized and thick-skinned. It is now and it was then. There is continuous pressure to win amid second-guessing by players, fans, the media, and in Lambeau's situation — the board of directors. Coaching in the NFL is not for the fainthearted.

Lambeau came across to his players during this time as tough, heartless and overly demanding, yet he was able to mold and lead 25 energetic, burly, rowdy, undisciplined young men into a cohesive team with a single-minded purpose — to win. Spirited, dynamic, decisive and impatient. Lambeau's qualities may not have been those of the perfect leader, but they were ideal for being a pro football coach. Perhaps most important of all was Lambeau's insatiable desire to win. He had a gnawing hunger not to be just good — but great. He could define success in easy terms for his players to grasp. He made sure they could see it, touch it, feel it and point to it. He had the rare ability to show the players that vision of success. He might not have been skilled at designing plays, but he drove his team to achieve. He made winners out of losers or he dumped them on the wayside. He had no tolerance for a losing attitude. Only winners stayed on the team or new ones joined them. Those players who would not or could not adapt to a winning attitude were cast aside. Some players could not understand this approach and therefore called Lambeau heartless and non-caring towards his players. It wasn't so much that he did not care for his players — he cared for winning more. Oliver Kuechle, sportswriter for the *Milwaukee Journal* wrote this about Lambeau's desire to win: *"As coach, Lambeau was born with a raging desire which nothing but total victory would satisfy. 'Win, win, win' was the one philosophy he knew. The businessman Lambeau was imminently successful, too. In his early coaching years, he was one of the best in the large insurance company he worked for. His office in Green Bay was plastered with diplomas for his selling efforts. In his very early years he was a successful men's clothing salesman."*

Pro football is a game played by gifted athletes where victory usually goes to the team that displays the greatest emotion and desire. Lambeau personally displayed such an excitable passion for winning that it rubbed off on his players, particularly during games. Lambeau dominated during this period not only because he had good athletes. His players simply wanted it more than the other teams.

The 1936 championship team Lambeau put together was basically the same as the 1935 club that had shown so much promise with their 8-4 record. With a cunning eye for talent, Lambeau somehow always found young players who responded to his motivational techniques and played with a determination and desire that is so important in football. Green Bay became an assembly line, a factory to develop the perfect football machine. As players aged or got injured, Lambeau would cut or trade them. He would never become emotionally connected with any player except Hutson. Lambeau's dogged determination to scout players in the off-season from coast to coast and his persuasive skills to convince them to come to remote Green Bay were two of his greatest contributions to the success of the Packers. However, his ability to sign anyone from anywhere would change in 1936. The NFL had a problem because more and more of the college players were going to the highest bidder. The clubs with the most money got the better players. At its February meeting, the league decided to have a draft of the college seniors of that year. Bert Bell, who was at that time the owner of the Philadelphia Eagles, promoted the idea that the team with the worst record would take their pick first and on up the line. The Packers had the eighth pick that first year and Lambeau chose Russ Letlow, a guard from San Francisco.

While some of his former players may have downplayed his game-to-game play design, Lambeau consistently came up with a unique strategy that often caught the other team off guard and led to a Packer victory. At practice, during games and off the field — Lambeau was in charge and his players knew it. He insisted that they dress well on road trips. During this period he obtained green blazers for the team to wear when traveling to games away from Green Bay. Lambeau would always attempt to arrange for the team to travel "first class." They usually stayed in the best hotels in Chicago, New York and elsewhere. He also told them what to eat — or not to eat — providing them early in the season with a recommended diet to follow. He was very specific about the players staying away from fried foods. He practiced what he preached; he was always careful about what he ate, even long after he was finished with coaching.

Always known as a sharp dresser who was overly concerned with his own appearance, Lambeau often alienated his players with his continual habit of going after women — even when he was still married or the women were married. Single players often complained they had to compete with him for women when they were on the road or in Green Bay when Lambeau was between marriages. They would try to engage a young woman in conversation at a bar or restaurant, and the next thing they knew, Lambeau appeared. More often than not, he came away with the date — not the player. Lambeau would constantly display an insatiable need to win women's hearts — whether it be for a more permanent period or for one night — from early in his life to the end.

Janice Johnston, wife of Chester (Swede) Johnston, a back through the 1930s, would recall: "Among the ladies, he had a very nice personality. He had dimples when he would smile and had a little gray in his hair. He was charming." Harry Jacunski played for the Packers from 1939 to 1944 during the time in between Lambeau's second and third marriages. He would say later: "Curly was a ladies man. He actually competed with the players for some of the women in Green Bay."

As a coach, Jacunski saw Lambeau as a perfectionist who demanded excellence. He would say: "As a coach, Lambeau was enthusiastic, very upbeat, very demanding of his players. However, he could also get the players upset at him, as he often would fine them when they didn't perform the way he wanted them to. If they would miss a block, a tackle, drop a pass he would often fine them. This was very upsetting to the players." Jacunski also said that during the time that he played: "Curly wasn't really a strategist, he was more of a motivational type coach. The plays that he would draw up were basically done by his assistants. Curly concentrated more on disciplining the team as opposed to drawing up plays." While some players said Lambeau got a lot of help from his players designing plays, Hutson countered that Lambeau frequently came up with new plays for him and Herber to use for upcoming games.

Herm Schneidman, a back during a good part of this period of Lambeau's success, recalled an example of Lambeau's emotional sideline ravings that often motivated the team to victory: "I don't remember the year, but we were playing the Bears in Chicago and we were down a few points with about three minutes to go. Lambeau started going up and down the sidelines yelling, 'I want that ball, get that ball.' He started to put guys in and we kicked off and he kept yelling, 'I want that ball.' One of the Bears caught the kick-off and half the team hit him, he fumbled and we got it. I don't know if Hutson scored a touchdown or Hinkle, but we won that game."

Sometimes the motivation went from the psychological to the physical. A bonehead play or other costly mistake often prompted Curly to attack his own players. Tim O'Brien was a Packer trainer and recalled: "In 1936 he drafted Darrell Lester, an All-American center from TCU. In 1938 he centered the ball to Herber and it flew over his head into the end zone for a safety. The Packers lost 2 to 0. After the game, Lambeau was a wild man. He came in the locker room and pounded on Lester's chest and said, 'I want you to hit someone even if you hit the referee, but hit somebody.'" Lambeau did not confine his confrontations to the Packers' locker room. Scott Hunter, a Packer quarterback from 1971 to 1974, told a story relayed by his college coach, Paul "Bear" Bryant: "Coach Bryant had caught a train to Chicago and hitchhiked to Green Bay to see his old Alabama teammate, Don Hutson, in the fall of 1936. Hutson found out Lambeau was driving to Chicago the following Monday to do a radio show with Halas to promote the upcoming Bear game and asked Lambeau if Bryant could ride with him to catch the train back to Tuscaloosa. Lambeau said yes. On Monday they took off in his new Cadillac. Just on the south side of

Milwaukee, a young Wisconsin state trooper pulled Lambeau over for speeding. Curly told the trooper who he was and then tried to bribe him with a $10 bill. The trooper asked Curly to step out of the car, that he was under arrest for doing that, and then a scuffle broke out between the two. About that time, two Milwaukee policemen arrived, recognized Curly and got the two separated, cooled things down and got the trooper to let Curly go. With that he got back in the car, and Coach Bryant said Lambeau's expensive suit and silk tie were all askew and it was a funny sight. Coach Bryant knew not to laugh though or Curly would put him out on the highway." Bryant, of course, would go on to create a legacy at Alabama and win six national championships.

No coaching from the bench. That was the league rule at the time. But it didn't stop Lambeau. The players on the field had to call the plays and a new man coming into the game couldn't talk in the huddle until his second play. Lambeau, however, designed a way of communicating from the sideline using certain hand gestures and other signals indicating plays. The 1936 season was also the first year Lambeau would have an assistant coach since they joined the NFL, Richard "Red" Smith, a former Packer. Most players said Lambeau was reluctant to allow Smith to do much of the coaching that year.

One aspect of Lambeau's job that he never delegated was negotiating player contracts. Nearly every Packer player came out on the short-end of trying to get a higher salary from year to year. Tim O'Brien, an assistant trainer for the team in the late 1930s, remembered a time when one of the players tried to get more money out of Lambeau: "I remember George Svendsen, a big center, came into the locker room while we were painting the training room. He came in and said, 'I'm going in to talk to the boss about a contract and if I don't get my way I'll throw him right over the Northland to the courthouse.' (Lambeau's office was across from the courthouse.) He came back in a half an hour and said, 'I got the same salary as last year and apologized for taking up his time.' That's how sharp Lambeau was." O'Brien could not get a raise for himself either. He would say, "I wanted a raise in 1949. He wouldn't give it to me. I was only making $50 a week. He wouldn't give me a raise so I quit!"

Lon Evans, a guard with the Packers from 1933 to 1937, remembered negotiating a contract salary from Lambeau: "I hardly knew where Green Bay was, and Lambeau offered me a job to play with the Packers for $80 a game. The owner of the Redskins, George Preston Marshall, offered me a job for $85. I told them I had already given my word to Coach Lambeau and my decision was final. The Packers matched the amount that the Redskins had offered me and finally Lambeau said he would raise it after three games if I was doing okay. The next year I got a raise to $150 for regular season games, the most I ever made."

Charles "Buckets" Goldenberg, a key member of the championship teams of 1936, 1939 and 1944, would say later: "Contract negotiations with Curly were like a three act play. You started out full of hope. Then Curly started to talk down your demands. At the end, you felt like a bad guy trying to rob the Packers. Lambeau used to have three sets of contracts. One he sent to the league — that was the official one. The second one was for club records. The third copy he kept under lock and key in his desk. That was the one he brought out when you asked for more money. 'Are you worth more than Hinkle or Hutson?' he thundered at me once when I asked for a raise. He opened up his desk and pulled out their contracts. 'Here's what Hinkle is getting and this is Hutson's salary. Do you think you should get more than they do?' It wasn't until afterwards that I found out that those contracts that Curly had locked up so well were phonies. He kept them around to whittle down a player's demands. After some of his hocus-pocus you were happy to get what you got the year before or maybe just a little bit more."

While Lambeau's autocratic style rubbed some players during their winning years, the team followed his lead. John Biolo, who played for the Packers in 1939 would recall, "I thought he was a pretty good coach. He wasn't a real popular coach, but I thought he was a real good coach and innovative for that time. He was very autocratic. For instance, he was famous for trying to date players' wives or their girlfriends, and if you didn't like it, you were gone the next day. If you played a poor game or bitched about his social life you could be cut. There were times when he was very relaxed and easygoing. But then there were times he would be madder than a stuck pig. He would chew you out, even to the point of embarrassing you. I think he had our respect because it was scared into us. Back then, cutting a player was a pretty easy proposition. You cut 'em and that was it." Only Hutson was exempt from Lambeau's wrath according to Biolo: "Lambeau treated Hutson with kid gloves. He was the only one though. Don would make practice sessions jovial. He would half-heartedly do the exercises and Lambeau would kind of look at him and smile. But anybody else and they caught the wrath of the Belgian."

Lambeau, like many NFL coaches of that period, had no tolerance for player injuries. Biolo would say later: "You didn't get hurt. Lambeau had very low tolerance on that score. If you were injured you were liable to get cut. Back then you couldn't do anything about it."

Lambeau's tough-minded, heavily disciplined coaching style led the 1936 Packers to a 10-1-1 record for the Western Division championship and an NFL title with a playoff win over the Eastern Division champion Boston Redskins 21 to 6 before nearly 30,000 at New York's Polo Grounds. The Bears finished in second place, but were undefeated late in the season when the Packers beat them in Chicago, 21 to 10. After that game, John Walter, sports editor of the Green Bay *Press-Gazette* wrote of the Packers: "One of the greatest teams that had ever stepped upon an American field." *Chicago Tribune* writer George Strickler called the Packers, "A greater football team than at any time since its three year championship reign teams in 1929, 1930, 1931." After the Bear game, Green Bay would win four straight and tie the Chicago Cardinals in the season's finale, while the Bears would play out the rest of the season at 3-2, finishing 9-3.

George Preston Marshall, who owned the Eastern Division champions, the Boston Redskins, planned on moving the team to Washington D.C. the next year because of poor attendance so he arranged for the game to be played in New York instead of Boston. Lambeau wanted to avoid the cold December weather in Green Bay, so he took the team to New York for their workouts several days before the game. They stayed at the Victoria Hotel and practiced at the Polo Grounds the first two days, then moved to Central Park to run through their workouts. It rained hard in New York for two days before the game, making the playing field a sloppy, muddy mess on game day, even though the sun was shining brightly at kickoff. It wasn't much of a contest. The Packers won easily.

Lou Gordon of the Packers recovered a fumble near midfield at the start, and on Green Bay's first play from scrimmage, Herber passed 42 yards to Hutson for a touchdown. The game was less than three minutes old. Earnest (Pug) Rentner boomed through for a yard for the Redskins' lone score in the second period. Smith missed the kick and the Packers held a slim 7 to 6 lead at the half. The Packers got a touchdown in each of the remaining periods. Milt Gantenbein took an eight-yard toss from Herber for the third-period score and Bob Monnett got the last one on a two-yard plunge. Not only were the Redskins playing without the benefit of hometown support, they had lost their ace back, Cliff Battles, early in the first period because of an injury. To make matters worse, their starting center, Frank Bausch, was thrown out of the game for fighting in the third quarter.

Basking in their latest title triumph, Lambeau and the team returned by train to Green Bay the following day. It was 10:00 p.m. when the train pulled into the station. Winning was now the expected in Green Bay. The Packers were greeted by a smaller and somewhat more subdued crowd than the ones that had greeted them during the previous championship years. Still, an estimated 10,000 loud and cheering Packer fans crowded around the train station. Lambeau and a few of the players made a short speech to the crowd in front of microphones set up on the station's wooden platform. The following night the team was treated to a special celebration at the Columbus Community Club. Dinner was attended by many out-of-town celebrities, including Arch Ward, Lambeau's friend and sports editor of the *Chicago Tribune* and Russ Winnie, who broadcasted the Packer games as radio announcer for WTMJ in Milwaukee. Don Hutson would recall later in a recorded interview: "It was the first time a Green Bay team had won the NFL championship since they started having a championship game. It was really something for them to win the title, after all they were just a little town, and they won it over teams that came from all the big cities, like New York, Chicago, Detroit and Boston. We came back by train after the game and we got to Green Bay the next day and, hell, the whole town was there to greet us. There was a lot of celebrating, a parade, and a banquet. The town was football-crazy and still is."[82]

Within a week of the victory banquet, Lambeau, his assistant coach Red Smith and most of the players headed to the West Coast for several exhibition games for some extra cash — both for the club and the players. Lambeau's contract also had a clause calling for a bonus from any exhibition games beyond the regular NFL schedule. They met the Brooklyn Dodgers in Denver and won 21 to 13. They played two more exhibition games on the West Coast against pick-up teams before meeting the Bears for two more games in Los Angeles. It was the usual grudge match between two teams who literally hated each other. Herber wound up with a broken nose when a Bear smashed him in the face, and Hinkle was involved in a fistfight with several Bears' players. The first game ended in a 20 to 20 tie, but the Packers won the second battle, 17 to 14.

While they were in Los Angeles, Lambeau met with MGM Studios and arranged to make a Pete Smith movie short about the Packers that allowed everyone to get another extra paycheck. There were a lot of ten-minute Pete Smith movie shorts shown in theaters prior to the feature film in those days. It was always a humorous episode that Pete Smith would narrate. With Smith as commentator, this film was called the *Pigskin Champions* and had its world premier in Green Bay in August. The short showed off a lot of the Packers' pet stunts, some of the trick plays and demonstrated why the Packers were national champions. It also displayed the ability of some of their stars. Arnie Herber was shown throwing a ball through a piece of plate glass from 60 yards back. Clarke Hinkle dropped a 60-yard punt on a small piece of board in the coffin corner. John Torinus would recall the shooting of the film: "They hung a piece of plate glass from the goal post and they told Arnie they wanted him to throw as many times as it was necessary for him to bust the glass. They said they would keep on shooting film until he was able to score. 'What would you do that for?' Herber retorted. He then stationed himself about 60 yards away and proceeded to throw the ball and broke the glass panel into smithereens on his first attempt."[83] Thousands of people from Green Bay and surrounding towns came to the premiere that had to be shown several times at a downtown theater in Green Bay.

During the late 1930s and early 1940s, the Packer players were a tight knit group. Many of the players and their wives spent time together and would often recall they "were just like a big family." Janice Johnston, the wife of Swede Johnston, would recall this trip to the West Coast: "We had a good time. We didn't make any money, but we had a lot of fun. We went out to the coast and we stayed at the Hollywood Plaza. It wasn't expensive compared to today. We stayed there for quite a while. One day we were taking a walk and there was a Gilbert Hotel on the back street. Swede said, 'Let's go in and see what they get for the rooms.' So we did and decided to move there for the rest of the time. The other fellows found out we were there and they all came over. Curly and

Red Smith came also, so we were all together. It was fun! The wives would go to the rooftop when the fellows were away and have a picnic. We also went to Tijuana and had a big time. This was after the season, when they won the world championship in 1936. They made a Pete Smith movie short. We got to meet a lot of movie stars. Curly got all of us onto the MGM set."

Lon Evans, a Packer lineman during this time period would say later: "Many members of the team and their wives would get together and go out to eat at night. Oftentimes, we would drive to Sturgeon Bay which was famous for its seafood, or places like May Drurry's that served delicious chicken dinners. We would make the trip, four to five couples, and have such a good time seeing the bay. It was also fun to go downtown to the taverns for fish fries featuring lake trout. All the townsfolk turned out and were so friendly to the Packers, their team. It was like a big family gathering." Hutson would say: "There wasn't much to do in Green Bay, but we did it together. Some of us would see movies together, or to fish fries on Friday nights, or just hang out at my bowling alley. We spent a lot of time doing things together." Lambeau seldom took part in these get-togethers. He and Susan lived in an apartment outside of Green Bay, and the two of them would often go out to eat alone or with Lambeau's friends who were not players or Packer board members.

Before the start of the 1937 season, the Packers would play the college All-Stars in Chicago's Soldier Field. A team of graduating senior players chosen by fans around the nation had been meeting the NFL champions in August every year since 1934. "The man in charge of this affair was Arch Ward of the *Chicago Tribune,* the same promoter usually given all the credit for originating the idea of major league baseball's All-Star Game series, which was first played in the summer of 1933 at Chicago's old Comiskey Park. Ward had served several years as publicity man for the football team at Notre Dame during his student days there, during which time he had labored in the service of the legendary Knute Rockne.

"The idea of a summer football game, to capitalize on the presence of thousands of visitors attending the nearby Chicago's World Fair, was not something that had come suddenly to the *Tribune's* promoter when he was allegedly approached by Chicago's Mayor Kelly. In reality, in the summer of 1933 Soldier Field of Chicago had already been the scene of a college All-Star football game staged by other promoters, advertised and played as being a part of the festivities for the Century of Progress. That game had been a

match-up between two squads of recently graduated college players, staged as an East against West showdown; and the rosters of the
two teams were loaded with prominent All-Americans and other
outstanding football names, many of whom were on their way to
careers in professional football."[84]

Lambeau had his team go through easy two-a-day workouts
two weeks before taking them by train to Chicago the day before
the game. "It was no secret that Lambeau was far from pleased
with his club's state of readiness. He could not get them up for an
exhibition game against a bunch of college seniors. George
Strickler of the *Chicago Tribune* had been at the Packers' training
camp for two weeks and told his readers that, 'the attitude of the
men leaves much to be desired. They have evinced no concern
over Wednesday's contest. There still was no explanation for the
apparent apathy with which the Packers regard the collegians.
They have been reminded time and again that they represent the
smallest city ever sent into the game...the most important game of
their careers.'

"The Packers did have their share of support from other sportswriters, including Steve Snider of the United Press, who wrote,
'The Packers have to be given whatever edge there is. They are
experienced as a team. They know the All-Stars cannot be regarded lightly since twice they have held pro teams to ties.' An un-
bylined story in the *Chicago Daily News* noted, 'The Packers must
be figured as favorites to win. They may not be in top physical condition, but they are more experienced. But the collegians look
capable of offsetting much of their defensive weakness by their
own aerial attack.'"[85]

Lambeau had ordered new uniforms for the game showing off
green jerseys with large, ten inch gold numbers on the front and
back, with gold helmets and pants. However, the jerseys and pants
were made out of satin and did not breathe well on the hot August
night of the game. The players complained years later about the
new uniforms that made it seem they were playing in their own private sauna that sapped them of energy as the game wore on. True
enough. But it's more likely the Packers' numerous interceptions
and fumbles were the main reason Green Bay lost, 6 to 0.

The game would draw huge crowds from the year of its inception, and this game between the Packers and the College All-Stars
was no exception. Nearly 85,000 crowded into Soldier Field.
George Strickler of the *Chicago Tribune* wrote the following: "A

chastened Green Bay Packer football team dressed in silence and slipped away from Soldier Field last night with its only manifestation one of disgust…The opinion that they had given a better demonstration of football than their professional predecessors was small solace…None was willing to discuss the chief reason for the Packers' failure — the air of detachment which characterized the team's preparation for the game. This indifference toward the All-Stars held over until after Tinsley had scored. Then it was too late." Lambeau had little to say after the game. Later he would admit it was one of the most embarrassing losses in his entire coaching career. His Packers would meet the College All-Stars again in 1940 and 1945 and the outcome would be much different.

Lambeau threw out the 'hot' uniforms he designed for the All-Star game and went back to the Packers' traditional blue and gold combination. The team would keep this color scheme of blue jerseys with gold numbers and shoulders, gold pants, and blue socks until Lambeau left the team in 1949. The Packers and Bears were tied for first place late in the 1937 season (the same year the famous ivy was planted at the base of the outfield wall at Wrigley Field), before Chicago pulled away to take the Western Division championship with a 9-1-1 record to Green Bay's second place finish of 7-4-0.

While President Franklin D. Roosevelt was continuing to pull the country out of the depression, Joe Louis began his twelve years as a heavyweight champion in 1937 by knocking out Jim Braddock. Lou Gehrig batted .354 to lead the Yankees and the American League. However, the country was still trying to shake itself free from the crippling depression. By the time Roosevelt took office in March 1933, the United States economy had hit bottom. Banks and businesses had failed by the thousands. Farm prices had reached new lows, and hundreds of thousands of farmers faced the loss of their land through foreclosure. About 13 million Americans — one-fourth of the work force — were without jobs and income of any kind. Roosevelt had no master plan to end the depression, and he was no revolutionary. His New Deal was largely a matter of try this, try that, and stick with what seems to work. Five days after Roosevelt became President, Congress began a special session called the "Hundred Days." It passed nearly all the bills he submitted during this period. Roosevelt, a superb speaker, also began a series of radio broadcasts called "fireside chats," explaining his administration's actions. The New Deal established subsidies and conservation programs, one of which was the Emergency Conservation Work (ECW) Act, more commonly known as the Civilian Conservation Corps (CCC). With this action, he brought together two wasted resources, the young men and the land, in an effort to save both.

By September 1935 there were 500,000 men located in 2,600 camps across the nation building fire towers, roads, planting trees and building recreational parks. Due to programs such as this, by the late 1930s the nation was beginning to climb out of the depression.

Off-season, 1937. Lambeau had a dilemma. If he wanted to take full advantage of Hutson's uncanny ability as a receiver, Lambeau concluded he would have to replace Herber as the team's primary passer. Although he was only 28 years old, Herber had been playing for eight years and had taken a physical beating. He was missing game time and losing some distance in throwing the bomb. At the NFL draft in Philadelphia in February of 1938, Lambeau made the shrewd selection that would assure him two more Packer championships. He chose Cecil Isbell, an outstanding passer with Purdue, as his number one draft choice. Although Isbell, with his black, wavy hair and handsome looks, would have a relatively short pro career, he would team up with Hutson to become the best NFL passing combination for the next five years. Lambeau was once asked to name the best passer he had ever seen. He didn't hesitate. "Cecil Isbell," he said. "Isbell was the best, with Sid Luckman of the Bears a close second and Sammy Baugh of the Redskins a long third. Luckman wasn't as versatile, and Baugh couldn't compare on the long ones. Isbell was a master at any range. He could throw soft passes, bullet passes or long passes."

Isbell played with the Packers from 1938 through 1942, and then retired at the peak of his career to go into coaching. But in his five years, a brief span for a superstar, Isbell left a lasting impression on his teammates, rivals and in the record book. His records are all the more amazing when one considers that he played both in college at Purdue and in the pros with Green Bay under an extreme handicap. In his first Big Ten game against Northwestern, his left shoulder was dislocated when he fell on it after a tackle. Isbell would recall later: "The trainer came out and popped it back in, and I continued in the game. On the next kickoff, I went down to make the tackle and it went out again. They put it back in place on the field and I finished the game. After that, they decided I should have a chain on my left arm, so I couldn't raise it too high. That way, the shoulder never went out again. I wore the chain in practice and in games, both at Purdue and with the Packers."

Isbell and Hutson would hook up on passing routes other teams found difficult, if not impossible to stop. Isbell would recall how Hutson could outmaneuver anyone trying to cover him: "He'd charge off the line with his head down like a bull out of a chute. But he had great eyes and fine judgment and could see what was going on around him all the time. Most teams would try to beat him up on the line, not letting him get out, but he was tough to box in. He would follow the ball all the way, right into his hands. I've studied the movies on him closely and when the ball got to him, his hands would go absolutely limp, he'd be so relaxed. He never fought the ball. He just guided it into his hands with his eyes. With his great concentration, nothing else mattered."[86]

When Isbell retired from the Packers after only five seasons, he was at the peak of his pro career, but said he didn't want to wait until he was washed up and have Lambeau cut him. He would say later: "I'll tell you why I quit after only five seasons. I hadn't been up in Green Bay long when I saw Lambeau go around the locker room and tell players like Herber and Gantenbein and Bruder that they were all done with the Packers. These were good players who had given the team good service for years and they had no money in the pot. But there was no sentiment involved. I sat there and watched, and then I vowed it would never happen to me. I'd quit before Lambeau came around to tell me."

Isbell's departure hurt. Lambeau would miss Isbell's ability to run the team on the field, as well as his skills as a passer and runner. Isbell would recall: "When I was with the Packers, I called the plays. The quarterback was the blocking back so the tailback gave the signals. Lambeau would call a play once in a while, but mostly he was too excited. Oh, I had help. If Hutson or Hinkle got tired, they would tell me to call someone else's number." A few years after Isbell's retirement, Hutson would call it quits. Lambeau was not able to come even close to replacing these two astonishing athletes, and it would mark a decline in the Packers' fortunes that would eventually cost him his job.

Isbell had his own opinion of Lambeau as a coach during his playing time with the Packers: "As a coach I thought Lambeau was a fine organizer, but he really didn't spend much time on football fundamentals. He was more of a motivator and had a great deal of enthusiasm for the game that rubbed off on us."

Lambeau made one other important addition to the Packers that summer when he signed a giant of a lineman from Nashville, Tennessee that would make a huge difference both on offense and defense for the next eleven years. Acting on a lead from a friend, Lambeau was able to sign the 6-foot, 7-inch, 280-pound behemoth, Buford Ray, who went by the odd nickname, "Baby." No one drafted the big tackle that had just graduated from Vanderbilt, but Lambeau was able to bring Ray to Green Bay instead of Chicago as Halas also was after him.

When Lambeau spoke at the annual Green Bay Packers, Inc. stockholders meeting that summer, he said he was enthusiastic about many of the talented new players joining his cast of proven veterans. He claimed his new additions were the best in the history of the team. In between trips to the East Coast with his wife, Susan, where he was trying to make a player trade with some Eastern clubs and the West Coast, where he had begun to dabble in real estate, Lambeau found time to golf with his son, Donald, at Green Bay's Oneida Country Club. Donald graduated from Green Bay East High School that year and was to enroll at Fordham University in the fall.

Before the start of the 1938 season, Marcel Lambeau supervised the construction of additional seating at City Stadium to increase the capacity to 25,000. The Packers' locker room was also increased in size somewhat from the dingy, tiny, crowded room they had used for years. The visiting team, however, still had to dress either at the downtown hotel and bus to the stadium in full uniform, or use the East High School locker room next to the stadium. City Stadium also had finally installed men's and women's bathrooms by that time. Lambeau insisted the team continue to play at least two league games a year at State Fair Park in Milwaukee where seating capacity had been increased to hold 30,000 for the Packer games.

George Calhoun, although no longer the *Press-Gazette* sports editor, was still secretary for the club and handling the publicity for the Packers. Starting in 1938, Calhoun began sending out a weekly one-page sheet titled *Green Bay Packer News* that contained various Packer tidbits. He sent it to 75 newspapers throughout Wisconsin and surrounding states with the hope of keeping the Packers in the news year-round. The team now had Packer ticket outlets in 300 communities in Wisconsin, Minnesota and the Upper Peninsula of Michigan. Packer popularity was growing each year. The success the team would experience over the next two years would reach enormous proportions.

1938 once again saw Green Bay basking in championship glory. With an 8-3 record, the Packers won the Western Division championship, earning the right to the playoff game against the Eastern Division champions, the New York Giants. Newspapers again hyped up the playoff game as "David" Green Bay, smallest city in the NFL, going against "Goliath" New York, the largest. Nearly 1,000 people crowded around Green Bay's train station on a cold December evening to see the Packers off to New York five days before the championship game. There was the Lumberjack Band, shrieking factory whistles, blasting automobile horns and shouts from the football-frenzied citizens of the city. The Packers had lost to the Giants, 15 to 3, in New York before nearly 50,000 at the Polo Grounds just weeks earlier.

Lambeau, nervously pacing back and forth on the station's wooden platform, was confident his Packers could beat New York in the playoff. "If the mental attitude of the players means anything, we'll win," Lambeau declared. "They're ready for the Giants. They're anxious to get at them again." Lambeau declared that his entire squad would be ready for service on Sunday. Don Hutson, injured the previous week, was still limping, but Lambeau had hoped that he would be available to play.

When they arrived in New York, the team checked into the Victoria Hotel and within hours had started their practice session in Central Park. Hutson's injured knee kept him from practice, but Lambeau had him spend time with the team in an attempt to keep his injury a secret from the Giants.

The Packers all but pushed New York out of the Polo Grounds on game day, but the Giants, coached by Steve Owen, won the NFL title, 23 to 17, when a pair of first-period Packer punts were blocked and turned into scores. The largest crowd ever to see a championship game up to that time, 48,120, saw a bruising battle that belonged statistically to the Packers. The Giants turned one of the blocked kicks into a 13-yard field goal, and a few minutes later New York's Tuffy Leemans ran six yards for a touchdown. That gave the Giants a nine-point edge before the game hardly was underway. The Packers retaliated at the start of the second quarter on a 50-yard pass from Herber to Carl Mulleneaux, who carried the ball into the end zone. Lambeau from the sidelines, dressed in his tweed overcoat and dark fedora, would send Hutson onto the field from time to time to serve as a decoy, but the Giants ignored him because of his limp, and the strategy failed. The Packers dominated the game statistics as they collected 14 first downs to 10 for the Giants and gained 164 yards to 115 on the ground. In the air, the difference was even greater, the Packers piling up 214 yards to 97 for the Giants.

To add insult to injury, Lambeau experienced a most embarrassing situation during the game. Trailing 16 to 14 at halftime, Lambeau began to contemplate what he would say to the team in the locker room. Deep in thought, he lingered behind the players headed to the locker room and somehow made a wrong turn. He went out the door he thought was to the clubhouse and wound up on the street. Before he realized his error, the door slammed shut behind him and he was locked out. He frantically pounded on the door to no avail, and then raced to the nearest gate. But the guard refused to let him in. Swearing a blue streak, Lambeau hustled off to another gate. But no amount of pleading or threatening could get him past the next guard. Meanwhile, back in the locker room, the Packers were wondering what had happened to their coach. As the halftime minutes elapsed, the perplexed players couldn't agree on a revised game plan. By now, Lambeau had charged into the main gate, only to be stopped once again. Yelling at the top of his lungs, Lambeau attracted a big crowd, including some reporters. The sportswriters immediately recognized Lambeau and convinced the guards that he was indeed the Green Bay coach. By the time he reached the locker room, the second half was about to begin.

While the embarrassing incident and the loss were hard to shake off, Lambeau and the Packers would get an opportunity to change the championship game outcome the following year. During the off-season, Lambeau spent less time on the West Coast amid rumors he and Susan were having marital problems. Some said they were accusing each other of extramarital affairs. In the meantime, Marguerite was now employed at Prange's department store in Green Bay where she had worked her way into a supervisory role. Lambeau took Donald east in August to enroll him at Fordham University. The campus is situated on Rose Hill in the North Bronx section of New York City. The Packers had practiced on the Fordham football field on numerous occasions in past years when they were playing Eastern teams. One of the Fordham players who came over to watch the Packers practice in the mid-1930s and ask questions was a fellow named Vince Lombardi. Lombardi graduated from Fordham in 1937.

The big news on the world front in 1939 was Germany's attack on Poland and the start of World War II. On the home front, Clark Gable and Vivien Leigh starred in the well-known movie, *Gone with the Wind*. The average income in 1939 was $2,163, but you could purchase a new car for $680 and fill it up with gas for 19 cents a gallon. 1939 was rough overseas but very kind to the Packers. Compiling a 9-2 record, they won the Western Division crown again with a squad that has been called one of the best teams in Packer history. Even Lambeau himself often was quoted as saying this was his best team. Their backfield consisted of rookie Larry Craig, Arnie Herber, Clarke Hinkle, Joe Laws and Cecil Isbell. Milt Gantenbein and Don Hutson were the ends while Russ Letlow and Buckets Goldenberg anchored the line.

"Larry Craig of South Carolina joined the Packers in 1939. In Craig, a rugged individual with a build like Li'l Abner, Lambeau had found the perfect complement to Hutson. A solid 200 pounder, Craig played blocking back on offense and end on defense. This permitted Hutson to move to the secondary, a natural place for his speed and ball-hawking ability. This unquestionably lengthened Hutson's pro career, for his slender build was not meant for the pounding at defensive end. Hutson laughed about it. 'Craig is my defense and Isbell is my offense,' he said."[87]

While Lambeau's Packers were winning the Western Division championship for the second year in a row, George Halas and his Bears finished second, just one game back. The Packer-Bear games seemed to be increasing in intensity with each passing year, and 1939 was no exception. "Halas leveled accusations of spying and cheating at Lambeau as the Bears practiced in Green Bay before the September 24 game at City Stadium. Halas noticed the windows of nearby houses were full of binoculared onlookers as the team practiced. Halas actually went so far as to question some of the residents, all of who claimed that they were 'bird watchers.'"[88]

The Packers ended up winning the game 21 to 16, but players from both teams were ejected for fighting. Several players had to leave the game due to injuries and players from both teams had run-ins with the officials. After the game Halas was crying about the Packers using illegal pass plays and he upset Lambeau who was quoted in the *Press-Gazette* as saying, "The Bears are the last team in the world to talk about unfair tactics. We have tolerated the Bears' rough, dirty play long enough and now I'm going to demand Halas either apologizes for what he said or try to prove them." Of course, Halas neither apologized for his remarks nor tried to justify them.

Halas would get his revenge when the Bears beat the Packers later in the season in Chicago, 30 to 27. Fistfights abounded between players on the field and in the stands where over 40,000 jammed Wrigley Field. "One particularly belligerent Bears' supporter made the mistake of picking a fight with none other than former Packers' end Lavvie Dilweg. According to *Press-Gazette* writer Dick Flatley's account of the incident, Dilweg got the best of the grandstand fight. Flatley wrote that the Bears' fan realized picking the fight, '…was an error of ways, the lesson of which was learned painfully.'"[89]

As Western Division champions, the Packers were again scheduled to meet the Eastern Division first place team, the New York Giants, in early December. "This playoff game would be played at Milwaukee's State Fair Park where Lambeau, after consulting with Oliver Kuechle of the *Milwaukee Journal*, decided to play the game in Milwaukee and to charge a top ticket price of $4.40, an unprecedented high in professional football. State Fair Park was sold out two days after tickets were put on sale. A crowd of 32,279 was on hand for the rematch, including 6,000 in seats on the automobile racing track."[90] Lee Joannes, the president of the Packers' board of directors, agreed with the decision to play the championship game against the Giants at State Fair Park in Milwaukee instead of Green Bay. Joannes was the owner of Joannes Brothers wholesale grocers and the switch of game site so upset Green Bay people that some of the retailers refused to accept groceries from the Joannes Brothers Company.

The move made both the Green Bay residents and players angry. As a result, the Packers played inspired ball and shut out the Eastern champions, 27 to 0. It was Lambeau's fifth world championship, four more than Halas. So rugged was the Green Bay defense that the Giants gained only 70 yards rushing all afternoon. A cold 35-mile-per-hour wind slapped down their passing game to a measly 98 yards. About the only satisfaction the New Yorkers got was that once again they held Hutson scoreless. But it was his catch of a 15-yard pass from Herber that set up the first touchdown.

The score came on a Herber-to-Milt Gantenbein toss of six yards. Cecil Isbell threw 20 yards to Joe Laws for another marker in the third, and Ed Jankowski plunged a matter of feet for the third Packer touchdown. Paul Engebretsen and Ernie Smith each kicked a field goal.

The crowd braved a cold, cloudy, blustery day to attend the game, giving the Packers a record gate of more than $80,000 as Green Bay recorded the first shutout in NFL championship game history. Members of the New York press complained about what they called deplorable conditions. What raised their ire so was the rickety press box atop the grandstand at State Fair Park. As the press box swayed in 35-mile winds, the writers feared for their lives. They also complained about a 'monumental traffic jam' after the game, and took pity on fans seated on folding chairs set up in the racetrack. 'For a day at least, professional football dipped back into its unsavory past and did itself uncalculated harm' wrote an indignant Stanley Woodward of the New York *Herald Tribune.*

"Seats cost up to $4.40 each, track seats $3.30 each. *Milwaukee Journal* writer and sports editor R.G. Lynch scoffed at complaints about the press box, but agreed about the $3.30 seats on the track, which he called 'the worst gyp this town has seen in a long time.' The Giants' staff said the top price was double the highest price charged at the Polo Grounds. Minimum wage in this period was 40 cents an hour and the *Milwaukee Journal* daily newspaper cost three cents and the Sunday newspaper ten cents.

"WTMJ's Russ Winnie was the voice of the Packers, while the national broadcast announcers were Red Barber and Harry Wismer, announcers for the Giants and the Detroit Lions. The game was dubbed the 'Dairy Bowl' in honor of Wisconsin's dairy industry. But as the *Milwaukee Sentinel* observed the next day, while about 200 empty bottles were picked up after the game, 'Not one was a milk bottle.'" [91]

After the game that night, another large crowd waited for the Packers when they arrived by train. The usual banquet was held the next night in downtown Green Bay. But, the year did not end on an entirely high note for Lambeau as his father, Marcel, passed away shortly before at the age of 63. Marcel would not see his son's last national championship five years later. But neither would he witness his fall from grace.

7

The Last Hurrah

While Lambeau was experiencing success with the Packers during this time, his marriage to Susan was heading in another direction. Susan, only 32 and eleven years younger than Curly, wanted more from her marriage. With each passing year since their wedding in 1935, they spent less time together. They had an apartment in DePere, a suburb of Green Bay, and a place they rented in Los Angeles, but in the last year, they were seldom in the same place at the same time.

Curly was completely absorbed in the Packers from August through the end of December each year. Social life during the football season simply didn't exist. There was his usual routine of scouting the bowl games in January, the NFL meeting in Philadelphia in February and negotiating player contracts throughout the winter. Curly and Susan spent most of the winter months in Los Angeles when he wasn't traveling and returned to Green Bay in the summer. When they were first married they often traveled together. More recently, Susan stayed behind in Los Angeles.

Early in the marriage, Curly often took Susan to hot spots such as the Hollywood Pladium and the Mocombo to mingle with the movie stars. Lambeau loved Hollywood as it had become the center of the motion picture industry with its mild, dry climate and vast variety of natural scenery. Within 200 miles, moviemakers had their choice of gorgeous, scenic backgrounds. Huge sound stages abounded as Hollywood began the production of sound films in the late 1920s

Lambeau tried to use his movie connections to land Susan some kind of role in a film, but to no avail. While she was extremely attractive, she had no acting ability and settled for the few modeling jobs she could get during the depression. Los Angeles' economy, like that of so many other cities, wilted in the grasp of the Great Depression of the 1930s. But its population continued to grow as thousands of jobless and homeless people drifted into the area, hoping their luck would change. The city's economy recovered and reached new heights following the outbreak of World War II in 1939. Hundreds of thousands of new residents flocked to the city to work in aircraft factories, shipyards and other war plants.

Summer, 1940. Curly and Susan were drifting further apart. When he came to Green Bay in July, the chatter in town was that Lambeau was seeing other women. Out of sheer loneliness, Susan also began to go out with other men while she stayed behind in Los Angeles. Their marriage would soon be over, and Lambeau was planning ahead for the time he would be single again. Although Susan was unaware of it, Curly had a contractor begin building an elegant home on the shoreline of Green Bay. When finished, it would have three bedrooms and a large paneled great room with a massive fireplace surrounded by an oak mantel. The entryway would have a large capital "L" engraved in the flooring. The outside of the house was a mix of limestone and cedar siding. It was typical ostentatious Lambeau.

By 1940, Green Bay had become Wisconsin's fifth largest city with a population of just over 46,000. But like the rest of the nation, it was still trying to crawl out from the depression. The beginning of the decade saw extreme social and economic conditions. According to the 1940 U.S. census, only one out of five Americans owned a car, one in seven had a telephone and only fifteen percent of the college-age population attended college. The Depression's grip was closing tighter. Only 75 percent of American households had a refrigerator or icebox, 60 percent lacked central heat and three out of four farmhouses were lit by kerosene lamps. When World War II started in September 1939, many Americans still believed that the United States could stay out of it. The nation stopped all arms shipments to warring nations. Later, it allowed the Allies to buy arms for cash, but by 1940 Great Britain and China were running out of funds. Roosevelt then urged the nation to become "the great arsenal of democracy." Hitler's 1939 blitzkrieg in Poland and the staggering Nazi sweep through Western Europe and Russia in 1940 and 1941 gave a tremendous push to Green Bay and the surrounding area's industry. The United States shifted from neutrality to combat, working frantically to shore up Hitler's enemies while building its own military power. By the end of 1941, war contracts had pushed business volume to the highest level in seven years.

Prior to the NFL season that year, the Packers were scheduled to meet the College All-Stars in Chicago in August. Lambeau did not want to experience another embarrassing loss to the graduating college seniors like the 6 to 0 defeat his Packers had tasted in 1937. Even before the practice sessions started, he began to mail letters to the players with specific instructions of what they should be doing to get in shape. He wrote, *"Don't be foolish enough to think you can get into condition after practice starts. If you fail to report in shape, you not only handicap yourself in your efforts to make the team, but you will seriously retard the progress of the squad as a whole. The well-conditioned player is seldom injured. The fellow who is out of shape generally suffers injuries, fatigue as a result of poor condition, and is responsible for most football injuries."* Other instructions Lambeau gave them were: *"Number one, work out in football shoes whenever possible. Be sure your feet are ready for strenuous work when you report. Number two, concentrate on ankle, knee and foot calisthenics. Get your feet and legs into condition. Dancing is all right, but the hours are bad. Hiking and running, particularly sprinting, are better. Number three, avoid bad habits. Keep regular hours, get nine hours of sleep a day."*[92]

At the Green Bay Packers, Inc. stockholders' meeting in July, Lambeau added a new title to his name — vice president. He was now head coach, general manager and an executive right next to the president, Lee Joannes. For all practical purposes, Lambeau had almost complete control of every aspect of the Packer operation. There was little he could not act upon without approval from the Packer executive committee or board.

Lambeau received a new five-year contract from the Packer Board that paid him $10,000 annually, plus an additional $1,000 a year for office expenses. In addition, the contract called for Lambeau to receive 25 percent of the Packers' net proceeds from the *Chicago Tribune's* All-Star game. He would also get a percent of the net after expenses from the NFL playoff games and any exhibitions.[93] In a good year, with all incentives paid off, his annual salary could have reached $20,000, an exceptionally high income during the 1940s when the average was under $3,000. He was probably the highest paid NFL coach at the time, with the exception of George Halas, who owned the Bears and took out the club's profit for himself.

In early August, Curly pulled his team together and began to prepare for the All-Star game. "By 1940, Lambeau had done some fine-tuning on his team, and the arrival of blocking back Larry Craig in 1939 had permitted the Packers to switch Hutson to defense where he was extremely effective. Even more important-ly, Arnie Herber was phased out as the team's leading passer. Lambeau rated Cecil Isbell ahead of both Chicago's Sid Luckman and Washington's Sammy Baugh as the league's best passer. The key offensive backs were Isbell and Herber at tailback, Hinkle and Ed Jankowski at fullback, and Andy Uram along with veteran Joe Laws at wingback. The primary receiver of course was Hutson, with the secondary pass catcher being big Moose Mulleneaux. "In retrospect, this 1940 Green Bay outfit may have been one of the best Packer teams of all times."[94]

George Strickler, the *Chicago Tribune* sportswriter covering the Packers at their training camp in Green Bay wrote, "The Packers were a very fine football team. It came prepared for battle, capable of victory, and full of respect for the College All-Stars." What Strickler did not report was that Lambeau had not only whipped his players into tip-top physical shape, he had also designed numerous new passing plays. He had determined the team would be going into this game throwing more passes. On the night of August 29, a record crowd of 84,567 fans filled Soldier Field to witness a spectacular offensive show. The two teams exchanged touchdowns before the Packers took a 28 to 21 halftime lead and then Green Bay won going away, 45 to 28. Isbell had con-nected with Hutson for two touchdowns and Mulleneaux for anoth-er score. Herber, now a backup to Isbell, passed to Hutson for a final touchdown in the romp with the All-Stars. Lambeau had his revenge and would say later the win was his most satisfying victory.

When the *Milwaukee Journal* sportswriter Oliver Kuechle once asked Lambeau what in his long coaching career he consid-ered the most satisfying experience he ever had, Lambeau would reply: "The most satisfying game we ever won was the All-Star game of 1940. Maybe this sounds funny for me to say, but I believe pro football turned the corner in that game. You see, pro football had not yet caught on all over the country. There were a lot of detractors, especially among college people. They called the pros lazy and uninspired. There were some, including a few good college coaches, who kept insisting that a well-coached college team could beat a pro team any day. The 1940 game changed all this. We scored more points than the pros had scored in the six previous games combined and for the first time opened the eyes of those who for so long had refused to accept pro ball for what it was. No game as I look back now ever gave me more satisfaction than that, for what it did for all pro ball."

Lambeau went into the 1940 season with high expectations that were never reached. The Packers were projected to battle the Bears for first place in the Western Division that also consisted of the Detroit Lions, Cleveland Rams and Chicago Cardinals. The five teams in the Eastern Division were the Washington Redskins, Brooklyn Dodgers, New York Giants, Pittsburgh Steelers and Philadelphia Eagles. They rounded out the ten-team National Football League that year.

The Packers finished second in the Western Division with a 6-4-1 record with two of the losses coming from the Bears who finished in first place with an 8-3 record. Prior to their first meeting at City Stadium in Green Bay, Halas sent Lambeau a sarcastic wire saying to the effect, "Take it easy on my Bears. We have many injured players!" Lambeau knew it was a ploy and warned the team about Halas, the Bears and the importance of the Packer-Bear rivalry. It did not do much good as the Bears humiliated the Packers 41 to 10 at City Stadium for the worst defeat in Packer history up to that point.

Halas had cleverly implemented new plays that caught the Packers off guard. Defensively, the Bears picked off seven Green Bay passes. Lambeau was concerned that other teams had spotted something in the Packer defense and offense, so he and his coaches, along with Hutson, took the train to Chicago the next Wednesday to scout out the Packers' next opponent, the Chicago Cardinals. They were more worried coming home because the Cardinals beat the Bears 21 to 7.

Hoping to mystify the Cardinals, Lambeau and his coaches cooked up some special plays. The ploy worked and Green Bay beat the Cardinals in Milwaukee, 31 to 6. At mid-season, the Bears were on top of the Western Division. The Packers were right behind them. 45,000 people jammed Chicago's Wrigley Field to see the latest edition of the Packer-Bear rivalry. It wasn't pretty for Green Bay as the Bears won a tough game, 14 to 7, and took over first place in the Western Division with three games to go.

The following week, Lambeau again broke the ice for professional teams when he chartered two airplanes to take the Packers to their next game in New York. It was the first time any NFL team flew to a game. However, it was a rather eventful flight in more ways than one. Because of the weight (poundage) in the plane, they were forced to land in Cleveland to re-fuel. While they were on the ground in Cleveland, they were told that bad weather in New York was backing up air traffic at LaGuardia airport. With this happening, Lambeau decided to take a train to New York for the rest of the trip. Bitter defeat awaited as the Packers lost to the Giants at the Polo Grounds, 7 to 3.

After winning the Western Division championship, the Bears met the Eastern Division champions, the Washington Redskins, for the NFL title. Simple words cannot describe what happened that day. As long as football is played anywhere in the world, the Chicago Bears' public massacre of the Washington Redskins, 73 to 0, in Griffith Stadium on December 8, 1940, will be mentioned. The Redskins came into the National Football League title contest as the favorite because Sammy Baugh, their great passer, was having his finest year and also because the Bears had lost to the Redskins, 7 to 3, less than a month before in a regularly scheduled game.

Washington came to the championship game with a 9-2 record, the Bears had an 8-3 card, and the 36,034 paying spectators were expecting an even battle. But what the fans did not know is that the Bears had become infuriated by bulletin board material at its finest. The remarks were attributed to George Preston Marshall, the talkative, egocentric owner of the Redskins, following the Washington triumph over Chicago in November. On that day, the Bears had protested the validity of the lone Redskins touchdown. They kept up their protests even after the game was over. Marshall called them "cry babies and front-runners." It was a major mistake that Halas used to his full advantage. He had the Bears whipped into a frenzy by game time and a rout was on. To add a bit of frosting on the cake, Marshall pulled another bonehead act that further infuriated Halas and the entire Bear team.

When Marshall, in a long raccoon skin coat, took his seat behind the Redskins bench to courteous applause from the crowd, he waved politely and confidently, much as a politician might. Then he lifted one of the song sheets he had distributed to the crowd to tell them: Okay, it's time for the pre-game song (Marshall believed strongly in all the pomp associated with the game) and proceeded to lead the crowd in song — "Who's afraid of the Chicago Bears, Chicago Bears, Chicago Bears; Who's afraid of the Chicago Bears, Chicago Bears, Chicago Bears..." and so on, until the crowd sensed there wasn't a voice in the house afraid of the Chicago Bears. Halas and the team were seething, waiting for the game to start so they could begin tearing the Redskins limb from limb. Lambeau watched the scenario play out and took mental note that Halas was intense enough about winning — don't ever do anything to further that intensity.

During the summer of 1941 while Americans were reading in newspapers and listening to radio broadcasts about the events unfolding in rapid-fire action on the other side of the Atlantic, Curly was in the process of finalizing his divorce to Susan. The British were now fighting Germans in North Africa and Greece after France had fallen to Germany. Tensions rose in the United States when an American merchant ship, the *Robin Moor*, was torpedoed by a German submarine and again when the *USS Reuben James*, a destroyer, was sunk off Iceland. President Roosevelt declared a "Limited National Emergency," the peacetime draft was expanded and "Uncle Sam Needs You" signs began appearing in public places everywhere. Daniel Topping, husband of Sonja Henie and now the new owner of the Brooklyn Dodgers football team, was drafted at the age of 29. Topping planned to apply for an exemption because as he stated, "Who would manage the box office while I'm away?" He eventually received an exemption due to stomach ulcers.

Another draftee, actor Jimmy Stewart, entered the Army. His salary of $21 a week probably didn't stretch quite as far as the $6,000 a month he was making as an actor. New York Yankee fans breathed a sigh of relief when diminutive rookie sensation (he was only 5 feet, 5 inches) Phil "Scooter" Rizzuto won a draft deferment because of dependents. Rizzuto batted .347 at Kansas City of the American Association the past season, and big things were expected of him with the Yankees. The Yankee's Joe DiMaggio had his unbelievable and record-setting 56-game batting streak stopped on

July 17 as his team ran away with the American League race. Lou Gehrig, a former Yankee teammate, passed away that summer at the young age of 37. Boston Red Sox slugger Ted Williams was still batting over .400 in August, and Elmer Layden, 37, one of the famed "Four Horsemen," surprised everyone by resigning as football coach at Notre Dame to become commissioner of the National Football League. His new salary of $20,000 a year was twice what he had received in South Bend. A new car went for less than $700, while gasoline was still only 19 cents per gallon.

Big Bands were doing their best to keep the mood positive and upbeat in the country and dominated popular music. Glenn Miller, Tommy Dorsey, Duke Ellington and Benny Goodman led some of the more famous bands. Eventually, many of the singers with those Big Bands struck out on their own. Bing Crosby's smooth voice made him one of the most popular singers, vying with Frank Sinatra. Dinah Shore, Kate Smith and Perry Como also led the hit parade. Be-Bop and Rhythm and Blues grew out of the Big Band era toward the end of the decade. These were distinctly black sounds, epitomized by Charlie Parker, Dizzie Gillespie, Thelonious Monk, Billy Holiday, Ella Fitzgerald and Woody Herman.

"Radio was the lifeline for Americans, providing news, music and entertainment, much like television today. Programming included soap operas, quiz shows, children's hours, mystery stories, fine drama and sports. The goal of most sports announcers was to do baseball on radio. The job was virtually year-round. You would go south in March and stay with the team until the end of the World Series. Football was a sometimes thing. It was just the weekend. It encompassed four months of the year, and that was all. The football season ended late in November, around turkey time. The difference between baseball and football was evidenced in the men who made their reputations doing them. Bill Stern and Ted Husing were rapid-fire announcers with exciting voices. A fellow like Red Barber was a soft-spoken, laid-back broadcaster — like baseball. Baseball is a relaxed game to watch. You pay attention, lean forward with each pitch, and then sit back. A baseball game is a relaxed two-and-one-half hours in the sunshine. Football is a clash between gladiators. Those who best broadcasted the sport reflected football as war."[95]

While Lambeau's draft picks from the college seniors were not much in 1941, one of the choices turned out to be a real prize. Lambeau used his lowly number seven choice to take a running back from little Gonzaga University, Tony Canadeo, known as the 'Grey Ghost of Gonzaga.' It would turn out to be the best seventh pick Lambeau would ever make. Canadeo would spend twelve years as a productive Packer player and another 40 years as a member of the team's board of directors, creating the longest association anyone has ever had with the team. One of the most popular of all Packers, he still ranks as the number three rusher in club history, was only the third rusher in the NFL to gain 1,000 yards in a single season and was inducted into the pro football Hall of Fame in 1974.

In early August, Canadeo checked into the Astor Hotel in downtown Green Bay with most of the other single players and settled in before reporting to the Packers for the start of training and pre-season games. Having signed a standard contract earlier in the year that called for $175 a game (roughly $3,000 annual salary — not bad, considering Joe DiMaggio made $5,000 in 1941), Canadeo knew that the contract language, like all player contracts of those days, made it clear there was no salary guarantee. He could be cut at any time and payment would stop at that point.

The people of Green Bay literally "worshipped" their Packers during this period. They were enthralled that "their" Packers from a small Wisconsin town of 46,000 could actually compete against the "big city" teams such as New York, Chicago, Detroit, Philadelphia, Cleveland and Pittsburgh. Many of the players rented rooms from local families or stayed at one of the two hotels in town, the Astor or the Northland. The fans would see them at restaurants, shopping at the local clothing stores or just walking the streets, hanging out in the hotel lobby or coffee shop. The players were their heroes that took on the "city slickers and kicked their butts."

These were, indeed, heady times to be a player. Hero worship abounded. Young women adored them and would go out with them at the drop of a hat. With his divorce now in process, Lambeau openly dated other women. The players, while enjoying the attention and adoration, generally did not let it go to their heads. Almost without exception, they enjoyed camaraderie with their fans and engaged in small talk and conversation just like you might have with a friendly neighbor. Lambeau, however, was different. He was beginning to distance himself more and more from the people in Green Bay. "Standoffish" is how the locals described him and they began to grumble about it at the coffee shops, bars and restaurants.

While researching his four-volume Packer history, author Larry Names came across an episode in early September of 1941 that involved Lambeau, Susan and Arnie Herber. Although now divorced, Susan showed up in Green Bay eight months pregnant. Since he was convinced the child was not his because he had evidence of her indiscretions in Los Angeles, Lambeau put the word out that no one on the team could see her. He refused to see her even though Susan insisted the child was Curly's. He denied it and said it was a result of her fooling around. It was Susan's intent to force Curly to pay child support as well as the medical bills when it came time to deliver.

When she couldn't pay her rent the Northland Hotel, where she was living, put her out. No other hotel would accept her, so she turned to Arnie Herber's wife who took her in. When Curly found out, he insisted Herber ask Susan to leave their house so she could return to Los Angeles. Herber would have none of it and, when he refused, Lambeau released him from the team, telling the *Press-Gazette* that Herber could not control his weight so he had to cut him. Names said: "Herber was still on the roster in pre-season. Lambeau told him that if he didn't get her out of his house by Monday, he would fire him. Arnie and his wife said that they couldn't throw her out, she had no place to go, had no money and they weren't that kind of people. Curly fired him."

Janice Johnston, wife of Packer Swede Johnston, was in Green Bay at the time and recalled, "Susan had a little boy who looked like Curly. He had little fat hands. He was cute. I think he was named after Curly, but I'm not sure. Susan stayed with Herber's wife who was an attorney. Her mother came and she was staying in one of the apartments over the drugstore across from the Northland Hotel." In the book, *Packer Legends in Facts,* where each season of the Packers is chronicled, it simply states in 1941, "Arnie Herber was released in a surprising move just before the beginning of the regular season."

Herber, although only 31, had slowed down somewhat and did struggle with his weight. Lambeau knew he could release Herber because Cecil Isbell was going to be the number one passer on the team anyway. Isbell had taken over Herber's spot as the Packers' primary passer, reducing Herber's playing time. Nevertheless, it came as a surprise when the popular Herber, an eleven-year veteran, was cut just before the start of the season. The explanation that "he weighed too much" didn't wash. The loss of Herber was not felt as the Packers and Bears battled for first place throughout the 1941 season and wound up at the end of the schedule tied for first place.

Lambeau had not lost his passion for winning and kept the pressure on his players throughout the 1941 season. George Svendsen, a center with the Packers from 1935 through 1941, would recall: "Lambeau was a prime egoist in a way, but a positive guy who never thought he would lose. He always thought he could win, and when you look back at his record, he could. He knew how to handle all the players. He put a lot of faith in the ballplayers. In 1941, we had a brain trust — myself, Hinkle and Hutson — a players' council that met with him before games. We were like assistant coaches. The credit for the Packers' innovative passing attacks should go to Lambeau. His pass patterns were ingenious. He could attack a defense like nobody ever saw. He was the first to use the pass the way it is today."[96]

At the time of the Packers' last game of the regular season against the Washington Redskins on November 30, 1941, the Japanese Navy was steaming toward Hawaii. The Packers finished their season at 10-1 while the Bears (9-1) had one more game to play. If the Bears lost to the Chicago Cardinals, the Packers would be the Western Division champions. If the Bears would win, they would be tied with the Packers and there would be a playoff between the two teams. On the morning of December 7, 1941, Comiskey Park, home of the Chicago Cardinals, was packed for their game against their cross-city rivals, the Bears. Also in the stands were Lambeau and some of his Packer players to scout the Bears in case of a playoff. Would the following Sunday see them traveling back to Chicago for a playoff game or staying at home and hosting the New York Giants for the championship? That question would seem trite by halftime. No one at the game was prepared for the entire world to change that day. The announcement came over the PA system early in the third quarter: "Ladies and gentlemen: The Japanese have bombed Pearl Harbor." The crowd sat in stunned silence.

Tony Canadeo had traveled to Chicago with Lambeau, and like many others, didn't even know where Pearl Harbor was. "We were sitting in Comiskey Park, the Bears were playing the Cardinals. At about the third quarter, someone who was listening to the radio said Pearl Harbor had been bombed. Everyone was saying, 'Where the hell is Pearl Harbor?' I didn't even know where Pearl Harbor was," Canadeo remembered.

After the game, George McAfee of the Bears remembered, "We went over to a Cardinal player's apartment and listened to all the news on the radio." "My wife was at the game. She said people just sat there stunned, with no one talking. After that, we just sort of went through the paces," Bears' halfback Harry Clark said. After the announcement, the game's outcome seemed trivial. The Cardinals put up a good fight, but in the second half the Bears scored two touchdowns and won, 34 to 24, forcing a playoff with Green Bay. Back in Green Bay, fans listened to the radio, hoping for a Cardinal win. They were informed that Pearl Harbor is in Hawaii, then a territory of the United States. The Packers' contingent returned from Chicago at midnight, and Lambeau and his only assistant, Red Smith, had the team on the practice field Monday afternoon.

Now the Packers and Bears had to play a game at Wrigley Field to determine the Western Division champion and the right to play the New York Giants for the world championship. Hundreds of Packer fans crowded around the train station along with the Packers' famed Lumberjack Band on the Saturday before the game to give the team a noisy send off. In Chicago, the team stayed at their usual spot, the Knickerbocker Hotel. First to retire were Don Hutson and Smiley Johnson. "Hutson hits the hay almost every night by eight o'clock," said Packer Line Coach Red Smith. "Friday, however, generally is his night to howl. Then he'll probably stay out as late as 8:15."

The next day, on a cold and windy December Sunday, the Packers were no match for the powerful Bears before a crowd of 43,425 at Wrigley Field. They lost, 33 to 14. The sub-freezing temperatures and strong winds contributed to a loosely played game with eight fumbles, seven interceptions and a total of 15 penalties called on both teams. Two weeks after the attack on Pearl Harbor, the NFL got a taste of problems in the offing at the league's championship game. Just over 13,300 fans turned out at Chicago's Wrigley Field. There were about 43,000 empty seats as the Bears bludgeoned the Giants, 37 to 9.

By the spring of 1942, the manpower shortage was becoming apparent as players enlisted or were drafted into the armed forces. A league survey in May found that 112 of the 346 players — 32 percent — on the league's ten teams in 1941 were already in the military services. "Naturally, we're proud of that record," said Commissioner Elmer Layden, "and I believe it is additional proof of the worthwhileness of football." Complicating pro football's manpower problem was the fact that few college seniors could look forward to playing immediately, since most would be taken by the military soon after graduation. Layden said, "We're planning our regular schedule. But everything we decide today may have to be abandoned tomorrow. While we believe professional football has a definite place in the recreational program of a nation at war, nothing connected with it should or will be permitted to hinder the war effort."

After Pearl Harbor, there was no question: America would join the war. Recruiting stations were soon jammed with eager young men, and people rushed to buy defense bonds. By February 1942, more than five million volunteers had emerged to help local community war efforts. Industry had moved into high gear, churning out so many tanks, planes, guns and ships that their efforts jump-started the listless economy. The attack on Pearl Harbor was a singular moment in modern American history, a penetration of our borders by a hostile force. It had the effect on the country that a burglary has on the family home: people never felt quite safe again.

While federal officials pined for a militant march to urge the country on, the most popular song of 1941 — indeed, of the entire war — was Irving Berlin's "*White Christmas*," a sentimental ballad sung by Bing Crosby. It became the mantra of homesick soldiers and their loved ones who gazed from windows, eager for their return. The mood throughout much of the country was like that of an ad hoc task force — inexperienced, but ready to tackle an ugly job. In February, before addressing the nation in a memorable "fireside chat," President Franklin D. Roosevelt suggested that people buy an atlas to acquaint themselves with the geography of the war. The 1942 popular movie, *Casablanca,* starring Humphrey Bogart and Ingrid Bergman, provided Americans with a view of the war that gave it an added dimension.

Americans began rationing gas, coffee and, later on, leather shoes. Coastal "blackouts" became commonplace, and everyone knew that the "Bataan Death March" wasn't a John Phillip Sousa anthem. And though rationing was an irritant, it was also a daily reminder that the nation was at war. In fact, practically every inconvenience, every shortage, every small sacrifice — meatless Tuesdays, gasless automobiles, ketchup-less hamburgers — was justified as a contribution to the war effort. Few wartime measures had so great an impact on the home front as food rationing. Sugar and coffee were the first items to be rationed, starting in 1942. The next year processed foods — soups, vegetables, canned juices — were added to the list, followed by meat, fish and dairy products. Shopping became a complicated and often frustrating experience.

All professional and college sports experienced a drastic decrease in the number of players during the war. Baseball was the hardest hit. More than 5,700 men played in the major and minor leagues in 1941, and more than 4,000 of them eventually served in the military. Over 600 players from the NFL would serve before the war was over in 1945. The 1941 season was almost over before the Pearl Harbor attack, but the raging war in Europe was already exacting a toll on baseball. Hank Greenberg, the American League's most valuable player in 1940, was the first major leaguer to enter the service, after playing in only 19 games in 1941.

By the summer of 1942, the NFL had lost a third of its players to the service. The Packers were no exception. Particularly painful was the loss of fan favorite, Clarke Hinkle, who was called to the Coast Guard. Although he turned 30 in 1942, Hinkle was not past his prime. He left the game as the NFL's top rusher at that point, having gained 3,860 yards. In all, Green Bay lost 16 other veteran players to the war that year, including Guss Zarnas, Hal Van Every, Moose Mulleneaux, Smiley Johnson, George Svendsen and Ed Frutig. The Packers also lost services of 18 of Lambeau's 20 college draftees. John Walter, sports editor of the *Press-Gazette* that year, reported that approximately 100 NFL players from the year before were now in the Armed Forces.

Going into the 1942 season, the Bears were still considered the most powerful team in the NFL. They had won the championship game against the Giants and had lost only one game in 1941. And their draft losses were not that extreme, having lost only regulars George McAfee and Norm Standlee. Lambeau was not sure what kind of competition the Packers could give the Bears in 1942 since their draft losses were heavy. Nevertheless, they still had the best receiver in the NFL in Don Hutson and an excellent passer in Cecil Isbell. Lambeau decided during the 1942 training camp that he would throw caution to the wind and emphasize even more passing that season.

And pass they did — with record-breaking efficiency. Isbell became the first quarterback to throw for 2,000 yards in a single season. His 24 touchdown passes also set an NFL record of that time. Hutson shattered a number of receiving marks — many his own — by catching 74 passes for 1,211 yards and 17 touchdowns. Their efforts and those of others, such as Andy Uram and Lou Brock, provided the Packers with the league's top passing offense. The 1942 team passed on nearly 50 percent of their plays as they gained 2,400 yards through the air and only 1,374 on the ground.

The new replacement for Hinkle wound up being the club's leading ground gainer. Ted Fritsch, who wasn't even drafted by the Packers in 1942, would go on to become one of the most popular Packers ever. He had attended college in Stevens Point, Wisconsin, and although he earned all-conference as a fullback his junior and senior years, Lambeau did not think enough of him to include him in the draft. Fritsch got his chance with the Green Bay Packers only because the Packer backfield coach that year, Eddie Kotal, a former Packer, had been his coach in college. Once he got to Green Bay, he proved he belonged. Just because he came from the tiny town of Spencer, Wisconsin, attended Stevens Point State Teachers College and wasn't even picked in the 20-round draft of 1942 didn't mean he was a sub-par athlete. Quite the contrary. He led the team in rushing three times and was an all-pro fullback in 1945 and 1946.

As the 1942 season unfolded, predictions that the Bears would be the team to beat proved true, as they finished undefeated (11-0), while the Packers finished second in the Western Division (8-2-1). The two Packer losses came from the Bears, 44 to 28 and 38 to 7, leaving no question about the Bears' superiority that year. (Chicago eventually lost to the Washington Redskins in the championship game, 14 to 6.)

Professional football, like baseball, deteriorated during World War II with the armed forces taking many of the top stars. Competition in 1942 maintained essentially the high quality of the pre-war teams, but by 1943 the rosters were decimated and the infusion of young talent into the National Football League all but stopped. Like baseball, pro football was urged by President Roosevelt to continue. It did, although there were such developments as the Philadelphia Eagles and Pittsburgh Steelers combining to form one team called the Steagles in 1943; the Cleveland Rams disbanding for the 1943 season; and the Chicago Cardinals and Steelers combining as one club for 1944. Because the amalgamated club lost all ten games, it was universally known as the Card-Pitts (as in carpets). Attendance plunged to 887,920 in 1942, the lowest since 1936, and failed to regain its 1941 level until 1945.

In early spring of 1943, Curly's son Don, now 23 years old, married his high school sweetheart, Nancy Leight, who was 18 years old. The couple spent their honeymoon in the house by the bay that Lambeau had built the year before. Nancy would recall: "It was the most unique house that he designed. We couldn't get out of Green Bay due to freezing rain so we spent our honeymoon with the housekeeper and dog." While Nancy had a good relationship with Curly, the same could not be said of his son. Nancy said: "Curly was not a good father. He and Don did not get along at all. He would come to see me, and then Don would come home and find out he had been there to see me, but not when he was there and he would get mad as hell. He would call all of Don's friends and meet them at the country club. It hurt Don terribly. Curly was warm, vibrant and bright — as long as you weren't his son. If you were his son it was tough. Don could never live up to his reputation and the divorce from Marguerite hurt while he was in high school. There was nothing dull about Curly, ever. He was always looking for a good time. He cheered you up. My mother was a good friend to him. She never lost track of him. When I was young, he and Marguerite would be at our house all the time. We had a player piano and he sang — he had a great voice. He even did blackface at the Strand Theater when he was young. He had a sense of humor like you couldn't believe."

As 1943 dawned, the war was now into its second year for the United States and the NFL was losing more players. To deal with the shortage of quality players, the league cut its team players from 33 to 25 in 1943 and then voted to permit unlimited substitutions. Until 1943, a player could enter a game only once each quarter, except in the fourth quarter when two players from each team could be brought in twice. Some retired players rejoined their old teams during the war. One of the most illustrious was Bronko Nagurski. He came out of retirement from his farm in Minnesota and returned to the Bears just for the 1943 season. The Bears also lost their coach, George Halas, to the service in 1943.

In Lambeau's college draft, there were three players that would have an impact on the Packers: Dick Wildung, a tackle from Minnesota; Irv Comp, a halfback from St. Benedictine; and Bob Forte, a halfback from Arkansas. Wildung, who would enter the service and join the team in two years, and Forte would become good performers for years, while Comp would compete for a starting spot in the backfield. "In early April, Dan Reeves shocked everyone by withdrawing the Cleveland Rams from the league for the coming season and possibly for the duration of the war. Cleveland's roster of players was then divided among the remaining nine teams by drawing names out of a hat. It was also decided that the Philadelphia and Pittsburgh franchises would merge for 1943 and play as the Phil-Pitt "Steagles" for lack of a better name. This left the NFL with eight clubs, four in each division, balancing the schedule to ten games with each team playing a round robin slate within its division and playing each team in the other division once."[97]

1943 was tough on Lambeau in other ways. Isbell and Hutson had told him in August they were retiring and would not return for the 1943 season. The loss of both would have been absolutely devastating to the Packers. Isbell did not return, becoming the coach at Purdue, his alma mater. Fortunately, with Lambeau's urging, Hutson changed his mind and returned before the season started, but got off to a slow start. Beset with grief, first at the loss of a younger brother in the Pacific theatre and then with the sudden death of his father, the 30 year-old veteran was not the Hutson of previous years. His preoccupation with civic and personal affairs contributed to his slower pace at the start of the year. He had difficulty securing adequate help to operate his thriving Green Bay bowling alley, was busy as chairman of the Brown County Red Cross drive and served on a civic committee to study the possibilities of Green Bay obtaining its own airport. The soft-spoken loner, however, never complained openly. While he seemed somewhat aloof, the Packer veterans who had played with Hutson for years knew he was painfully bashful and was a team player in every respect.

The *Press-Gazette* was doing its part to keep the public's mind off the war with extensive coverage of the Packers. Ray Pagel was now the sports editor, and Art Daley was one of the sportswriters who covered the Packers. Newspapers were at least five inches wider than the papers today, allowing for large banner headlines to run 17 inches across the top of the page. The *Press-Gazette* often ran huge eight column heads and six column wide pictures highlighting some aspect of the Packers' accomplishments. Packer coverage was bigger than ever. A.B. Turnbull, now publisher, made sure his reporters understood what kind of a slant to give Packer articles. Daley said: "The way A.B. put it to us was that we are privileged to have a team like that in Green Bay, so do everything you can do to promote them. That was repeated many times to sportswriters. You don't cover the Packers the same way they cover the Bears in Chicago. It's different." Turnbull made it clear to his staff there would be no negative comments made by any of the writers about Packers players, coaches or their performance. That trend would continue up until Lombardi would arrive in 1959. Negative comments wouldn't be necessary because a championship dynasty was in the making. In keeping with the charitable mood of the time, the Packers and *Press-Gazette* worked out an arrangement so that 700 paper carriers could get into the games free. They had their own special section in one of the end zones. George Calhoun was still handling the publicity for the Packers in addition to his job as wire service editor for the *Press-Gazette.* His publication, *Packer Football News*, now had nationwide circulation. It was a bulletin issued weekly throughout the year and went to sportswriters, radio announcers and servicemen all over the United States and elsewhere. Many former Packer players and fans requested the bulletin be sent while they were in the nation's armed forces. They said the gossip about the Packers and other pro teams made good reading. One of the items that year mentioned Lambeau's benevolent side. The children in orphanages in and around Milwaukee were great followers of the Packers. Whenever the team played in Milwaukee, Lambeau had a block of tickets set aside and threw in refreshments for the day. The orphanages had their own football team and during halftime entertained the fans with plenty of football, plain or fancy.

    The Packers were not expected to give the Bears much of a battle for the Western Division title in 1943. With all the teams crippled with veteran players serving in the military, who could say for sure just how the season would unfold? As it turned out, the Bears still had enough talent to take first place (8-1-1) for the fourth straight year and then whip the Redskins for the championship (41 to 21) before a wartime crowd of 34,320 at Wrigley Field. The Packers came in second again in the Western Division with a 7-2-1 record, but they did play the Bears tough, tying their first game at City Stadium 21 to 21 and then losing at Wrigley, 21 to 7, when the Bears scored two touchdowns in the second half.

    With the certainty of the draft looming over a few of the Packers' heads at the beginning of 1944, the nation was entering its third year at war. So many millions of men were going into uniform that scarcely a home in the country was not affected.

Although people at home were humming that year's most popular songs, *"Sentimental Journey"* and *"I'll Walk Alone,"* they were faced with irritating and bewildering changes. There were rationings and shortages. New automobiles or refrigerators were not to be had. Women put on coveralls and went to work in factories or joined the armed forces. The mood of the nation was "Let's get it over with." Significantly, there were no rousing songs to compare with *"Over There"* of 1917. For a time, people sang, *"Praise the Lord and Pass the Ammunition,"* but the song probably owed its popularity more to its bounce than to its patriotic sentiments.

By 1944, another three Packers, including offensive backs Andy Uram and Tony Canadeo, had replaced their Packer uniforms with those of the military. The three new inductees brought the number of Packers serving overseas to 27. "The Bears were still the hardest hit of the two teams. Stars Harry Clark, Danny Fortmann, Bill Geyer and Bill Osmanski all left for the war. George Halas was still in the service, leaving co-coaches Hunk Anderson and Luke Johnson with a roster of veterans, rookies and old-timers all scrambled together. Even Sid Luckman was not spared. As a Merchant Marine, Sid was usually away during the week, but he generally got to play on Sundays. His backup was the 35 year-old Gene Ronzani (a name we will see return with the Packers — but not as a player), who had retired in 1938. In 1944, a total of 43 Chicago Bears were away at war."[98]

Don Hutson said he wanted to retire again and didn't sign until September 1, two weeks before the first game. Lambeau sweetened the pot a bit and offered Hutson more money as an assistant coach. He took the position. Other than Hutson, this year's team was mostly older veterans, draft-deferred players and some who came out of retirement. Guard Buckets Goldenberg at 33 years old did not really want to punish himself with another year. He, too, retired, but then came back after the Packers' first game and finished another stellar season. Lineman "Baby Ray" at age 33 and old Pete Tinsley were back, as was Center Charley Brock, giving Green Bay a solid line. A fairly good backfield was made up of Larry Craig, 33 year old Joe Laws and Lou Brock. Also returning were Ted Fritsch and Irv Comp. It was a competitive team in 1944, but not with the same talent and depth as some of its predecessors.

Fortunately for Lambeau and the Packers, all the other teams in the NFL and particularly the Bears had nowhere near the talent they had before the war. The 1944 season was one of the worst for the NFL as it was a terrible time for recruiting football players. "Greasy" Neale, the coach of the Philadelphia Eagles, despaired about his prospects. In September, the Eagles' general manager, Harry Thayer, said that Neale had cut his own salary from $12,000 to $3,000 because the team would be so poor. During the 1944 season, teams again combined because of the shortage of players. The Chicago Cardinals and Pittsburgh Steelers merged in the Western Division along with a new franchise at Boston, called the Yanks. The Cleveland Rams returned to the Western Division after suspending the 1943 season.

The unusual 1944 season schedule gave the Packers the first five games at home, three in Green Bay and two at State Fair Park in Milwaukee. They won them all, mostly by lopsided scores. Green Bay opened for the first time at State Fair Park in Milwaukee. Milwaukee had been a good second home for the Packers. They had won 17 of their last 18 games there, including 16 straight between 1935-1942. Overall, the team was 18-4 in Milwaukee since it began playing home games there in 1933. They then went on the road for the remaining five games and went a decent 3 and 2. Finishing the year at 8-2, the Packers won the Western Division and met the New York Giants for the championship. Leading the Giants was a face all-too-familiar to Packer fans — Arnie Herber. Lambeau had said Herber was washed up when he cut him in 1941. Coming out of retirement "Flash" led the Giants to an 8-1-1 record.

As Lambeau and his Western Division champions readied to leave for Charlottesville, Virginia for a week of pre-title game practice in warmer weather, American B-29's were bombing Japan. In a companion strike, nine ships and a Japanese troop convoy were sent off Leyte. Gasoline and food ration cards were still in effect as were transportation problems, which delayed the Packers' departure for Charlottesville. They were delayed a day trying to get their train out of Green Bay. When they finally arrived in Virginia they had two workouts a day, squad meetings and films of the previous Giants' games every day. Lambeau had good reason for spending so much time in preparation. His team had lost to the New York Giants four weeks earlier, 24 to 0, before a large crowd in New York of 56,481 fans. This championship game was played on December 17, 1944 and drew 46,000 at the huge Polo Grounds. Back in Wisconsin, Packer fans had the choice of two radio broadcasts of this game. Harry Wismer was broadcasting the game on WTAQ and Russ Winnie, the voice of the Packers, was describing action over Milwaukee's WTMJ.

This was Lambeau's twenty-sixth year of coaching. He still didn't want much to do with the T-formation that George Halas had updated and put into NFL play in the early 1940s. Lambeau decided to put Don Hutson in as more of a decoy and stuck with the running game. Their young fullback, Ted Fritsch, scored two Green Bay touchdowns. Joe Laws also chewed up a lot of yards on the ground, gaining 74 yards in 13 carries in this game. "I only used two plays for myself that day," said Laws. "I used a half-spinner in the middle and a trap over the guard. I'd keep my eye on Larry Craig, the Packers' blocking back, and then whichever way he took the guy he was blocking I'd go the other way. At our quarterback meeting the night before the game Curly said we're going to throw all caution to the wind. You have permission to call anything you want." The Packers beat the Giants, 14 to 7.

A large crowd of Packer fans crowded the tiny Chicago Northwestern depot platform once again to meet the team after their championship victory. The celebration went on through the evening and into the early morning hours by some of the more rambunctious fans. The 1944 championship marked the last time the Packers would win one until a coach by the name of Lombardi led Green Bay to a championship game 17 years later. This season would also be the year before the Packers' decline from power in the NFL. No one knew it at the time, but the glamour years for Curly Lambeau were over. The championship of 1944 would be his last hurrah.

1

Lambeau was a star for Green Bay East High School where he lettered in football four years.

In his senior year, Lambeau's high school yearbook reflected his captivating personality.

Lambeau (center) also excelled at track in high school.

As captain and coach of his high school team, Lambeau (far right with football) would lead his team to an undefeated season his senior year.

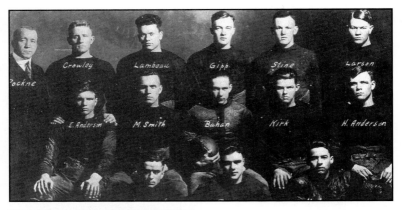

Lambeau (top row, third from left) played one season (1918) at Notre Dame for legendary coach Knute Rockne. The famed George Gipp (fourth from left, top row) was his teammate.
Notre Dame Archives

Curly and Marguerite, high school sweethearts, were married in 1919, the first year the Packers were formed.
Tom Murphy, private collection

The first Packer team, 1919. They outscored their opponents 565 to 12 and won 10, lost 1. Lambeau, coach and captain, is holding the ball, center, just behind the first row. George Calhoun, team manager is far right, back row.
Packer Hall of Fame

In the first few years of the Packers' existence they played at Hagemeister Park in Green Bay, which was basically an empty lot near East High School. *Top:* Photo shows fans in 1919 standing behind ropes stretched around the field. *Below:* By 1920, Lambeau's father, Marcel, and his construction company built wooden bleachers and a seating capacity for 1,000 on one side of the field. Chicken wire was placed around the field and admission of 50 cents was charged.
Stiller-Lefebvre Collection

By 1922, the Packers were established members of the new professional
football league and playing before crowds of nearly 2,000 at
Hagemeister Park. *Top:* Lambeau shown passing which became his
trademark in an era when few teams passed more than four or five times
a game. *Below:* For two years, starting in 1923, the Packers played
their home games before crowds nearing 4,000 in an old wooden baseball stadium, Bellevue Park. Hagemeister Park was dug up to make way
for a new East High School. *Stiller-Lefebvre Collection*

The 1921 Acme Packers, the team's first year in the NFL. Curly is center and his younger brother, Rummy, is far left in a topcoat. Note the patchwork uniforms, common for all pro teams of the time. *Stiller*

Lambeau played with the Packers from 1919 to 1928 and was their leading performer in the early years. He did most of the team's running and passing. *Packer Hall of Fame*

George Calhoun was the sports editor of the Green Bay *Press-Gazette* in the 1920s and publicity director for the Packers for nearly 30 years. His writing built the Packers and Lambeau into 'larger than life' characters. *Packer Hall of Fame*

Thousands of Packer fans took the train from Green Bay to Chicago for the Bear and Cardinal games starting in the 1920s through the 1940s. Special cars on the train, such as the one shown here, were set up as a bar.

Two of Lambeau's best performers: Johnny Blood, excellent runner and receiver and hell-raiser (left) and Clarke Hinkle, one of the finest all-around players in Packer history.
Packer Hall of Fame

Green Bay's City Stadium in 1927. Curly's father, Marcel, was responsible for building stands through the years at City Stadium.
Stiller-Lefebvre Collection

Lambeau's handsome ▶
appearance coupled
with his outgoing per-
sonality made him an
appealing interview
for newspapers and
magazines. This pub-
licity photo was taken
in 1931, the year the
Packers won their
third consecutive
world championship.
Packer Hall of Fame

◂ Lambeau's 1929 undefeated Packer team, the first to win a world champi-
onship. They would also win world championships in 1930 and 1931.
Lambeau is far left, front row. Other players are left to right, back row: Cal
Hubbard (T); Hurdis McCrary (B); Tom Nash (E); Bernard Darling (C);
Claude Perry (T); Red Smith (G); Verne Lewellen (B); Roger Ashmore (T);
Johnny "Blood" McNally (B); Jim Bowdoin (G); Lavvie Dilweg (E); Jug
Earp (C). Front row: Curly Lambeau (B); Paul Minnick (G); Bo Molenda
(B); Roy Baker (B); Eddie Kotal (B); Red Dunn (B); Dick O'Donnell (E);
Mike Michalske (G); Bill Kern (T); Whitey Woodin (G); Carl Lidberg (B).
Stiller-Lefebvre

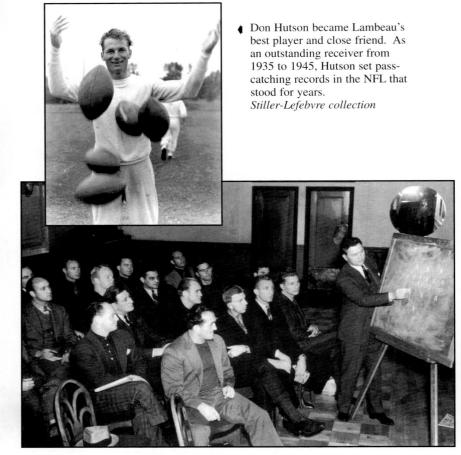

◀ Don Hutson became Lambeau's best player and close friend. As an outstanding receiver from 1935 to 1945, Hutson set pass-catching records in the NFL that stood for years.
Stiller-Lefebvre collection

◆ Lambeau plots out strategy in a pre-game meeting in a New York hotel, preparing for the NFL championship game in December 1936 against the Giants. Front row includes Charles "Buckets" Goldenberg (left) and Don Hutson (far right).
UPI-Bettman

Four players from the championship era pose with Lambeau and assistant Red Smith at training camp in 1937.
Arnie Herber and Mike Michalske are on the left, Milt Gantenbein and Hank Bruder on the right.
Lefebvre

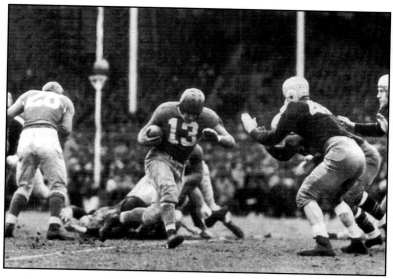

↞ The Packers beat the New York Giants 27-0 to win the 1939 NFL title. The game was played at State Fair Park in Milwaukee to gain a larger crowd than the Packers could obtain at Green Bay's City Stadium. It was an extremely unpopular move with Green Bay fans, but a huge financial success for the team.

The playing field at ▸ State Fair Park was set up inside the race track and folding chairs were set up on the track to boost attendance to over 32,000 to see the 1939 NFL championship game. Packers first score seen here on a pass from Arnie Herber to Milt Gantenbein. *Courtesy of State Fair Park*

City Stadium as it appeared in the 1940s. Wooden bleachers then held nearly 25,000 and a playing surface considered the best in the National Football
League at the time. East High School is on the right and the East River
winds around the stadium at left. The Packers had their locker room
beneath the stands, but the visiting teams did not. They usually dressed for
the game at a hotel in downtown Green Bay and took a bus to the game and
would use the high school locker room and gym at halftime.
Stiller-Lefebvre Collection

11

▲ Lambeau poses for photo during training camp
in late 1930s. The Packers trained on a field
next to City Stadium in Green Bay from the
1920s through the 1940s.
Packer Hall of Fame

Lambeau at the height of his coach-   ▶
ing career with the Packers in the
late 1930s and early 1940s.

▲ Two of Lambeau's best players in the early 1940s, Don Hutson, number 14,
and Tony Canadeo, number 3, in a game against the Rams at City Stadium.

12

- Packer fans turned out by the thousands to greet the team when returning home by train. This was the scene after the 1944 NFL championship victory against the Giants, 14 to 7, at the Polo Grounds in New York.
Green Bay Press-Gazette

- The sixth and last world championship Packer team of 1944. Lambeau, (top row, far left) next to Hutson, coached the team to an 8-2 record during war-depleted talent.
Stiller-Lefebvre Collection

◄ Don Hutson (left) was promoted to assistant coach in 1944, although he continued to play. Lambeau (center) and George Trafton were coaches in that last championship season of Lambeau's.
Charles Brock collection

◀ In 1945, Lambeau met and married the beautiful and wealthy California socialite, 49 year old Grace Garland.
Courtesy of Mary Hoyt Gough

◄ One of the homes Grace and Lambeau lived in was on the waterfront in Malibu Beach. She also owned property in Thousand Oaks and Seattle.
Courtesy of Mary Hoyt Gough

◀ In 1946, Lambeau convinced the Packer board to purchase Rockwood Lodge, 14 miles northeast of Green Bay for player housing and training facility.
Packer Hall of Fame

➤ Curly and Grace lived in one of the small houses on the Rockwood Lodge grounds.
Courtesy of Mary Hoyt Gough

◀ Grace, Curly and Grace's daughter, Jane, pose for a photo during an open house at Rockwood Lodge in 1946.
Packer Hall of Fame

Lambeau purchased Rockwood Lodge and converted it into a one-of-a-kind training and team housing complex, the likes of which the NFL had never seen. A practice field was marked out on the spacious lawn in front of the lodge **(above)** and a tackling dummy was set up along side another practice field **(below)**. The field became unpopular among the players because the playing surface was so hard it caused shin splints. Lambeau would also receive criticism from the Packer board for the amount of money it took to remodel the facility. *Courtesy of Tony Canadeo*

◄ Lambeau had Hollywood connections that allowed him to arrange for actress Margaret O'Brien, a big movie star at the time, to visit the Packer team at Rockwood Lodge for a publicity shot. Bob Forte and Jug Girard are kneeling to Margaret's left and Ted Fritsch in the dark shirt bending over at her right.

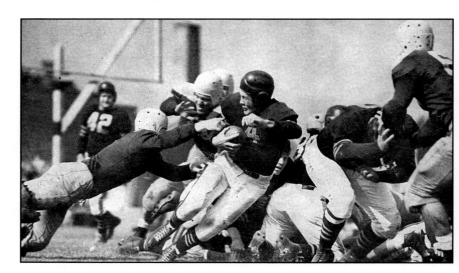

◄ By 1947, the Packer-Bear games were still bitterly competitive battles, but neither team would be champions again for years.
Wide World

17

George Halas, coach and founder of the ▶
Chicago Bears, and Lambeau were
extremely competitive during the many
years they coached against each other.

◆ The Bear-Packer games were always fearlessly fought battles, with
player fights a customary occurrence. This is the playoff game in
December for the Western Division championship in 1941 at Wrigley
Field. The Packers lost 33-14, one week after the Japanese attack on
Pearl Harbor, launching the United States into World War II.

By 1946, Lambeau's
Packers had begun to
slide as the war was
stripping NFL teams
of the better players.
On the sidelines,
Lambeau, with his
customary game day
cigarette, watches in
dismay along with
his assistant coach,
Walt Kiesling.
Packer Hall of Fame

Lambeau and assistant coach Don Hutson show their frustration during a
game in 1947 that saw the Packers go 6-5-1, but would lose four games by the
slim margin of four points or less. Victories in those close games would have
given the Packers a 10-1-1 record and first place in the NFL Western Division.
Green Bay Press Gazette

The Packers played two games each season at Milwaukee's State Fair Park, often before large crowds such as their game against the Los Angeles Rams in 1947. The Packers won 17 to 14 before 36,613. The 1947 season was a heartbreaker. The team finished the year at 6-5-1 and third place in the division, but they easily could have taken first place if they had not lost four games by four points or less.

One of the close losses of the 1947 season came against the Western Division champion Chicago Cardinals, 21 to 20 at Comiskey Park. Ted Fritsch intercepts a pass from the Cardinals' Paul Christman while Bill Dewell tries to tackle him. Lambeau would coach the Cardinals three years later and Dewell would be one of his assistant coaches.

◆ During the time between 1936 and 1944, Lambeau was at his coaching best. He had matured into a seasoned strategist, motivator and recruiter. He found the players he wanted, negotiated their contracts, set up exhibition games, handled team travel arrangements, and basically ran the Green Bay Packer organization. During this nine year period, his Packers would win 75 percent of their regular NFL season games, win the Western Division championship four times, place second five seasons and take three world championship. The Packers' record during this remarkable span was 73-21-4. No other NFL coach came close to matching Lambeau's success during this period.

Before the 1949 season, ▶
Curly and his assistant
coach, Charley Brock,
relax in front of the
Rockwood Lodge.
Packer Hall of Fame

◀ Packer coaching staff gets ready
to view game film during the
1949 season. Left to right: Tom
Stidham, Bob Snyder, Lambeau,
Charley Brock and Don Hutson.
Packer Hall of Fame

The opening game of the 1949 ▶
season against the Bears would be
indicative of how awful the team
would be when the Packers failed
to complete one pass in a 17-0
loss. Jug Girard is shown here
running for a long gain.
Green Bay Press-Gazette

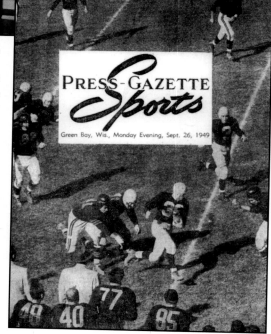

PRESS-GAZETTE
Sports

Green Bay, Wis., Monday Evening, Sept. 26, 1949

▲ Lambeau lost favor with three key members of the Packer executive committee in 1949. Shown here at Rockwood Lodge (left to right): A.B.
Turnbull, publisher of the *Press-Gazette* and first president of the corporation; Lambeau; President Emil Fischer; Bert Bell, then commissioner of
the NFL; and Attorney Jerry Clifford, who would become Lambeau's
chief adversary.
Green Bay Press Gazette

Late in the 1949 season, the   ▶
Packer board voted to keep
Lambeau as coach in a heated
and controversial meeting.
Posing for pictures immediately
after the session: Lambeau
(left) strikes a smile along with
Board members John Moffatt,
Harvey Lhost and Bill Servotte
Packer Hall of Fame

◀ However, once the photo shoot
was over, Lambeau donned his
hat and coat and headed for
the door with a much more
concerned look. Right in front
of Lambeau is board president
Emil Fischer and Art Daley,
Press-Gazette sports editor.
Press-Gazette

A dismal Lambeau looks on from the sidelines at the Packers final game in 1949 against the Lions in Detroit. The Packers finished at 2-10. It was to be Lambeau's last game as the Packers coach. *Chicago Tribune*

Packer stars of yesteryear put their uniforms back on to help the team raise money on Thanksgiving Day, 1949. Left to right, back row: Tiny Engebretsen, 1934-41; Herb Nichols, 1919-20; Curly Lambeau, 1921-30; Jug Earp, 1922-32; Lavvie Dilweg, 1927-34; Verne Lewellen, 1924-32; Johnny Blood, 1928-36. Front row: Charley Brock, 1939-47; Don Hutson, 1935-45; Arnie Herber, 1931-41; and Joe Laws, 1934-45. *Press-Gazette*

➤ Having resigned from the Packers in 1950, Lambeau became head coach of another NFL team on the decline, the Chicago Cardinals. Left to right: Cecil Isbell, a former Packer; Lambeau; Billy Dewell, and Phil Handler rounded out the Cardinal coaching staff. It was obvious Lambeau had lost his heart for football that year.

Lambeau threw many ➤ a tantrum on the side- lines coaching the Cardinals the next two losing seasons. He would resign in 1951 with two games left and the team in total disarray. *Press Gazette*

25

Lambeau and his third wife, Grace, would be celebrities in Chicago when he first took over coaching the Cardinals. The luster wore off fast when Lambeau could not turn the team into winners. *Courtesy of Mary Hoyt Gough*

Charlie Trippi, talking to Lambeau on the sidelines at Comiskey Park, was a star performer for the Cardinals, but had a falling out with Lambeau that eventually split the team apart in 1951. *Courtesy of Mary Hoyt Gough*

◀ Mary Jane Van Duyse, a 27 year old model and Golden Girl that performed during Packer halftime programs, met and started dating Lambeau in 1960. "The first time I met him I was extremely impressed. I thought he was so handsome," she would say.

➥ Mary Jane appeared with Lambeau in 1960 on his weekly television program, *Ask Curly Lambeau*, where he discussed the Packers and fielded questions from viewers.

One of Lambeau's favorite pastimes in the early 1960s was fishing in the waters of Green Bay from his 27 foot power boat nicknamed "Lazy."

Lambeau's summer home in Fish Creek, located on eight acres at the northern tip of Door County, Wisconsin, was purchased in 1956. He would host many parties in the large, 100 year old picturesque property. It would be destroyed by fire in 1961.

After fire destroyed the main building, Lambeau remodeled the carriage house on the same property and lived there during the summer months.

Curly and Mary Jane were constant companions during the summer and fall when Lambeau was living in Door County. "Nobody my own age interested me after I met him," Mary Jane said.

Performing during halftime at Packer games, Mary Jane often got specific instructions from Lombardi regarding what she should wear and what numbers to perform.

Lambeau would propose marriage to Mary Jane, but being a devout Catholic, she turned him down.

29

Fritz Van, a well known and popular sports announcer in the Green Bay area headed up a movement to bring Lambeau back as Packer head coach in late 1958. It was Van who introduced Lambeau to his sister, Mary Jane.

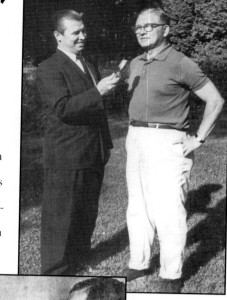

Lambeau (second from left) at ceremonies honoring his installation into the Wisconsin Hall of Fame in Green Bay in 1962. With him are (from left) George Strickler, assistant sports editor of the *Chicago Tribune*; Vince Lombardi, and Pete Rozelle, commissioner of the National Football League. Lombardi disliked Lambeau and often avoided having their picture taken together.

Lambeau is surrounded by five of his greatest stars at the Green Bay Elks Club Banquet, April 26, 1965 honoring six Packers in the pro football Hall of Fame at Canton, Ohio. Left to right: Mike Michalske, Don Hutson, Lambeau, Cal Hubbard, Clarke Hinkle, and Johnny Blood. This is the last known photo of Lambeau before his sudden and unexpected death five weeks later.

◆ One of Lambeau's proudest moments was when he was inducted into the renowned Pro Football Hall of Fame in 1963. He was one of 17 to be inducted with the inaugural enshrinees.
Packer Hall of Fame

The evolution of the Packers' City Stadium to Lambeau field. *Top:* City Stadium as it appeared in the late 1920s. *Middle:* City Stadium as it looked from the mid-1930s through the mid-1950s. *Bottom:* The new City Stadium, built in 1957, was dedicated Lambeau Field in 1965. This is how the stadium appeared at that time.

◄ Lambeau was pictured with Lombardi on the front cover of the 1965 Packer yearbook. Lombardi was so mad at Art Daley, editor of the yearbook, for putting their picture together on the yearbook he refused to talk to Daley for months.
Green Bay Press-Gazette

8

Fall From Grace

After winning the NFL championship in 1944, Lambeau would slip from being an honored and revered coach to one of disrepute and humiliation. Over the next five years, several key factors would lead to Lambeau's fall from grace with his players, the board of directors and the Green Bay populace in general. The descent began gradually. By 1949, he was in a free fall.

Much to the consternation of Packer Board members and to the disappointment of citizens in and around Green Bay, California was playing a larger role in Lambeau's life. Observers felt Lambeau was there far too often and was not spending enough time in Green Bay tending to his Packer duties. After his marriage to wealthy widow Grace Garland in 1945, Lambeau did extend his stay on the West Coast each year and made far fewer appearances on behalf of the Packers in Wisconsin. The team was literally unraveling. Don Hutson's retirement at the end of the 1945 season was a sharp blow. With his most proficient scorer gone, Lambeau was unable to replace him with anyone even close to his talent. In addition, Lambeau had no skilled passer to replace Isbell, who had retired several years earlier. The passing game — the very essence of his offensive strategy — no longer existed.

A new pro football league, the All-America Football Conference (AAFC), began in 1946 and with backing from extremely wealthy owners, took many of the more talented college players. Many of Lambeau's college draft picks from 1946 through 1949 were less than mediocre because too many of the athletes that Green Bay wanted went to higher paying AAFC teams. The Packer talent would become more inferior to other NFL teams.

During this period, Lambeau fell out of favor with his backers by alienating some board members and men who had been his chief supporters for years. He had quarreled with the Packers' board president, Lee Joannes, off and on for years. Joannes, finally tiring of the stressful situation, resigned his presidency. Emil Fischer, a Green Bay businessman, assumed the top position on the board. Fischer and Lambeau also had a troublesome relationship that created discord almost from the beginning. Fischer, although successful in business, had no clue about running a professional football club. When Lambeau named replacements for Dr. W. W. Kelly as team physician and George Calhoun as Packer publicity director in 1947, he created three bitter enemies in Kelly, Calhoun and their close friend, Jerry Clifford. All three were influential and persuasive members of the Packers' executive committee. They would go out of their way to seek revenge against Lambeau. Furthermore, with City Stadium holding only 25,000, the Packers could not draw the same kind of home crowds as other NFL teams in Chicago, Detroit, Los Angeles, Philadelphia, Pittsburgh, New York and Washington, D.C. The Packers began to see their profits slip away to the point that midway through the 1949 season the club was on the verge of bankruptcy.

With all of these negative circumstances coming into play, the Packers began to lose at an unparalleled pace from 1946 through 1949. The result would be an ignominious end to the extraordinary 31-year relationship between Earl Lambeau and the Green Bay Packers.

During the winter of 1945, Lambeau met and began to date glamorous 49 year-old Grace Garland, a wealthy California socialite. Grace, single at the time, had been married several times, including to William Garland, a wealthy West Coast entrepreneur and Gregory LaCava, a well-known Hollywood movie director. Garland died and left a large fortune to Grace and their daughter, Jane. LaCava also provided a lavish lifestyle and numerous movie celebrities as social connections. Grace had an older son, Warren, who had left home and was on his own.

"LaCava entered films during World War I as an animator for Walter Lantz on such animated films as *"The Katzenjammer Kids."*

LaCava gained a reputation as a surefooted comedy director, responsible for such classics as *"My Man Godfrey"* and *"She Married Her Boss."* LaCava was equally proficient in other fields as well, turning out the dramatic *"Stage Door"* and the bizarre political fantasy *"Gabriel Over the White House."* LaCava is also supposed to have directed some scenes in several of the films of his close friend W.C. Fields when Fields couldn't get along with the directors assigned to him. However, there is no official record of it,"[99] although letters from Fields to Grace were found in her personal belongings after her death.

Grace and LaCava were neighbors on Malibu Beach where they got to know each other. After their marriage, LaCava had Grace's house expanded to four stories with a large, ostentatious pool on the oceanfront. It would be one of several elegant homes in which Curly and Grace would live after their wedding. Grace was an extremely attractive brunette who, with her twelve year-old daughter Jane, found the handsome Lambeau charming, lovable and attentive. Jane desperately wanted a father who could provide her the emotional security she needed. Curly quickly won Jane's heart with the unique and thoughtful gifts and attention he would give her, including a baby elephant that Jane kept on a ranch at Thousand Oaks, along with horses and chickens.

Jane would later say that Curly was the best dad she ever had and commented on how gentle and considerate he was of her and Grace. When traveling frequently with Curly and the team and attending practices, the threesome often went out for dancing and dinner. Many of the younger Packers would playfully tease Jane on the game trips they made together. Jane's favorite Packer was young Don Wells, a handsome, 6 foot, 2 inch end who played with the team from 1946 through 1949. When Lambeau heard Wells had playfully asked Jane to marry him, he insisted the players knock off that kind of teasing.

Grace, who had lived in the Los Angeles area for over 20 years, socialized with other wealthy and famous personalities from the entertainment and business world. This would be an entirely new and provocative adventure for Lambeau. Grace's friends would become his, and her social affairs involved him. Their lavish style of fast-paced living would be about as far removed from the commonplace and humdrum Green Bay as it could be. The seductive West Coast influence would sway Lambeau's behavior back in his hometown in the years ahead. Grace's social connections included actors Jennifer Jones, W.C. Fields, Jane Russell, Donna Reed, the Joe Kennedy family and numerous other well-known personalities.

Lambeau and Grace first met during a chance encounter at the Roosevelt Hotel in Los Angeles. He was staying there while on a scouting trip to the West Coast, and she was a guest while in between shopping and parties. Calling her "his little bird," Lambeau gave her a bird in a cage on one of their early dates. She would say later, "He was very romantic and swept me off my feet. Frankly, I found him simply fascinating and refreshing from other men I had known in my life up to that time." The relationship thrived with Lambeau's determined pursuit, and the two were married in August of 1945 at the Little White Chapel in Las Vegas.

Housing options were certainly no problem for the new couple. They would split time between the house Grace owned on Malibu Beach, her second home in Palm Springs, her smaller house in Seattle, a ranch in Thousand Oaks, Curly's cottage in Green Bay or Rockwood Lodge where the Packers trained. Malibu, located near Los Angeles and Santa Monica, features a beautiful beach with 22 acres of coastline and secluded canyons inland. The beaches and mountains of Malibu inevitably look familiar to first-time visitors. In part, this is due to that fact that large tracts of the Malibu Rancho were sold in the 1930s and 1940s to movie studios. Most "Westerns" were shot in the Santa Monica Mountains, as was "Mash" in the 1970s, while the "Gidget" films of the 1950s used Malibu's scenic beaches. Grace and Jane also owned a 700-acre chicken ranch in Thousand Oaks, several miles northeast of Malibu.

Curly, with unlimited funds at his disposal, was now rubbing shoulders with an entirely different group than ever before. Although he had spent the better part of 15 years in the Los Angeles area, he now socialized with well-known movie directors and producers, actors and actresses, as well as members of the West Coast media. With his reputation as an extremely successful and popular football coach along with a charming personality, Lambeau fit right in with this group of socialites. The differences between the glamorous, glitzy and shallow Hollywood company he kept and the more conservative, moderate and staid Green Bay "common" people were dramatically pronounced. It seemed to some of the people of Green Bay that Lambeau was becoming much more influenced by his Hollywood surroundings. Viewed through his hometown lens, Curly's behavior grew more and more ostentatious and often boorish throughout the late 1940s.

If World War II staggered the NFL by diluting its product, it didn't deter certain entrepreneurs from realizing the potential of pro football. Seeing that the American public was becoming enamored with the game, wealthy men from coast to coast tried to parlay that interest into financial gain by joining the NFL. But one by one, they were rejected. Frustrated in their attempts to break into the NFL, a group of wartime power brokers met in a hotel room in St. Louis on June 4, 1944, and discussed the possibility of forming their own pro football league. Arch Ward, the visionary sports editor of the *Chicago Tribune* who had organized the Chicago College All-Star Game and baseball's All-Star Game, chaired the meeting that included representatives from Buffalo, Chicago, Cleveland, Los Angeles, New York and San Francisco. By the end of that day, the group had laid the foundation for a proposed league and chosen its name: the All-America Football Conference.

Unknown at the time, this new professional football league would eventually become a factor in Lambeau's undoing as the Green Bay Packer coach and vice president. In the spring of 1945, however, the entire country was looking forward to better times. It was a time of optimism for the American people. The forces of the United States and its allies had landed in Europe and were pressing toward German territory. In the Pacific war, the United States took back the Philippines from Japan and bombed Japanese cities. It was clearly just a matter of time before the war would be over.

By March 23, Germany's important industries had been captured; in April, the great industrial Ruhr was captured, and with it an entire German army group of 400,000 men. German forces in Italy surrendered on April 29. The Nazi government for what was left of Germany capitulated, and it was all over on May 8. "Give me ten years and you will not be able to recognize Germany," Hitler had said in 1933. It was certainly not recognizable in 1945. Some three million Germans had been killed in Hitler's battles, a like number had died from other causes, over four million were missing, and the maimed were everywhere. The nation was in chaos: cities smashed, bridges wrecked, railroads cut to bits. The Allies applied themselves to the minimum tasks of keeping the Germans from starving, and began the rehabilitation of the nations Hitler had enslaved. But the big job was still the unfinished business in the western Pacific.

The nation's leader all during the war, President Roosevelt, was not to celebrate with Americans on V-J Day. Just weeks before, ill and exhausted, Roosevelt died of a cerebral hemorrhage at his retreat in Warm Springs, Georgia. Franklin Delano Roosevelt, thirty-second President of the United States, died on April 12, 1945. American forces in the Pacific were then methodically clearing Okinawa against Japanese resistance, as the new Commander-in-Chief, Harry Truman, took over. President Truman would not have an easy time. As was the custom of the time, he had been limited as Vice President to presiding over the Senate and attending ceremonial functions. This man, who shortly would have to decide whether to use the atomic bomb, did not even know on April 12 that such a device existed: "...last night the whole weight of the moon and stars fell on me," he told the press. "Please pray for me."

World War II claimed the lives of 20 NFL men: 18 active or former players, an ex-head coach and a front office worker. Probably the best active player killed was the New York Giants' tackle, Al Blozis, a 6 foot, 6 inch, 250-pound tackle. He was killed by machine gun fire in France, six weeks after playing in the 1944 NFL game against the Packers. In all there were 638 NFL players, management and coaches who served in the war. In all, 69 were decorated.

By the 1945 season, players from the service began to trickle back to their teams. The player limit went back to 33 and the fans returned, too. In 1942, the total attendance for NFL games had dropped under 900,000 and remained low through the war years. In 1945, the ten NFL teams played for a total of 1,918,631 fans, an average of 28,636 for the 68 games, including exhibitions. During the war, playing the National Anthem had become a ceremonial prelude to NFL games. Commissioner Layden announced that the anthem would continue to be played. "It should be as much a part of every game as a kickoff," Layden said. "It must not be dropped simply because the war is over. We should never forget what it stands for."

As the late summer of 1945 unfolded, Lambeau and Grace traveled to Green Bay where he began to get his Packers ready for the annual All-Star football game. "Once again, the roster of the All-Stars would include former college stars currently in the military, with no less than 36 of the players still on active duty at game time. A significant change was the moving of the game site back to Soldier Field in downtown Chicago, after a two-year term at Northwestern's Dyche Stadium,"[100] where the All-Stars would meet the NFL champion Green Bay Packers on August 30. It would be Lambeau's and the Packers' third appearance in the football classic. "On August 29, the Packers arrived in Chicago and checked into the Knickerbocker Hotel. The Packers had ascended to the 1944 NFL title with a narrow 14 to 7 win over the New York Giants the previous December. The pro champs featured a very capable, but certainly not dazzling, cast of players that included the likes of Don Hutson, Irv Comp, Herman Rohrig, Lou Brock, Roy McKay and Ted Fritsch."[101] Lambeau was not pleased with his team's preparation for the game. When he initially pulled the team together three weeks before the game to begin practice, he warned the players, "Many of you fellows have played on All-Star teams before this one and since coming into pro ball you have met a lot of men who were your teammates on these college squads. We, too, are inclined to look down our noses at these kids. Well, here is a year we must train and work as though we were going into a league championship game. Just look at what the All-Stars have this year. If you haven't been reading the papers, you might just as well realize now that this is one of the best All-Star squads ever put together."[102]

When he arrived with the team in Chicago, he said, "'We're behind schedule, they don't know their assignments well enough. We haven't come close to reaching the efficiency we will need to beat the All-Stars.' The Packers had held only closed practices at their camp, so no one really knew what their state of readiness was, except that with Hutson available things couldn't be too bad. The odds-makers seemed to think so too, as the Packers were installed as 7 to 5 favorites."[103]

A record crowd of 92,753 jammed Soldier Field the night of the game to witness a Packer victory, 19 to 7, highlighted by Hutson's interception and 85 yard return for a touchdown. "After the game, Keith Brehm of the *Chicago Herald-American* wrote, 'Hutson remains today as football's greatest pass catcher and scorer. Charlie Trippi was voted the Most Valuable Player award for the All-Stars, as nearly all the sportswriters voting agreed that the Georgia halfback, 'ran, passed and kicked brilliantly.'"[104]

Lambeau was optimistic about the 1945 Packers repeating as Western Division champions. Don Hutson returned, along with talented Irv Comp, Ted Fritsch, Joe Laws (who was now the oldest Packer at age 34) and Larry Craig. Vets Charley Brock, Baby Ray, Tiny Croft and Pete Tinsley anchored the line. Two draft picks, Clyde Goodnight and Nolan Luhn, both ends from the University of Tulsa, would become solid receivers for the Packers throughout the remainder of the decade.   Before the 1945 NFL schedule opened, Lambeau was given a new contract that ran through the 1949 season.   He was quoted shortly afterward in the *Press-Gazette:* "There have been rumors in the past about the Packers moving out of Green Bay. I had been born in and living in Green Bay all my life and have no intentions of moving. My home is here and will always be here. To date, the executive committee and I have always worked in harmony. They have been generous in giving me the right to vote and I appreciate it. I will always give 100 percent to protect the interests of the Packers."   Lambeau was attempting to ward off some of the rumors beginning to surface in Green Bay about his "going Hollywood," as the locals would say.

By the time Japan surrendered in August 1945, the returning NFL players often had rude awakenings. One of those getting a military discharge and back to football was Ed Frutig, who played with the Packers in the 1941 season before being drafted. "Frutig was discharged from the Navy in September 1945. He recalled: 'I contacted Curly Lambeau of the Packers and joined them in Washington for the next to last exhibition game before the regular season. The next week we played Detroit. He had his team all set by then, but I think he wanted to see what kind of shape I was in. He put me in the game and called a long pass play — the kind that Don Hutson was awfully good at, and I couldn't get under it. I was in terrible shape. After we got back to Green Bay, he called me in and said, 'You've been traded to Detroit.'"[105]

With the Packers' Lumberjack Band, under the direction of Wilner Burke, playing the merry strains of the team's fight song, "Go! You Packers Go!," the newest championship banner was raised at City Stadium. It was opening day, 1945. Optimism was high as the banner took its place alongside others from the championship years of 1929, 1930, 1931, 1936 and 1939. The team played well enough in the first half of the year (4-1) before going 2 and 3 the rest of the schedule to finish 6-4-0. Green Bay finished in third place in the Western Division behind the Cleveland Rams (9-1-0) and the Detroit Lions (7-3-0). It was the first time they failed to finish in either first or second in the division since 1934. The downhill slide was officially on.

At the same time, the Bears finished 1945 at 3-7 for their first losing season in 15 years. Although the Packers and the Bears both had sub-par seasons, their rivalry was as strong as ever. Frequent player fights broke out in a game in Chicago won by the Bears, 28 to 24. The Packers' Irv Comp was knocked out, and Roy McKay received a broken nose and lost several teeth from a punch thrown by an unidentified Bear. After the game, Lambeau voiced his displeasure with his team's lack of aggressiveness. He warned his players that the next week during practice he would fine them if they didn't put out more than they did in the Bear game. Lambeau was particularly upset with some of the older players' performance, however, his constant threats of fining players had much less impact with World War II vets than it had before the war. One player said later, "It got to be a real pain in the ass and really turned a number of vets off to Lambeau."

Green Bay began a decline in 1945 that worsened each year through 1949. The team and Hutson in particular did have one last shining moment. On October 7, the Packers rang up 57 points — a team record — and hammered the Lions, 57 to 21. Hutson, 32 years old and in his eleventh season, caught four touchdown passes and kicked five extra points in the second quarter alone to set an NFL record. He kicked two more points after touchdowns in the game and left professional football having scored a team and then-NFL record of 823 points. Unfortunately, 1945 would also be remembered as Don Hutson's last year. When he finally retired after eleven years, Hutson held every Green Bay and nearly every NFL pass receiving and scoring record. He left with 488 catches for 7,991 yards. Joe Laws would also retire after the 1945 season. Known as "Tiger" to his teammates, the popular Laws played halfback, fullback, returned kicks and punts and played defensive back for twelve seasons.

Their decline swelling, the Packers took hits from all sides, especially from the competing pro league, the All-America Football Conference. Good players Lambeau may have drafted went to the other league. Indeed, the AAFC fared well in the player war with the NFL. Of the 60 players on the College All-Star team in 1946, 44 opted to play in the AAFC. About 100 men who had played in the NFL jumped to the new league. A classic example of Lambeau's difficult task of signing his draft choices came in 1946 when he tried to sign John Strzykalski who played for Marquette in the early 1940s. Strzykalski was born in Milwaukee and graduated from South Division High School before going on to Marquette. Coming out of Marquette, he was chosen by Lambeau in the first round of the 1946 NFL draft, but chose to sign with the 49ers in the

All-America Football Conference. Strzykalski starred at Marquette in the 1942 season as a freshman/sophomore halfback. He was called up to active duty in February 1943, but continued to star on the gridiron, playing for the Second Army Air Force team in Colorado Springs, Colorado. When he left the service after the war, he was the subject of an AAFC controversy after he signed a contract with the Cleveland Browns in January 1946 for an $8,000 salary. The 49ers protested, and the AAFC office negated the contract, ruling that Strzykalski was already on the 49ers' reserve list. Shortly before that, the Packers had made him the sixth overall pick in the NFL draft. Lambeau was still hoping to get Strzykalski into a Packers' uniform. "We haven't given up hope by any means," Lambeau said in a *Milwaukee Journal* story appearing January 30, 1946. Hope for the Packers eventually faded, though, and Strzykalski signed with the 49ers. Many returning NFL stars were offered big raises to jump to the AAFC. Chicago Bears quarterback Sid Luckman said before the season, "They have been hounding me for several weeks, and their offers have been fabulous."

The AAFC began to play in 1946 with eight teams — the New York Yankees, Brooklyn Dodgers, Buffalo Bisons, Miami Seahawks, Cleveland Browns, Los Angeles Dons, San Francisco 49ers and Chicago Rockets. The Browns, led by legendary coach Paul Brown, became Cleveland's team when the Rams left town for sunny Los Angeles. The competition from the new league drove players' salaries up and complicated the college player draft with a bidding war. It also caused a few veterans to leave their NFL clubs. For instance, the Cleveland Browns signed Ted Fritsch, the Packers' fullback from the previous four seasons, during the winter. After some maneuvering on the part of the Packers and the Los Angeles Rams, he was able to return to Green Bay. Once back, he had a good season, scoring 100 of the team's 148 points that year.

Tony Canadeo, now back from the service, and Irv Comp also received inquiries from AAFC teams, but neither was interested in leaving Green Bay. Canadeo was just happy to be home with his wife, Ruth, and son, Bobby. The three of them moved back into the Savoy apartments along with several other teammates. Nevertheless, most of the team lived at the Packers' recent purchase, Rockwood Lodge. Earlier that year, Lambeau had sold the Packers' executive committee on the idea that since there would be a housing shortage with all the veterans returning from the service, the Packers should provide their own lodging and training facilities.

Lambeau bought the lodge, located about 14 miles northeast of Green Bay, from a group of individuals who had purchased it from the Norbertine Fathers in 1937. The Packers paid $32,000 for the facility and put $8,000 into remodeling and another $4,000 for six prefabricated houses for the married players unable to fine a home. After purchasing the forty-room, fifty-five acre estate, Lambeau immediately converted the lodge into a one-of-a-kind training complex, the likes of which the NFL had never seen. A practice field was marked out on the spacious lawn in front of the lodge, but looks were deceiving. It didn't take long before the players complained that the practice field was extremely hard.

"More trouble began when the Packers' executive committee discovered that the practice field did in fact have only a thin layer of topsoil over hard ground and rock. Players began suffering shin splints, sore feet and leg injuries. Eventually, the entire team would have to be bused back into town to practice. 'It was a hard field,' Canadeo confessed. 'It was built on the rock ledges along the bay. We used to call it the shin splint special.' The hard field notwithstanding, Canadeo defended Lambeau's decision to buy the lodge. 'Curly was before his time. Hell, they all have training camps now. I think he did the right thing. Housing was hard to get. Us town kids were able to live at home and just commute to practice. But if you came from out of town, you had a hell of a time trying to find a place to live. He got housing for a lot of married guys who didn't have it.'"[106]   Dick Wildung, an outstanding offensive and defensive player for the Packers in the late 1940s and early 1950s, recalled his experience with Rockwood: "It was a terrible place to practice football. Right under the dirt had to be all rocks. We had shin splints and everybody's legs were in terrible shape after practicing on that damn thing every day."

Most of the players and their wives would be living at Rockwood Lodge that year. The "Rock," as it was known, was a large and beautiful stone building. The single players lived six and eight in a room, sleeping in army-style bunks and ate specifically prepared meals in a huge dining room. Players with wives lived in the little prefab houses surrounding the lodge, named for former Packer greats. At its heart, the lodge offered a spacious living room complete with a huge stone fireplace, a coffee table and soft chairs all around. There was a classroom area for players to get their blackboard sessions from Lambeau and his assistants.

It was not unusual for the wives and girlfriends, as well as a fair number of people from Green Bay, to drive out to Rockwood Lodge to watch the team practice. Ruth Canadeo thought back to those trips to the lodge and practice sessions: "We were fortunate because Tony could live at home...a lot of players lived at Rockwood Lodge. He went to practice every day, and I would take our son Bobby and go watch. I was there the day Tony dislocated his shoulder. I heard him hollering out there, 'Get it back!'" Ruth also had her own thoughts about Lambeau: "He could be a charmer. But he was very strict as far as the wives traveling with the team or interfering with practices. There was no question — he was in charge! I don't think any of us disliked Curly...we were afraid of him, actually. He was the boss and we tried to stay clear of him. I was afraid of him." Tom Miller, as well as most players of that period who enjoyed playing for Lambeau, said, "It was easy to get along with Curly. But the wives? I don't think they disliked him as coach. They disliked his way of living. Curly was quite the ladies' man."

The expenses Curly and Grace ran up for decorating one of the cottages on the Rockwood grounds irritated the Packer board. "The financial committee threatened to resign over the bills which were being presented by Lambeau for decorating the cottage that he and his wife were occupying. The decorating had been done by Marshall Fields in Chicago."[107]

Lambeau's personal life became a public obsession with board members and Green Bay citizens alike griping openly. Chuck Johnson, in his book on the history of the Packers, wrote: "Lambeau was also criticized for his personal life. He had been married three times and divorced twice and he left Green Bay in the off-season to winter at Malibu Beach in California. Had this been New York City, for example, Lambeau's personal life would have been his own, but in the small Wisconsin city, failure to conform made him the object of personal attack. Mimeographed letters were distributed in the bars of Green Bay, referring to Lambeau as 'the Earl of Hollywood.' Some of Lambeau's players would later defend their coach, "A lot of people around town thought Curly had gone high hat on them," a player recalled. "They couldn't understand that pro football had changed. It had got so complicated that it was no longer a part-time occupation for the coaches."

While Lambeau may have liked having most of his team located at Rockwood Lodge where he had more control, the players weren't crazy about it. The fans definitely didn't like the team so far away from town because they didn't see the players nearly as much as they had in the past. One of the best-known Packer fans during the 1940s was Sue Wallen. She worked the front desk at the Astor Hotel in Green Bay where many of the Packers stayed in previous years. Every player missed her when they moved from the Astor to the Rockwood Lodge. Not casually, but deeply. Each one told stories about things she had done for them. They said it wasn't the same because they were not living at the Astor Hotel where they came down every morning and talked to Sue behind the desk. Sue was a pretty blond-haired woman with bright, sensitive blue eyes. She had not only seen every Packer game played since 1919, but she knew all there was to know about every player. A few years previously, the hotel changed management and Sue was going to be fired. The Packers rose up in revolt and threatened to tear the owner apart if Sue left. When Lambeau wanted the address of a Packer player, he often called Sue. During the war, Sue corresponded with dozens of players…letters came in from all over the world. The first thing a Packer said when he met another Packer far from home was, "Have you heard from Sue?" Sue Wallen listened to their foibles, sent them money, gave them advice and helped them all with warm affection.

The Pro Football Hall of Fame in Canton, Ohio, has an old magazine article written by Jack Sher in December 1946, entitled, *"Packers of Green Bay, Story of a Great Town and a Great Team."* Sher described the mood in Green Bay when the Packers played the Bears: "On the Saturday afternoon before the game, I sat in the Loop Café on Adams Street hating the Bears. I have no idea why I hate them; the Bears have never done anything to me. But a week of living in Rockwood Lodge with the Packer players and circulating among the local citizens has done something to my sanity. On the sidewalk in front of the café, Joe Laws, who sparked the Packers to a championship in 1944, stood talking with his father and another ex-Packer. Across the street in front of the Astor, the players who would go to the game tomorrow began gathering in little groups. When they were spotted by a group of Green Bay people, elderly couples, businessmen, working girls, and kids, some were keyed up, solemn and angry. The Packers had lost three exhibition games and now the people demanded to know why. They got dozens of reasons, but none satisfied them. Some people went so far as to say that Curly had lost his touch that had made him a great coach. Others griped that Curly could always think for himself, but now he doesn't breathe without asking Hutson about it first. Many were resentful because Hutson wasn't playing, while others advanced the theory that Lambeau was trying too hard...trying to play the game from the sidelines and sending in too many substitutes with instructions. In a sense, the town tirades against Curly Lambeau were a tribute to him. They tell you that the people of Green Bay know that 'as Curly goes, so goes our Packers.' They know that Curly is the blood and bones and chemistry that hold the Packers together. Lambeau with his peculiar foibles is still the man who took Green Bay out of the backwoods and with courage and heartache put it on the national football map. They expect him, with fierce love and pride in the town and team, to keep the Packers out in front."

The Packers opened their training camp in August of 1946 with their largest number of players. There were 57 in total, with 27 of them veterans and 30 rookies. Don Hutson had retired and was now a full-time assistant coach. Lambeau was picking up players any way he could get them. Tom Miller, a 6-foot, 2-inch, 210-pound end who had played with the Philadelphia Eagles and Washington Redskins, recalls an incident that put him in a Packer uniform. "When I came to Green Bay with my new wife who was from Green Bay, I needed a haircut. My father-in-law took me to the barbershop in downtown Green Bay and Lambeau was there with a towel over his face getting a shave. The barber asked, 'Curly do you know Tom Miller from the Redskins?' Curly asked 'What are you doing here?' I told him this is my father-in-law and I married his daughter who came from Green Bay and we were here visiting. It wasn't too long after that my contract was signed with the Green Bay Packers. I had no problems with Curly at all. He was awfully good to me. Hell, I wasn't a very good player."

New faces abounded but one thing stayed the same in Green Bay. There was still an unusually strong camaraderie among the players — and among the fans, for that matter. Few of the men of yesteryear played for the money. They played because they loved football. They hated the long, grinding practice sessions and the rigid training hours, but the games made up for those times. As one former player explained, "What we had at the Packers, was spirit. One time in a game, a Packer fullback walked up to a husky rebel player throwing a half-hearted block at him. The Packer whirled him around by the shoulders and growled, 'You ought to be ashamed to wear a football uniform. The next time you hit me, put your heart into it.'" The Packers off the field acted like family. Various families would gather in the huge living room of the Rockwood Lodge after the kids were in bed and would talk and play games. They made the place seem much more like home than was possible. On nights when husbands and wives would go to the movies in town, the single men on the ball club would often sit with the babies. Many of the players had ties with each other that began long before they joined the Packers. The two ends, Clyde Goodnight and Nolan Luhn, played together at Tulsa University.

Predicting where the teams would finish the 1946 season in the standings was pure guesswork. The war had interrupted so many players' lives and conditioning, it was almost impossible to judge a team's potential regardless of what veteran returned to his club. However, one thing was certain: Green Bay had lost a huge part of their passing game with Hutson's retirement. Although Clyde Goodnight and Nolan Luhn were decent receivers, they were not in the same class as Hutson. But then, who was? In addition, Irv Comp was not as good a passer as his predecessors, Cecil Isbell and Arnie Herber. It would be painfully evident that the Packers' famous and immensely effective passing game was gone. The Packers gained only 841 yards passing all year, less than half of the team's total rushing yardage. The team had gained 1,536 yards passing last season compared to 2,407 in 1942, illustrating how far the passing game had fallen. Comp only completed 29 percent of his passes. No one else did much better, with a total team completion of 30 percent and only four passing touchdowns all year. Goodnight and Luhn were the leading receivers, each with an anemic 16 all season. Hutson had often caught that many in one game.

Despite the Packer slide in 1946, Lambeau often displayed his old fire and passion. Nolan Luhn was a rookie in 1945 and recalled, "He always wanted to win. He always spoke of winning, at all costs. He gave a pep talk my rookie year at Green Bay. I'm kind of high-strung and halfway between his pep talk just before the game, I jumped up and headed for the door. I almost got out before he caught me. He said, 'Hey, I'm not through yet!' So I went back to sit down. This was in the locker room when we played the Chicago Bears at Green Bay. That was my first pro game. On the sidelines during the game he would pull off his coat and throw it on the ground, kick it and then pick it up. The fans just loved it. He smoked on the sidelines, too. He had this cigarette holder that was about six inches long that he used all the time. I thought he had a good personality. A little bit of a sense of humor, but come about Thursday, Friday and Saturday, he was just as quiet as he could be. Didn't talk to many people. He would go off and get lost by himself. We would have a meeting and he was quiet. He expected you to be quiet."

Lambeau continued to use player fines as a way to discipline. Luhn would say later: "Curly fined some players $500 or $600 for eating pie on the train coming home after losing to Washington. He didn't believe in eating the pie because we lost. He took losing very hard. If we lost a game, the following day he would get on his boat and go up the bay and sit all day. He would show up for practice about 9:30 Tuesday morning. You wouldn't see him at all on Monday. Never showed up. He wanted to win everything. I went tobogganing one day and looked downhill and saw Curly parked there in his Cadillac. He told me that I could get hurt and I was under contract and he would fine me $100 if he caught me doing that again. He also fined players $100 for going into a bar, even to make a phone call, unless he said 'lid's off.' That was his expression when we won, he would tell us, 'lid's off.'"

Lambeau stubbornly stuck to his single-wing, or Notre Dame box formation, while most of the other NFL teams had converted to the much more effective T-formation. The closest Lambeau came to altering his Notre Dame box formation was something he started to use called the "Quick Opening V Formation." That was better suited for quick openers, as opposed to the slower developing formation they used from 1941 through 1945. Without a passing attack and running from an outdated formation, the Packers struggled to a 6-5 season, finishing in third place in the Western Division. The downward slide continued.

Most humiliating to the players were the two losses to the Bears. In the first game of the 1946 season against the Bears at City Stadium, a huge crowd of more than 25,000 was on hand. The newspaper coverage was the heaviest in the history of the Packers. Writers were jammed three deep into the City Stadium press box, but it wasn't much of a game. The Bears completely outplayed the Packers, 30 to 7. Even the overly optimistic Art Daley of the *Press-Gazette* had a tough time making the team sound good in this lopsided loss. "I have nothing to say," read the austere post-game statement from Lambeau. Curly told reporters he was disgusted with his team's inability to execute the fundamentals of football — blocking and tackling. The locker room aura was proof enough.

Press-Gazette reporter Lee Remmel reported that "You could hear a pin drop" in the Packers' locker room and that the players talked "in hushed tones that would have done credit to a morgue."

Still, the Packers were in the race for the championship for about half of the season. After losing to the Bears and the Rams in the first two weeks, they won three in a row. Before that, they had a re-match with the division-leading Bears on November 3. A large crowd of 40,321 turned up at a wet and muddy Wrigley Field to see the two archrivals go at each other again. Lambeau made sure the Packers played a much different game than the one they opened the season with against the Bears. For two quarters, the Packers battled the Bears to a standstill. The Bears won only when Ted Fritsch was hammered by a vicious tackle, coughed up the football and Chicago's Ed Sprinkle scooped it up and sloshed 30 yards through the mud to score their only touchdown. Though the Packers had played hard and had outplayed the Bears, they suffered a tough loss, 10 to 7, and were eliminated from the race.

"Two reasons for the decline were difficulties making the T-formation function properly and Don Hutson was no longer playing end. 'Curly never recovered from the loss of Hutson,' a player of the time recalled. 'Lambeau tried to have ends like Nolan Luhn and Clyde Goodnight do the things Hutson had done and they couldn't. No one else could, either. There was only one Don Hutson. Curly just couldn't realize that he was gone as a player and that he would have to adjust his offensive patterns and play accordingly.'"[108]

As mentioned earlier, another incident took place that year that would come back to haunt Lambeau; he terminated Dr. W.W. Kelly as team physician and hired Dr. Henry Atkinson. The move so infuriated Kelly, who was now in his 60s and had been the Packer team physician since 1921 that he turned on Lambeau and openly became his outspoken enemy. Since Kelly was also on the Packer board, he would get his opportunity to even the score in a few years. Kelly never tried to hide his resentment of Lambeau's move to replace him. On one occasion during a home game when Kelly introduced an all-time Packer team at halftime, not once during the entire program did he mention Lambeau's name. "The oversight was not without precedent or repeat, however. Lee Joannes, in executive committee meetings, never referred to Lambeau by name any more, only as 'the man in the gray suit.'"[109]

Art Daley became the *Press-Gazette* sports editor in 1946 after serving as sports reporter for several years. Daley had his own rec-ollections of Lambeau that year: "My impression was that on the field he was strictly a holler guy. I distinctly remember him and Baby Ray out in the old stadium. He would be hitting him on the back and pushing him in the game. I often called him on the phone for interviews. I recall after a game we had lost to the Bears and he was really unhappy about it. I asked him what happened. He said, 'Uram fumbled. Andy lost the game for us.' That's the way it was. He would pick out a player, find a scapegoat a lot of times. He was really not a coach in the sense of X's and O's — all he had was this briefcase. He would always have that around him. But that's all he had. He was not a coach who designed plays. Don Hutson flat out said that Curly was not that type of coach. He was an enthusiast, a salesman and a good holler guy."

Daley also recalled some of Lambeau's 'rules' he enforced on the players: "When they were out at Rockwood Lodge, Curly would always tell them what to eat and what they couldn't eat. He had a thing about ketchup; he didn't want you to eat ketchup. Bruce Smith, a running back, loved ketchup. The trainer, Jorgenson, tried to tell Curly that this guy had been eating ketchup since he was six years old and it wasn't going to hurt him. And the 'sex thing' was there, too. Bob Forte used to say that 'Curly wouldn't let them do anything the night before.' When they were on the train to Chicago to play the Bears, it had to be absolutely quiet on the train."

Americans were now starting their second post-war year in 1947 and eager to get back to normal. The nation's economy was heating up. Instead of tanks, airplanes and guns, the country was manufacturing cars, stoves, refrigerators and home furniture at a record pace. The upbeat and optimistic mood of America was the best since before the war. People were singing the first phrase to a popular tune, *"Zip-a-Dee-Doo-Dah"* and listening to the haunting melody of *"Autumn Leaves."* The new look for girls and young women featured full skirts, v-necks and spiked shoes. Kids were nuts about a new radio show, *"It's Howdy-Doody Time,"* while their parents tuned in to the popular *Art Linkletter* program. The average annual income for Americans was now up to $3,031, and they could buy their own three-bedroom home for around $6,500, a new car for just over $1,000 and put gas in it for 23 cents a gal-lon. For the first time in years, Hollywood was finally producing non-war related movies. Films like *Gentleman's Agreement, Lassie* and *A Streetcar Named Desire,* featuring a new actor by the name of Marlon Brando, were most popular in 1947.

Meanwhile, the folks in Green Bay wanted their Packers back on top in the NFL — and they wanted it *now.* The fans also followed their minor league baseball team, the Green Bay Blue Jays. Playing on that team was a young infielder who also happened to be a local radio sports announcer, Earl Gillespie.

Off the field, more turmoil was in store for the Packers when team president, Lee Joannes resigned in July. He had held the job since 1930, and for 18 years he had provided solid leadership, playing a major role in guiding the organization through the Depression and the financial difficulties in the 1930s. But in recent years, he and Lambeau were often at odds. Emil R. Fischer was elected by the board of directors to replace Joannes. The change in leadership would have a dramatic impact on Lambeau within a few years. Fischer was the president of the Atlas Warehouse and Cold Storage Company in Green Bay and had been on the board of directors since 1936. He was not considered Lambeau's ally.

One of the first actions Fischer took was to reduce Lambeau's all-inclusive control of the Packers. He increased the board of directors from 22 to 25, and then expanded the executive committee from nine to a cumbersome twelve members. With the urging of Jerry Clifford, who was an open enemy of Lambeau, he divided the executive committee into subcommittees that essentially took over responsibilities Lambeau had previously held. They had committees for contracts and publicity, finance, grounds and legal affairs. In short, all the things that Lambeau took care of before were now taken out of his hands. Or, at least, the committee was going to be involved in the decisions he used to make by himself. He would be assisted with everything but coaching.

While Lambeau made no public derogatory remarks about the change, privately he was seething. "'I believe these men, all good businessmen, acted for what they thought were the best interests of the Packers, but the plan just won't work,' Lambeau said later. 'You can't run a football team if you have to go to this committee for that and that committee for this.' But the subcommittees were not dissolved. The struggle in the front office spilled over onto the field. Bob Forte, who played linebacker and often doubled as right halfback on offense from 1946 through 1953, spoke of this later, 'The players can't help but be affected by troubles in the front office. Management fights upset the coaches, the players and even the fans.'" [110]

This move might have been prompted by what the Packer board, Jerry Clifford in particular, considered runaway expenses by Lambeau and two unpopular moves he made involving Dr. Kelly and George Calhoun. John Torinus, in his book *The Packer Legend,* explained the expense side: "The executive committee began to be concerned about control of expenditures. In June of 1947, the committees decided from that point on it would meet weekly on Monday at noon to get a report from Lambeau as vice president and general manager. The executive committee was also divided into five subcommittees which were given control over the supervision of finances and other business matters such as grounds, contracts, policing the stadium and publicity."

Lambeau's replacing of Kelly as team physician struck most board members as a crass move. The change regarding Calhoun was even more distasteful to the board. Without any discussion with the executive committee, Lambeau replaced Calhoun as the Packer publicist with his friend, George Strickler, former sports reporter for the *Chicago Tribune* in March 1947. The saddest part of the change was how the 57 year-old Calhoun found out about the change. He discovered he had been replaced when he read it on the wire service in his office at the *Press Gazette.* This is the lead paragraph of the article that appeared: "George Strickler, who resigned last week as director of public relations for the National Football League, has signed a three-year contract as assistant general manager and director of public relations for the Green Bay Packers, it was announced today by Packer Coach Curly Lambeau." John Torinus, Sr., a close friend of Calhoun, said: "Calhoun was a bitter enemy of Lambeau from that day forward. George was surprised and deeply hurt. It broke Calhoun's heart. Cal wanted nothing to do with him after that point." Calhoun had been writing sports and promoting the Packers since the very beginning in 1919.

Larry Names, author of the four-volume Packer history, offered another insight: "There's a little bit more to the story. What I heard was that Strickler put the article on the wire. He jumped the gun. Curly never got a chance to tell Calhoun to his face. The other part of the story is Lambeau was procrastinating because he didn't have the heart to tell him. Strickler finally got tired of waiting and put the story out."

On the surface it might have appeared to be a logical move on Lambeau's part. Strickler, age 43, was an accomplished sports reporter with an excellent reputation, having held a top sports reporting job with the *Chicago Tribune* for ten years and the prestigious position of director of public relations for the NFL since 1941. Putting him into the Packer position of public relations with Calhoun still handling some of the mundane Packer news releases would seem like a good move for the Packers. But the way it was handled created a wound among his old supporting cast that had been behind him from the beginning — a wound that would never heal. Too many men on that board had the absurd notion that Strickler was an "outsider." The men he hurt still had enough influence to exact their sophomoric revenge. It would only be a matter of time.

As the Packers came together for the start of the 1947 training season in late July at Rockwood Lodge, Lambeau informed the players of his intent to switch from the single-wing, or Notre Dame box formation, to the T-formation. Dick Wildung, an outstanding lineman for the Packers for years, knew Lambeau made the right choice to change to the T-formation. He said, "We had to do it. I think the Packers and the Pittsburgh Steelers were the last two teams to go to the T-formation. The T is better for a pro football team. I always liked to play defense against the single-wing, but the T-formation, they hit much quicker. Although I liked Curly as a coach and a person, I think he fell behind in pro football. We were still playing that Notre Dame box when everybody had gone to the T-formation. I just don't think he stayed up with football at that time, but he was a good guy to play for."

In the off-season, Lambeau had obtained a T-formation quarterback from the Washington Redskins, "Indian" Jack Jacobs. No one knew much about the 28 year-old Oklahoma native who, although he played for the Cleveland Rams and the Redskins, had never seen much action. But Lambeau insisted he was familiar with the T-formation and was a potentially good passer, as well as a gifted punter. There was reason for optimism in the 1947 season. The players would often talk about how this could be a winning season for Green Bay and they could get back on top. It was a veteran club with a good crop of rookies. The NFL also increased the team limit from 33 to 35 for the 1947 season, which allowed the Packers to go a little deeper with the talent available. Although the competing pro football league, the AAFC, was still taking talent away from the NFL, there were still enough talented players to make for an exciting year in the NFL. The Packers, Chicago

Cardinals, Los Angeles Rams, Detroit Lions and Chicago Bears made up the Western Division while the Eastern Division had the Philadelphia Eagles, the Washington Redskins, Pittsburgh Steelers, Boston Yanks and New York Giants. There would be a twelve game schedule in 1947, compared to the eleven-game schedule in 1946.

1947, it turned out, would be a heartbreaker. The Packers played sound football and still finished the year at 6-5-1 and in third place in the Western Division, but they could just as easily have won the division. Unbelievably, they lost four games by four or less points to the champion Cards, 14 to 10 and 21 to 20, to the Steelers 18 to 17, and to the Bears, 20 to 17. Four heartbreaking losses could have gone in the Packers' favor and given them a 10-1-1 record and first place. Instead, the team finished a disappointing third behind the second-place Bears and first-place Cardinals. As disheartening as the 1947 season was, it was only the beginning. Disappointing skidded to dismal in the years to come.

"Indian" Jack Jacobs did turn out to be a decent T-formation quarterback, completing nearly 45 percent of his 242 attempts for 16 touchdowns. Nevertheless, he also threw 17 interceptions and fumbled five times at costly points in games. The defense was strong again in 1947, allowing the fewest points, 210, of any team in the NFL. Larry Craig had an outstanding year at defensive end while Dick Wildung, Ed Neal and Bob Forte were also exceptional on defense. All in all, the team should have had a much better record.

Ward Cuff, a graduate of Marquette, played with the Packers for the 1947 season after ten years with the New York Giants and Chicago Cardinals. It was Cuff who missed two short, critical field goals in the last seconds that led directly to two of the Packers' losses. When interviewed, it was obvious Cuff had no love for Lambeau: "The Notre Dame box single-wing, offensive formation the Packers used was out of date. Lambeau wouldn't change it and get into the more modern approach." Lambeau cut Cuff with two games remaining in the season, as said he recalled, "It was very unceremonious. He just came up one day and said, 'I'm going to cut you.'" Cuff's attitude toward Lambeau still rankles him. "Hell, Curly would often try to date the players' wives and because of who he was, being the coach and all, even succeeded in dating some of them. I don't think the players had any respect for Curly."

1948. More upsets. More heartache for the Packers. Lambeau's squad totally unraveled in the second half of their season to begin their decline into a black hole of defeats, despair and Curly's ignominious departure. In other 1948 upsets, Harry Truman defeated Thomas Dewey to become President (pictures showing Truman holding up the front page of the early edition of the *Chicago Tribune* with the huge headline **Dewey Defeats Truman!** have become part of American folklore); boxer Marcel Cerdan took Tony Zale's lightweight title away; and a little known California schoolboy, Bob Mathias, won the Olympic decathlon gold medal in London.

In October of 1948, Green Bay opened its first commercial airport. Service began at Austin Straubel Field in Ashwaubenon when a Wisconsin Central (North Central) Minneapolis-Chicago flight discharged two passengers and took on four from the temporary terminal in a construction shack. Lambeau arranged for the Packers to use the airport and fly to some of their away games in 1948, becoming one of the first NFL teams to use a DC-4 commercial airline.

Before the 1948 training season opened again at Rockwood Lodge, Lambeau would sign his number one college draft choice, Earl "Jug" Girard from the University of Wisconsin. Girard arrived at the University of Wisconsin in September of 1944 from his hometown of Marinette, which seemed to produce an inordinate number of talented football players. Jug might have been the best of all. He ranks with the finest all-around athletes ever to attend UW. He excelled at every sport he tried. Jug undoubtedly could have won nine letters, or maybe twelve, had he completed his eligibility. Following the 1944 football season, he dropped out of school and wound up in the army, returning to the campus in the fall of 1947.

Lambeau desperately wanted the popular, fun loving and talented Wisconsin boy who reminded him so much of Johnny Blood to join his 1948 squad. Unfortunately, so did the New York Yankees of the rival AAFC. Lambeau had to outbid New York in order to sign him and did so for $10,000, which at that time was an exceptionally high salary for a rookie with the Packers. As it turned out, Lambeau never did find a regular position for Girard that year. He would run the ball 13 times for a paltry 26 yards, throw 14 passes, complete only four and punt a few times. He did play a little defense, but that was never Jug's best position, to say the least. He would play a bigger role with the team in 1949 through 1951 before being traded to the Detroit Lions in 1952 where he had a decent career. The fact that Lambeau paid that kind of money to an unproven, undisciplined rookie did not sit well with many of the veterans who were making considerably less.

Once Girard joined the team, though, there wasn't a player who didn't like him. Damon Tassos, who played with the Packers in the late 1940s, said, "He was a good guy. He wasn't the greatest professional football player in the world. He played quarterback for us, kind of a scatterbrain, but a good guy. Jug was a good athlete, no question about it. Hell of a team ball player."

Girard joined the Packers too late in Lambeau's coaching career to appreciate the glory years. He would recall, "Lambeau was kind of tough and he was getting ready to pack it in. He had his day and we appreciated it. We didn't have too much (talent) besides (running back Tony) Canadeo, and he was getting past his prime. The team was pretty much done and gone with. Nobody said anything about it, but that was the general feeling."[111]

Before the 1948 training camp opened, Canadeo, who had led the Western Division in ground gaining the year before and was the Packers' leading ground gainer in the two seasons since he returned from the service, thought he deserved a raise. It was never easy to talk to Lambeau about money, tight-fisted as he was with players' salaries. Canadeo wanted more money than Lambeau was willing to pay. While they were having a conference, Canadeo finally said "enough" and walked out. Then it was officially stated that Canadeo was a holdout. "Of course," Curly said, "we'd like to have Tony with us, but we'll be all right at left halfback if he isn't back with us. It has always been and always will be our policy to pay players as much as possible and our aim is to give Packer fans a good football team." Canadeo was quoted in the *Press-Gazette*, "I don't want anything more than anybody else on the team, I just want as much as the fellows playing the same left halfback position! I was told that I would be traded if I didn't sign within 24 hours." Lambeau said that the team was having some financial problems and had even cut some operating expenses, although not salaries. Lambeau stated, "Our profit on the year's operation was as much as the increase that some of the players are asking. The only raises that we are giving are to a couple of men who made less than $5,000 last year and whose play certainly warranted an increase." Canadeo did eventually sign just before training camp opened, but he did not get a raise. He was making less than $8,000 a year at the time.

The narrow losses from the 1947 season may have given the impression that the Packers would still be strong enough in 1948 to challenge the Chicago Cardinals and Bears for the top spot in the Western Division.

That was perception, not reality. The Packers failed to challenge either team in 1948. Instead, they lost their last seven games and ended with a 3-9 record, finishing next to last in the division. It was the worst win/loss record in the history of the franchise and the first losing season since 1933. The 1948 team fell off in every major statistic from the year before: rushing and passing yardage was down 20 percent and scoring fell off by 44 percent as they put up 120 fewer points. The defense also deteriorated, allowing opponents to rush and pass for more yardage and score 80 more points than the 1947 team.

The losses piled up and the 1948 season rapidly fell apart. Still, Lambeau pushed his players. Perry Moss, a star quarterback at Illinois and a high draft pick of Lambeau's, recalled his rookie year in 1948: "At that time, Lambeau and Halas were the top guys in pro football. I was always impressed with him. He was a handsome, good-looking guy. He had a lot of energy and didn't like to lose. He was tough to beat. Really, I looked up to him and admired him. He was a tough, verbal coach. At halftimes at games when we weren't playing well, he'd get on us pretty good. I remember one incident where we lost a game to the Cardinals who beat us in Milwaukee in a close game and the first thing we did the next practice was to divide the team up 15 yards apart and we had head-on tackling."

There were several factors building up that contributed to the team's collapse. First, too many excellent and experienced veterans had left the club. Hutson, Laws and Goldenberg departed in 1945. Bill Lee and Russ Letlow left a year later. In 1947, Charley Brock and Milburn (Tiny) Croft called it quits. Just six players remained from the 1944 championship team heading into 1948. Losing such talent was problem enough. Replacing it was impossible. The draft hadn't been the answer. Only two choices from 1946 and 1947 played in 1948. "The 1944 draft was such a washout that only one player from it ever played for the Packers. To top it off, Green Bay lost its number one choices in a bidding war to the AAFC in both 1946 and 1947."[112]

The turning point of the season may have come after the fourth game, a 17 to 7 loss to the Chicago Cardinals in front of a large Milwaukee crowd of nearly 35,000 at State Fair Park. Lambeau was so upset with the team's performance that he held out a half game's pay from each player. After finding their checks lacking on Tuesday, the players turned around that Sunday and handed the Rams a 16 to 0 loss at City Stadium. Following that effort, the men expected an extra large check — pay for the Rams' game plus the missing pay from the Cardinals' contest. Lambeau, however, did not return the fines. Many of the Packers were service veterans or players who had been playing in the NFL for years, and this move by Lambeau struck them as "real chicken shit," as one player said. Morale hit rock bottom. He cut popular Bruce Smith that week, which also didn't help team morale. The team lost its final seven games to finish 3-9, one game ahead of the cellar-dwelling Lions. Only after the season was over did Lambeau return the missing money, but by then the damage had been done.

"'I'll never forget that day,' Bob Forte said later. 'We lost, 17 to 7, on a long run by Elmer Angsmann and a punt return by Charlie Trippi. After the game, we were in the dressing room at State Fair Park and Lambeau came around and told us that we'd been fined half a game's salary. We wanted to know what for. After all, the Cardinals were league champions and they'd barely beaten us on two long plays. 'For indifferent play,' Curly said. We couldn't believe it.'"[113]

"Perhaps statistics can best illustrate Green Bay's slide after Lambeau held their pay. The Packers gave up 77 first downs in the first five games then turned around and allowed 145 in the final seven. Opponents gained 728 rushing yards before October 24, then piled up 1,425 the rest of the way. And finally, after having surrendered just 83 points, the team gave up a whopping 207 down the stretch. Never before had a Packer team sunk so low. Unfortunately, such dreary performances, long the exception in the past, would become the norm in the following decade."[114]

Another poor decision made by Lambeau several weeks earlier may also have had an impact on the players' performance. In spite of a steady downpour at practice, he kept the team on the field for an intense two and one-half hours. Several of the players became sick. As a result of numerous injuries, less talent and some questionable decisions by Lambeau, who by now was also falling further out of favor with the Packers' executive committee, the season was a disaster. Still, it would get worse — rock bottom on the field and at the bottom line.

Green Bay's 3-9 record in 1948 was the team's worst season ever and Lambeau had to accept much of the blame for it. His irrational decision to fine the whole team five games into the season and then not return their money had been a dagger through the team's heart. Many also blamed the dismal performance on the team being removed from the townspeople. Businessman Jerry Atkinson of Prange's department store blamed the disillusionment on the Packers' living and practicing out of town at Rockwood Lodge, which actually had absolutely nothing to do with the won-lost record of the team.

The Green Bay Packers' losing ways were now beginning to show in the team's profit and loss statement. The executive committee met in December 1948 to review the financial situation. At the same meeting, George Strickler was stripped of his title as assistant general manager by the board. Tensions were at an incredible high. The next year would add considerably more tension and cloud a truly remarkable tenure for Lambeau.

9

Shameful Finish

When the Packer team of 1948 bottomed out at 3-9 in next to last place in the Western Division, Lambeau was somehow hoping to reverse the slide. It was not to be. In the months leading up to the 1949 season, the executive committee and Lambeau were nearly always at odds. Constant sniping evolved into a nasty power struggle, as though common sense had taken a back seat to unbridled pride by both sides. Lambeau's illustrious tenure as the Green Bay Packer coach would plummet to a pitiful, shameful finish and leave the team in disarray for years. Not until Vince Lombardi arrived ten years later and the board surrendered its choking grip on the coach would the Green Bay Packers return to their glory years.

On paper it looked as if the 1949 club might be able to hold its own. The ingredients seemed to be in place — a better than average offensive line, good running backs who had played together for several seasons, a decent if not spectacular defensive line, average line-backing and experienced defensive backs. They also had 14 new players on the 32-man squad, including Lambeau's number one pick in the college draft, quarterback Stan Heath from Nevada. Unfortunately, few would develop into impact players. The big question was how good or bad the passing game would be. Depth was another big question mark. Should the team suffer many injuries, it could cripple the team's chances.

Halfway through 1949, it was painfully obvious that the Packers were awful. They were seldom in any contest and won only two of their first seven games. The season's future was all too clear even in the first game of the year. A beautiful, sunny late September afternoon greeted the Packers on opening day. Perfect football weather. Packers vs. Bears. More than 25,000 enthusiastic Packer fans crammed into old City Stadium, buoyed no doubt by the optimistic reportage of Art Daley and Lee Remmel of the *Press-Gazette*. Wisconsinites who could not see the game in person would be listening to Bob Heiss call the play-by-play over the WJPG radio station originating from Green Bay. Fights between the Packers and the Bears flared up frequently. The Packers' Jay Rhodemyre, playing in the middle of the line on defense, received a blow to the head and was knocked out. Irv Comp returned the 'favor' to the Bears' Jim Keane who had to be helped from the field. More blows were exchanged when Canadeo was knocked out of bounds into the Bears' bench. Fans got into the spirit of the rough play at halftime when a group of kids mugged the Bears mascot and tried to remove his costume. A Bear field goal in the third quarter ended the scoreless tie. Johnny Lujack then threw two touchdown passes in the fourth quarter to cap off the 17 to 0 win for the Bears.

Canadeo accounted for all of the Packers' offense on this day as he picked up 92 yards in just eleven attempts, an average of over eight yards a carry. It wasn't nearly enough. Incredibly, the Packers didn't complete a single pass all afternoon — the first time that had happened in the history of the franchise. Jug Girard started as quarterback for Green Bay and his throws were high, low or wide as he went 0 for 7 with three interceptions. Indian Jack Jacobs replaced Girard and went 0 for 4 with rookie Stan Heath throwing two incompletions late in the game. After the game, Lambeau decided not to lace into the team, instead trying a motivational approach.

As soon as Lambeau reached the dressing room beneath the stands at City Stadium, he called the team together. "This is only one game," he emphasized. "Only one game. And there are eleven more to go. Your effort out there today was all right and if you keep it up, you're going to win a lot of ball games. This ball club started to come up for this game a little too late," he said. "Just a little more effort on the part of some of our veterans and we probably would have won. But, on the whole, the effort was good. We've come a long way since the beginning of the season," he rambled on, "and I think we can do even better if we just get down to work.

There won't be any practice until Tuesday, but then I want you to dig in and give it everything you've got. Forget about this one today and concentrate on the eleven games ahead of us and we're bound to do all right. When a ball club tries like this one did today," Lambeau assured them, "we (the coaching staff) won't criticize." Lambeau's talk was met with mixed reaction from the team. "Forget about this one — we'll get the Rams next Sunday," one veteran shouted. And another yelled a reminder, "Don't worry, we'll get 'em (the Bears) again in Chicago."

Was the spirit still there after the first game? The words probably sounded a little hollow after all they'd seen happen to their once-heralded passing game. As much as they tried to deny it, the passing attack was in tatters.

It didn't help the passing game when Lambeau cut Clyde Goodnight the next day. Lambeau said the receiver, who had been with the Packers five years and one of their leading receivers for the past two, had a bad knee and couldn't play up to his previous standards. (However, Goodnight went on to play two more seasons with the Redskins.) It was not a popular move with the players. One player told me, "Goodnight just got screwed by Lambeau. Clyde was making too much money and Curly just wanted to cut his salary. Whatever passing game we had went out the window with that move." What that player did not know was the board had demanded Lambeau to cut $24,000 off his payroll immediately. Goodnight was one of the highest paid members of the team and financially a logical choice. Lambeau said nothing of being forced to cut payroll to his players.

On the Friday after the Bears game, Lambeau made a rather startling announcement. He was turning the coaching over to his three assistants. He would devote his time to rebuilding the club and other duties connected to his position as vice president and general manager. He would confine his coaching, he said, to acting in an "advisory capacity." From now on, line coach Tom Stidham, backfield coach Bob Snyder and defensive coach Charley Brock would handle team workouts during the week and games on Sunday. Unfortunately, he did not put one of the three in charge. With nobody at the helm, the team would become a rudderless boat. Lambeau no longer had the stomach to coach this team. "How far we have fallen," he thought. His announcement caught the Packers' executive committee by surprise. They supported Lambeau's coaching change to the public, but behind closed doors they were upset that he made his latest decision without their prior knowledge. It also caught the players by surprise, setting a confusing tone on the team. Lambeau would be quoted the following day in the *Press-Gazette*, "I feel I can do the ball club more good under this arrangement. The duties of officer of a major league club, especially head coach and general manager, have increased so much in recent years it is impossible for one man to do justice in all three positions. My one aim is to have a solid, spirited organization and to build the Packers into a championship club again."

Board president, Emil Fischer, said: "It was a complete surprise to the executive committee, but Curly feels that he can be of greater service to the club under present circumstances and therefore we are in no position to demure." The news of Lambeau's change in status put the team into a funk, particularly because it came just two days before the next home game with the Los Angeles Rams. They lost by the humiliating score of 48 to 7.

No matter — Green Bay still loved their Packers. The fans' undying infatuation still lingered in spite of the once glorious champion's lifeless performances. Later that season, when the Packers' train pulled into Green Bay very late on Sunday evening after a loss to the Bears in Chicago, a crowd of more than 500 was waiting at the train station. The Lumberjack Band played "*On Wisconsin*" and other assorted marching numbers. Russ Leddy led the cheers when the Packers got off the train. As the crowd surged toward the ball club, one group spontaneously rushed up to Tony Canadeo and lifted him on their shoulders. They carried him down the station platform in tribute to his tremendous fighting spirit. Few ball players on a winning club experience this thrill, but in the minds of the crowd and those who saw or listened on the radio to Sunday's contest, nobody deserved the tribute more than Canadeo for his courageous effort in the loss to the Bears. The hollow demonstration lasted approximately ten minutes and then the crowd, brought together with the aid of the Minute Men and the Green Bay Quarterback Club, slowly dispersed into the dark night. It took the appearance of a group of friends visiting a very sick comrade who they knew had little hope of survival. They just wanted to be there with 'him' at the end.

Defeats continued to mount up. Team morale began to suffer even more. One of the players, Nolan Luhn, recalled: "Everybody was thinking, 'Let's just get this season over.' We went through earlier practices in pretty good shape, and then the coaches worked us a little extra hard. I think some of the older players worked themselves out during the week and they were worn out by Sunday. We didn't have the energy on Sunday to go out there and play." Rumors began to spread that Lambeau would soon resign. Newspapers in Chicago and a New York radio station said that Lambeau was going to quit the Packers and accept the general manager job with the Los Angeles Dons of the rival league.

Late in the season, the Packers traveled to Milwaukee for a game against the Pittsburgh Steelers at State Fair Park. Only 5,483 fans showed up in freezing weather to see the Packers lose another game, 30 to 7. On the train traveling back to Green Bay that Sunday night, assistant coach Charley Brock was bitter. "I think it was the worst ball game we've played all year," Brock declared. "Our blocking and tackling were terrible. Blocking and tackling is 90 percent of football — if you don't block and tackle, you don't win football games. Offhand, I can't think of anyone who played a good ball game," the all-time Packer center asserted. "Of course there were four or five who played their usual game — played their hearts out — but it takes eleven. We only showed spark once this afternoon and that was on the drive that we scored our touchdown. The rest of the time we didn't show any spirit — particularly in the fourth quarter."

The Packers were starting to have more problems beyond those on the field. They were having some serious financial problems, so serious that they weren't sure that the Packers could stay in the NFL. The NFL commissioner, Bert Bell, had to make a statement that he wanted Green Bay to stay in the league. The truth was that Green Bay might have to surrender its franchise. There were increasing rumors that Lambeau was going to quit his post with the Packers and accept a general manager berth the next season with the Los Angeles Dons competing in the American Conference. The Packers denied that Curly would be leaving for the Dons. His contract with the Packers at this time was due to expire January 1, 1950.

Late in the season, the board was applying more pressure to reduce expenses. Whatever expenses Lambeau was able to cut weren't nearly enough. By early November, the club was broke. They were $90,000 in debt and needed to raise cash in a hurry. In a recorded interview, Green Bay businessman Jerry Atkinson recalled a visit he received at his office at Prange's department store where he was chief executive officer: "I got a desperate call from

Emil Fischer asking if he, Curly and Frank Jonet could see me about a Packer situation. No sooner had they sat down in my office when Curly said, 'We're $90,000 in debt and need to raise $50,000 quick. We want to know if you will chair a campaign to get the cash we need within the next couple of weeks.' I was dumbfounded, but agreed to lead the effort to get the needed cash from the businesses in Green Bay. But, I also asked Curly if he would help raise some of the cash by having an intra-squad game on Thanksgiving Day and charging a fee to attend. Curly agreed and a few days later I had a meeting at the Northland Hotel where Fischer and Curly spoke to the businessmen about the need for quick funding for the Packers. When they were finished speaking, I asked if anyone in the room would help to please stand. The entire room stood up."[115] Lambeau himself took a voluntary salary cut to help ease the financial strain.

To raise the $50,000, the core group of businessmen and media in Green Bay quickly got more than 500 workers to make their contacts to businesses as soon as possible to get checks made out to the Packers. Another stock sale was commenced to rescue the team from further financial trouble. They were also going to pull in some Packer veterans to come in and perform during the halftime of the intra-squad game. The core committee that provided the push to raise the needed cash included Earl Gillespie, Art Daley, Bob Savage, Jug Earp, Frank Jonet, Lambeau, Jerry Atkinson, Emil Fischer and Green Bay Mayor Dominic Olejniczak. Numerous former players came to Green Bay, made speeches and encouraged the fans to raise the money to keep the Packers in the league. One of the all time favorites, Johnny Blood, came and spoke to several groups during the week.

Lambeau later that week caused a stir among the board members when he told them he knew four investors who would put up the $50,000 if the corporation would be converted to a for-profit rather than non-profit corporation. The board made it clear the Packer Football Corporation had to remain as originally conceived — a community non-profit corporation. Later, Lambeau would be falsely accused by a couple of board members of trying to take ownership of the team. That was not his intent, as the investors would only sink that kind of money into the Packers if they assumed ownership. Nevertheless, it would have been a way to rid him of the board under that arrangement.

Before the game with the Chicago Cardinals the following

Sunday, the Packers played an exhibition game on Thanksgiving Day at City Stadium to raise money. The players split up the squad into a green team and a gold team. Unbelievably, a crowd of nearly 18,000 ignored the cold and snow and paid to see the Packer intra-squad game in an effort to help raise $50,000. During half-time, some of the old Packer greats put on a show. Don Hutson, Jug Earp, Arnie Herber and Verne Lewellen were a few of the veterans who donned the Packers' blue and gold uniform one more time. Earl Gillespie described the special halftime show over radio station WJPG. A heavy snowfall kept some away, but there was enough paid attendance to raise sufficient funds to pay off some pressing debts.

The Girard "Blues" beat the Heath "Golds," 34 to 31, on the frozen and slippery field while the Lumberjack Band played, "*In the Good Old Summertime.*" Several of the old-time players, including Lambeau, posed for a picture on the snow-covered field at halftime. Just before going onto the field for the picture, Lambeau pulled on a helmet and stood there with many of the players who he had shared the victories of past Packer glory, all dressed in Packer uniforms looking trim and ready to play: Jug Earp, Lavvie Dilweg, Vern Lewellen, Johnny Blood, Charlie Brock, Don Hutson, Arnie Herber and Joe Laws. Past met present. For Lambeau, that cold, dreary day was a grim reminder of the glory that once was. There would be no glory for this 1949 team, only humiliation and degradation. "God, how it hurt," he said later.

Several of the players who participated in that special Thanksgiving Day fund raising game had mixed memories. Nolan Luhn told me, "It was a really cold day. I think there was snow and ice on the field. They took a road grader and cleaned it off. I don't remember how much money we made that day for the Packers, but I think we had a full house. The fans are like they are today; they want to keep the team in Green Bay." Damon Tassos recalled that the players just wanted to get the game over, "The weather was terrible. Real bad. It was slippery with ice and snow and we were trying to get the hell out of there." Canadeo remembered everyone was trying not to do something stupid and get hurt. He said, "That's the only game we ever played where nobody hit the ground! We faked the hell out of that game. It wasn't even as rough as a touch ball game or tag game. You got 'tackled' if someone looked at you sideways. But the fans really came out. I'm proud that we raised a lot of money from the game!" On one occasion when Canadeo came onto the field from the bench, players laid towels out. He got a standing ovation and the players bowed in mock honor to Canadeo.

The playful spirit of that intra-squad game would be short-lived. Later that week, there were still rumors about a riff between the Packers' executive committee and Lambeau. A Milwaukee newspaper said there was a determined effort to oust Lambeau as general manager of the Packers by the executive committee. As the players boarded the train to Chicago the following Saturday to play the Cardinals, there was no crowd to send them off. The players and coaches were alone as they boarded the train on a cold, gray November day that matched their mood. Their mood was reflected in their play the next day.

Lambeau called the squad together in the dressing room just before the game and said, as recorded by Lee Remmel of the *Press-Gazette*, "We have had some unpleasant situations. I think you have all heard about them. It makes for a bad situation on the ball club. It's unfortunate that it does exist, but it does. I think the stories going around Green Bay are highly exaggerated, but nonetheless it's still a bad situation." *(He was talking about the rift he was having with the executive committee.)* "For that reason," he continued, "now is a good time to find out who our athletes are and go out and win this game for the good fans of Green Bay. I expect everybody to do their best and we're going to go out and win this game. If we don't win, everybody puts out the best effort — that's all we can ask." He yelled at them, "Let's see some voraciousness out there. Good day to get voracious…let's rock 'em and sock 'em today. We can do a better job than we have." At halftime, Lambeau also gave another pep talk in a similar vein. Neither talk would motivate the team. His talent for motivating the team to play above their skills was no longer effective. The Cardinals (4-4-1) sped off to a 34 to 0 lead within the first 20 minutes of the game. Then the Packers responded with 21 points in ten minutes. But it wasn't nearly enough as the Packers lost again, 41 to 21, before a small crowd of 16,787 at Comiskey Park.

The Packers (2-9) would fly to Detroit to play the Lions (3-8) on December 11 in the last game of the year. It would be Canadeo's last chance to break the 1,000-yard mark. He got up that Sunday morning and looked out his hotel window to see that it was raining — not a good day for running the football. On the bus ride to Briggs Stadium, Larry Craig sat next to Canadeo and told him,

"This is my last game, Tony. My body is a wreck and my knee is shot. I'm going to give it hell today, but this is it!" Tony nodded. His own body hurt in what seemed a hundred places; his shoulder, back, ankles, and wrist all ached. As he looked out the bus window at the gray sky and rain coming down, he thought, what a fitting day to end our horseshit season.

As they got into their blue and gold uniforms in the visitor's locker room, Nolan Luhn and Dick Wildung were getting dressed next to Canadeo. "We'll make sure you get your yards today, Tony," they told him. As it turned out, Canadeo was about the only healthy back the Packers had for this game. Walt Schlinkman was out with an injury, while Ted Fritsch and Bob Summerhays were sick with the flu. What was left of their anemic passing game took a hit a few days before the game when, in another attempt to reduce expenses, Lambeau cut Ted Cook, their leading receiver.

The playing field was so dark that the lights were turned on at the start of the game. Only 12,576 fans (the smallest attendance on record for a Lions game) bothered to show up to watch two last place teams play in miserable weather. With support from his line and blocking backs, Canadeo managed to slosh his way through the rain and mud to gain 70 very tough yards and go over the 1,000 yard mark, breaking Steve Van Buren's old record of 1,008. He finished the season with 1,052 yards in 208 attempts for an amazing 5.1 yards per carry average. His outstanding accomplishment was somewhat overshadowed by Van Buren of the Philadelphia Eagles, who about an hour later that day shattered his own old rushing record and finished ahead of Canadeo in the NFL rushing standings with 1,146 yards. Green Bay lost to the Lions, 21 to 7, with the only Packer score coming on a blocked Detroit punt that a Packer recovered in the end zone.

Finally, mercifully, the 1949 season was over, but this was not like 1947 when the team lost many games by a few points. The 1949 team got hammered in almost every contest. They lost by lopsided scores of 48 to 7, 35 to 7, 30 to 10, 30 to 7, 41 to 21 and 30 to 0. They lost ten games by an average of 23 points. While their opponents were racking up an average of 27 points per game, Green Bay managed less than ten points a game, the lowest in the history of the Packers. The passing game that had been a question at the beginning of the season was far worse than they could have ever imagined. Between Girard, Heath, and Jacobs, they completed only 30 percent of their passes. They threw 29 interceptions and only five touchdowns. Rookie Stan Heath, the college star, who along with assistant coach Bob Snyder, was supposed to improve the passing was a complete flop, completing a pitiful 24 percent of his throws, with 14 interceptions and a quarterback rating of five. Ted Cook was the leading receiver with a meager 25 catches for the entire year. Nolan Luhn finished with only 15 catches. Canadeo would gain more than half of the team's total rushing yardage. The nightmare continued on the other side of the ball, too. Their defense against the rush was poor and against the pass, it was the worst ever in terms of passing yardage allowed. Opponents completed nearly 50 percent of their passes against the 1949 team.

The Packers had now hit rock bottom - total disarray, both on and off the field. The once-proud Packers were now a pitiful professional football team. Drastic change was in the air. A few weeks before that game with the Lions, in a rather bizarre meeting with the board, Lambeau's contract was renewed for another two years. Lambeau's contract as general manager and head coach, after many weeks of rumbling and rumors, was put to rest when he was verbally given a new two-year contract.

The board met with Lambeau at the courthouse for a heated four-hour meeting. About 25 interested fans and representatives of the press and radio gathered in the corridors waiting for the outcome. There was the assumption Lambeau would be fired or that he would resign. Among the waiting media were Lee Remmel, Art Daley and Earl Gillespie of the *Press-Gazette's* radio station, WJPG. The session started at 7:40 pm and was officially over at 11:25 pm. It was midnight when the last of the directors left. Twenty-one of the 24 directors were present to vote on Lambeau's contract and make financial recommendations. After the meeting, Emil Fischer, president of the board, announced that Lambeau would return to his head coaching position that he gave up in September in order to move up to the front office. Rumors still swirled that Lambeau might leave to coach the Los Angeles Dons, but everybody denied them.

John Torinus, who was on the Packer board at the time wrote in his book, *The Packer Legend,* "A climactic meeting of the Board of Directors was held on November 30, 1949, when the committee reported to the directors and recommended that the number of shares of capital stock in the corporation be increased to 200,000 and that a stock sale be held early in 1950. At the same meeting, Lambeau's contract extension came up for discussion, and it was moved and seconded that his contract be extended two years. Three members of the original 'Hungry Five' led the opposition and moved for a secret ballot on the extension. That motion was narrowly defeated, however, on a 12 to 9 vote, and the motion to extend Lambeau's contract was then approved by a vote of 18 to 3. The 'no' votes came from George Calhoun, Attorney Jerry Clifford, and Dr. W. W. Kelly. The only member of the original 'Hungry Five' voting for Lambeau was Lee Joannes, who did so reluctantly." After the season, lawyer Jerry Clifford became the spokesman for the anti-Lambeau faction, which also included former club presidents Lee Joannes, Dr. Kelly and George Calhoun. On December 22, Clifford called for a "complete reorganization of the club," saying it was "necessary." "I cannot be a party to asking the people of Green Bay to pour another $100,000 into what looks like a hopeless cause," Clifford said.

When Lambeau attended the NFL playoff game between the Eagles and the Rams in Los Angeles in mid-December, Bob Hope interviewed him at halftime over a nationwide hook-up heard back in Green Bay. Hope asked Lambeau: "You're going to be back with the Packers again next season, aren't you Curly? I see you have a new two-year contract." Lambeau answered, "You never know, Bob, you never know." The item also appeared in the *Press-Gazette* the next day. A little noticed item also appeared in the paper about the same time saying Mrs. Violet M. Bidwell, chairwoman of the Chicago Cardinals and widow of Charles Bidwell, was looking for a coach for her team: "The Cardinals are prepared to pay the highest salary in pro football to get a top flight head coach for 1950, and furthermore, I will not be pushed around in any deal in (the) formation of the new league. The league must be lined up to give an equitable schedule to the Cardinals or I'd just as soon retire from football. We must have (a new coach) before the first meeting of the new league January 19. This is big business. We're going to sign the best coach money can buy — if we have to pay him the highest salary in the league."

Deciding to stay in Green Bay instead of traveling to their home in Malibu Beach, Lambeau told Grace he was going to stay and fight for his lost power with the board. "On January 11, 1950, Lambeau stated his program: 'The Packers in this era of professional football cannot exist under the present arrangement of operation through committees and subcommittees. We must go back to the idea of a general manager with strong authority. The present arrangement is not only intolerable personally after two years of it, but also unworkable. I am going to fight for a change in every way I can and I know I will be acting for Green Bay's good.' Two days later, Lambeau asked that Don Hutson be made a member of the executive committee. 'We need a football man to substantiate the things I report on,' Lambeau said. But Lambeau's requests were flatly turned down and he was still waiting for his new contract so he could sign it.

"By late January, Lambeau still hadn't received his new two-year contract from the executive committee. When he was asked about this, Lambeau said he would work under the assumption that he would be the coach and general manager for the next two years, but he also expressed a need for harmony within the organization. He explained, 'No group of twelve men can get together once a week during the football season, for an hour and a half, including lunch, and run a professional football team. That can't be done. There are no miracle men.' He added, 'I can't possibly bring the corporation up to date in such a short time. I am not a brilliant man, but I certainly feel qualified to run our organization.' As a closer, he emphasized, 'We also must sell stock.'

"In a telephone conversation with a reporter from the *Milwaukee Journal,* Emil Fischer, who was vacationing in Florida, said that the delay in Lambeau's contract was due to his and Lambeau's absence from Green Bay, indicating that as soon as the two of them were in Green Bay together that it would be done."[116]

Another side of the story is that Fischer supposedly presented the contract to Lambeau when they were together in January at the league meeting in Philadelphia. It contained the same tight controls by the board as the old contract. "Curly took one look at it and tossed it back to Fischer."[117] Lambeau had decided he could not function with the board questioning his every move. Art Daley, sports editor of the *Press-Gazette,* was also at this meeting as a guest of Fischer. He told me, "We sure played a lot of poker. Fischer loved his poker. I know he and Curly must have had a fight over something because they didn't talk to each other the whole time and kept throwing 'daggers' at each other. We had dinner together one night and I thought to myself, 'Emil's not too bright — he sure as hell has pissed off Lambeau.'"

This may have been the last straw for Lambeau. While he was contemplating his next move, in an ironic twist of fate his beloved Rockwood Lodge burned to the ground. On January 25, 1950, a bitterly cold day, fire departments in and around Green Bay were called to Rockwood Lodge where a blaze had totally engulfed the Packer training facility. Unable to stop the raging flames, they watched the controversial lodge burn to the ground. Faulty wiring in the attic was blamed. The Packers had been trying to sell Rockwood Lodge for some time with no buyers interested, but the team collected $75,000 from insurance that helped heal some of the Packers' financial problems.

No sooner had the smoke cleared from the burning embers at Rockwood Lodge than Lambeau dropped his own incendiary salvo, sending his letter of resignation to Packer board president, Emil Fisher. He said, in part, in his letter: *"It is apparent that there is a growing reluctance to alter the policies under which the corporation has been operating for several years. Unfortunately, I have not and cannot now subscribe to these policies. The difference of opinion, honest though it may be, has brought about a dangerous disunity of purpose within the corporation. Therefore, I am resigning as vice president of the corporation and relinquishing the position of head coach and general manager effective January 31, 1950."*

Before his resignation was announced on January 30, Lambeau and Grace boarded the train at the station in Green Bay and headed for Chicago. Standing there in the cold, his shoulders hunched, coat collar turned up and hat pulled down against the frigid winds, Curly thought back to those many celebrated events on this same wooden platform. "Screw 'em," he muttered to himself as he climbed aboard. He sat with his coat and hat on, his coat still buttoned. He stared at the floor. Grace reached over with her hand and put it on his. He brushed it aside and continued to look blankly at the floor of the train as it lurched forward with a loud hiss. The only coach the Packers ever had was gone. Curly was 51 years old and over 30 of them had been as coach of the Packers.

"Curly quit the Packers!" Those words went sweeping through Green Bay on February 1 as people ignored the sub-zero weather and gathered in cliques on street corners, at luncheon tables and cocktail lounges around town to discuss Lambeau's resignation. The *Press-Gazette* had Lambeau's resignation splashed across the front page. The *Chicago Tribune* featured the story on their sports page. Green Bay apparently was less interested in the fact that Lambeau had accepted the head coaching position and vice presidency of the Chicago Cardinals. Instead, people focused the discussion on the fact that he had deserted the child he had helped bring into being 31 years ago and developed into a professional football power.

Lambeau's resignation became public property in Green Bay around eleven o'clock in the morning on the first of February, although it actually did not go into the mail to Emil Fisher until that same day. At his winter home in Miami Beach, Fisher said Lambeau's decision was not entirely unexpected. The officers and board members of the Packer Corporation met immediately to do several things. One, increase the board of directors again and increase the capital stock from 300 shares of common stock having no par value to 10,000 shares of common stock. They then adopted a plan for additional financing. There was a move to bring former Packer star Cecil Isbell back to Green Bay as coach, but he would join Lambeau as an assistant coach with the Cardinals. Within the week, Gene Ronzani, a former player for the hated Chicago Bears, for heavens sake, was named the new head coach.

Some of the petty board members wasted no time blasting Lambeau in the press. "Curly had outgrown Green Bay," said one member of the anti-Lambeau faction. "When things were going bad," said Lee Joannes, "we took all the grief and criticism. When the going was good, Curly got the credit," he whined. Lawyer Jerry Clifford, leader of the opposition and nitpicker of the team's expenses, as well as self-appointed 'savior' of the Packers, exulted, "We've had two good breaks in Green Bay in the last two weeks. We lost Rockwood Lodge and we lost Lambeau. If Lambeau had stayed for two more years we would have gone completely busted." Clifford detested Lambeau's private life and what he considered "excessive spending." What Clifford failed to mention regarding team expenses was that Lambeau had taken a voluntary cut in his own salary early in the season and that he had cut several of his better, higher-paid players at the insistence from the Board that he cut salaries from an already talent-depleted club.

Lambeau chose not to return the personal attacks. However, many of Lambeau's former players, while shocked and dismayed at the news, came to his defense. Said an ex-player: "Curly didn't have time to stop and chat with everyone on the street the way he used to. He had too much work to do. Some of the old-timers thought he was slighting them. They took it personally and looked for ways to get back at him." Buckets Goldenberg, once a Packer guard under Lambeau and a fan so perpetual he eventually became a member of the club's 45-man directorate, replied, "I don't see

how the Packers can last without him. He was the Packers."
Canadeo said in an interview: "He should have stayed and fought it
out. My God, look what happened after he left. They weren't for
shit until Lombardi came and straightened out the mess."

Oliver Kuechle, sports editor of the *Milwaukee Journal* and
close to the Packer situation for over 20 years during Lambeau's
tenure, wrote a summary sometime later: *"Whatever the basis for
the difference, however, personal or otherwise, the sum total was
the same. Here was one of the greatest little organizations in football, Lambeau's organization, no longer fighting jealously against
the big city rival on the field, and fighting successfully, but fighting
bitterly within itself. Something had to give. So Lambeau resigned
and the era ended. He was the Packers.*

*Through the first 20 years or so of the team's corporate histo-
ry all was serene. At all times in these happy years, Lambeau had
his head and was permitted to do what he wanted. Lambeau specifically ran the show and ran it well. At no time was there even the
faintest suggestion that they did not approve of what he did or that
his story would have the unhappy ending it did. Lambeau got rid
of Dr. Kelly as team doctor in 1944 and brought in the late Dr.
Henry Atkinson. He got rid of George Calhoun as publicity director and brought in George Strickler, now assistant sports editor of
the Chicago Tribune. He bought Rockwood Lodge as a training
base in 1946 and defended the purchase as an asset to the club
through more than one wild session with the executive committee
until it burned to the ground.*

*He squabbled with Joannes at the draft meeting in
Philadelphia in 1946 — and Joannes resigned at the next annual
club meeting in July of 1947. No longer did he have a winning
team to throw into the face of anybody who challenged what he did.
And no longer was there solvency in the corporation. The difficulties finally came to a head immediately after the 1949 season when
the board of directors met to consider renewal of Lambeau's five-
year contract. The ringleaders to oust Lambeau, of course, were
his old friends — Jerry Clifford, Dr. Kelly, George Calhoun and
Lee Joannes. In the vote, Lambeau scored his last Green Bay victory. His contract was extended for two years. The vote was 18 to
3. Dr. Kelly, Clifford and Calhoun cast the dissenting votes.*

*But the end had come. His contract, while supposedly an
extension of the old, contained a new clause of the time expected of
him in Green Bay — not California. And the new contract did noth-*

ing to restore any of the authority taken away from him earlier. The adventure of a small town football team in the big league came to an end. The world champion Packers who made Green Bay a household word. Few men anywhere have ever done as much for their home towns as Lambeau for his."[118]

Indeed, Lambeau was gone. Closing the final chapter on 31 years as a Packer and assembling the most wins of any pro football coach up until that time. In those 31 years, the Packers had only three losing seasons. No Packer coach will ever match, or even come close, to the long-term success of Lambeau. Only George Halas surpassed this NFL winning percentage during this time and his winning record was only one percentage point better than Lambeau's.

Six NFL championship flags hung limp at old City Stadium on that bitterly cold day in February. They were reminders of a distant past — of far better times. Thousands standing and cheering in the cold December nights at the train depot to welcome home their champion Packers in 1929, 1930, 1931, 1936, 1939 and 1944 were but a faded dream. The car horns, train and factory whistles, fire engine and church bells blasting and ringing out, celebrating the David-Goliath victories were now silent. The Packer victory banquets, all-night partying and dancing were now just a memory. There would be no more celebrating Packer champions — until a new hero would arrive ten years later.

There was a hushed stillness over Green Bay on that terribly cold winter day. The hometown hero was gone. Leaving with a most ignominious departure. No fanfare. No goodbyes. No "thank you Curly" for the Green Bay Packers and what their amazing accomplishments meant to this city and state.

No, there was just a discarded former and forgotten champion slinking away into the dark night, left alone with only memories. Most good. Some bad. It was the bad he most dwelled on as the train rattled toward Chicago. The infighting with the controlling faction of the board was so demeaning. "And my own pride," he thought. It had gone too far. He knew it could never be the same. The Packers were his team, his legacy. No other team could ever replace the Packers in his life. His passion for the game was gone. His heart, his emotions were no longer in the game. He just didn't know it at the time. There was a big piece of himself he left behind at that old railroad depot. What a shame. A shame this man could not have stayed with his beloved Packers and retired for what he deserved and earned — as a hero — if not a winner at the end, at least recognized for his outstanding accomplishments and contributions to his town. What a shame some of the small-minded, jealous board members could not realize that although they played a key role in raising money for the team in times of financial need, it was the coach and his players that played the game. And play the game they did. In winning for the most of three decades, the team made up of a band of overachievers, was a vibrant member of the NFL. The only reason these men of Green Bay would come to the financial rescue was because there was a team to save.

It was the team that was such a huge success. The players and their leader and their sacrifices that left them all with physical reminders for years. The board only made it possible for that success to continue. Boards and reporters don't play the game — players do. And winners are led by leaders who know how to win. Earl Lambeau, the local boy turned hero, in spite of all his human frailties, was a winner. What a shame it could not have been recognized when it was finished.

10

Road to Perdition

When they arrived in Chicago, Curly and Grace checked into the Knickerbocker Hotel where the Packers always stayed prior to any Bear or Cardinal game. A hotel of great character, the Knickerbocker's warm, friendly atmosphere had always afforded comfort and pleasure in days gone by. But now, the memories of happier times were much too painful. The next morning they moved across the street to the Drake Hotel. Lambeau was all business and next went to the Cardinal offices on LaSalle Street to visit Ray Bennigsen, team president. He immediately signed a two-year contract with the Cardinals calling for a base salary of $30,000 a year, plus a bonus, depending on the team's success and attendance at Comiskey Park. This new deal was more than he made in Green Bay and was considered a high salary in those days since the average household income was $4,000 a year. His title would be head coach and vice president. The vice presidency was Bennigsen's idea so that Lambeau could sit in on meetings of the new National-American League created with the folding of the AAFC. Bennigsen told Lambeau he could select three assistant coaches.

The Green Bay *Press-Gazette* and the Chicago newspapers played up the new Cardinal coach the next few days, particularly the *Chicago Tribune*, where Lambeau had a close friendship with sports editor Arch Ward. Naturally, there was a sharp difference in the angles taken by the Green Bay and Chicago papers. The *Press-Gazette* focused more on his failed relationship with the Packer executive committee and critical comments made about Lambeau. The *Tribune*, on the other hand, treated Lambeau's departure from the Packers after 31 years more as a fortuitous break for the Cardinals because they were able to land someone with Lambeau's stature to coach the team. In his *In the Wake of the News* column in the *Tribune*, Arch Ward wrote: "Under Lambeau's direction, the Cardinals, for the only time in their up-and-down history, except for the last regime of Jimmy Conzelman, will enjoy the type of leadership necessary to sustained success. Our association with Lambeau, which spans more than two decades, has been one of unbroken pleasantness. Some of those years he was cooperating enthusiastically in sending us All-Star talent. On three occasions he was an opponent — head coach of the team playing the All-Stars. With us or against us, he was a sportsman always, and with the possible exception of the Cardinals' official family, nobody is happier about his shift to Chicago. Curly now becomes overseer of such Cardinal greats as Elmer Angsman, Charlie Trippi, Mal Kutner, Pat Harder and others. He comes into a town that for years has been dominated by the Bears in professional football. It's a stern challenge. But the Belgian never was one to run away from a fight."

That afternoon at the Blackstone Hotel, Lambeau was introduced to the Chicago media as the new Cardinal coach. Wearing the horned-rimmed glasses he had been using the past year or so, he told them Phil Handler, who had been associated with the Cardinals for 20 years as player and coach, would remain with the club as one of his assistant coaches and chief talent scout. Bennigsen told the media that Lambeau would be in charge of the team on the field with no interference from him. "Lambeau will have a free hand on the field and that's no idle statement," Bennigsen declared. "I gave my word I would draw up no sure-fire plays for him."

Edward Prell, sports reporter for the *Tribune* quoted Lambeau in response to reporter's questions about his leaving the Packers: "I am sure I can do a better job with the Cardinals than at Green Bay," said Lambeau. "You need harmony to win. I intend to talk to every Cardinal player at the earliest opportunity. I will continue to use the T-formation offense; unless, after interviewing the players and watching them in action, I decide that the material would be more effective if it is sprung from another system. I have no set plans, as yet. It is my intention to do everything I can to make the Cardinals a winning team. If I find a line coach who, I think, can help make the Cards a winner, I'll sign him."

During the media gathering by telephone from Miami, Florida, Mrs. Violet Bidwill, chairman of the Cardinals' board of directors, congratulated Lambeau. Lambeau told the press that the Cardinals needed no clearance from the Packers or the league to enter into negotiations because he was not under contract and said he would dispose of his stock in the Packers' corporation. (It had no monetary value, since the club was a non-profit organization.)

Lambeau became the fourteenth head coach in the 30-year history of the Cardinals — a rich history in the NFL that went back even further than the Packers. As the Racine Cardinals — named for a Chicago street, not the Wisconsin city — they were 1920 charter members of the NFL, then called the American Professional Football Association (APFA). They became the Chicago Cardinals during the 1920 season.

The Cardinals had a certain amount of success in the early years of pro football, but nothing like the championships of the Packers. By 1933, Chicago businessman Charles Bidwill, Sr., bought the team. Two years later, player-coach Milan Creighton directed the Cardinals to a record of 6-4-2, their only winning season between 1932 and 1945. Jimmy Conzelman became the coach in 1940, but had little success (8-22-3) before leaving after the 1942 season. Under Phil Handler in 1943 and former Packer Walt Kiesling (the team merged with Pittsburgh because of wartime player shortages) in 1944, the Cardinals endured back-to-back seasons of 0-10. Conzelman returned to coach the Cardinals to a winning season in 1946.

The next year, Bidwill signed Charlie Trippi for $100,000 and added him to his self-proclaimed "Million-Dollar Backfield" of quarterback Paul Christman, fullback Pat Harder, and halfbacks Marshall Goldberg and Elmer Angsman. That group led the Cardinals to the 1947 NFL championship with a 9-3 record, but Bidwill was not there to see it. He died April 19 at the age of 51, leaving the club to his wife Violet. In 1948, the Cardinals repeated as champions of the West with an 11-1 record, but lost the title game, 7 to 0, to the Eagles in a blizzard in Philadelphia. Conzelman retired after the championship game of 1948.

Violet Bidwill married St. Louis businessman Walter Wolfner in 1949, and together they oversaw club operations. Buddy Parker and Handler co-coached the team and eked out one more winning season with a 6-5-1 record in 1949, but the Cardinals were definitely on the decline when Lambeau took over. Following the 1949 campaign, Parker left the Cardinals to join the Detroit Lions as backfield coach, leaving Handler, a long time member of the Cardinals, as the logical choice for the head coaching position. Much to Handler's surprise and disappointment, Lambeau was named head coach. While Handler would stay on as assistant coach, primarily because of Mrs. Bidwill's sentimental request, he and Lambeau never developed a good relationship. Handler would subtly undermine Lambeau with the players during their time together. Lambeau had problems on other fronts as well. Since he had moved so quickly in signing with Chicago, Curly did not have a good understanding of the role Mrs. Bidwill's husband would eventually play in running the club. Lambeau was not counting on the trouble that would unfold in the second year of his contract.

The day following Lambeau's media meeting, he and Grace rented a furnished apartment on Chicago's Lake Shore Drive. He also put in a call to Cecil Isbell, who had played with the Packers from 1938 through 1942, to determine his interest in one of the assistant coach positions. Isbell had left Lambeau and the Packers at the height of his excellent career to coach at his alma mater, Purdue, before coaching the Baltimore Colts from 1947 through 1949. Though his name had come up in the *Press-Gazette* as a possible Packer replacement for Lambeau, Isbell agreed to join the Cardinals. Within the next few days, Lambeau also hired a third assistant coach, Billy Dewell, who had been a Cardinal player since 1940 and retired after the 1949 season. Dewell had a good reputation as a receiver, having caught 178 passes to become the Cardinals' all-time pass receiving end.

While in Chicago, Lambeau also made a pitch to the Cardinals' starting quarterback for the last several years, Paul Christman. Now 32 years old, Christman, who had led the Cardinals in their championship years of 1947 and 1948, had said he was retiring to turn his attention to the sales position he held with Wilson Sporting Goods. Christman told Lambeau over lunch at the Balinese room at the Blackstone Hotel that he did not want to play in the forthcoming season. It was a letdown for Curly. Lambeau was hoping to convince Christman to return because the Cardinal quarterback situation would be grim. Jim Hardy was the only other passer of any quality on the team. "I'm not giving up yet. We need Paul and

I still think he'll play for us," Lambeau stated. Ironically, Lambeau would later trade Christman to the Packers for a draft choice two weeks into the 1950 season. Christman had decided to un-retire and return to the Cardinals, but Lambeau, disturbed at Christman's late decision, dealt him to Green Bay rather than take him back in Chicago.

With the business wheels in motion, Curly and Grace returned to Green Bay the next week to see his mother, sister and brothers and tie up some loose ends before flying to California. They would spend most of the winter on the ranch in Thousand Oaks, partying some of the time at their Malibu Beach home. Meanwhile, back in Green Bay, the perplexed Packer executive board members were frantically trying to find a replacement for Lambeau and fight off the rumors that Green Bay would be replaced in the NFL. "The National Football League and the All-America Football Conference had been fighting each other for those same four years, and one of the bones of contention between the two circuits was the Green Bay franchise. Why should a backwater burg in Wisconsin have a team in the NFL and fine cities — real cities — such as Cleveland, Dallas, Baltimore, and San Francisco, shouldn't? This question wasn't being voiced only by the football moguls from those places; owners in NFL cities such as New York, Washington, Philadelphia, Pittsburgh, and Detroit were also saying it."[119]

The NFL commissioner, Bert Bell, and other influential team owners like George Halas and George Marshall supported the Packers remaining in the NFL. While they publicly supported the Packers' place in the league, the truth was that, unless the Packers could stay afloat financially, everyone knew they would be finished. Frank Jonet, the secretary-treasurer of the corporation, said: "The one thing I would like to say is that this does not mean the end of the Packers. The Packers will definitely continue in Green Bay." In the meantime, the insurance money from the Rockwood Lodge fire and the thousands of bogus stock certificates sold in early 1950 put the Packers back in the black for at least another season. Rumors flew about who would replace Lambeau as head coach. The names of several candidates emerged but within a week of Lambeau's resignation, former Bear Gene Ronzani was given a three-year contract. Why Ronzani? When several members of the committee questioned Lee Joannes on whether any other prospective coaches were available, Joannes retorted, "We're not taking a chance on Ronzani, he's taking a chance on us. Hell, he doesn't even know if he is going to get paid."

Ronzani grew up 100 miles to the north of Green Bay in Iron Mountain, Michigan, where he excelled in high school sports before becoming a nine-letter man at Marquette. He played for the rival Bears from 1933 to 1938 before coaching for the Bears' minor league teams in Akron and Newark. The Italian Ronzani was 41 and single when he replaced Lambeau. As the board doubled its membership and increased their involvement in the Packers' activity — on and off the field — Ronzani's teams would go 3-9, 3-9, 6-6 and 2-9-1 during his sorry four-year reign. Pressure from the board caused him to resign during his final year, 1953.

Ironically, while Lambeau was carving a new life for himself in Chicago, the Packer board members most responsible for igniting and feeding the feud with Lambeau were all dead within a year. Jerry Clifford, who had been Lambeau's chief antagonist, resigned from the board before the 1950 season and was dead from a heart attack a year later; Frank Jonet, secretary-treasurer of the Packers for years, died a year later in 1951; and Dr. W. W. Kelly, who wanted Lambeau gone, passed away in August of 1951. George Calhoun, the publicist relieved of his duties by Lambeau, remained on the Packer board and continued to edit his *Football News* for years. He remained bitter about Lambeau's changing his position with the Packers until his death. After his retirement from the *Press-Gazette*, Calhoun was honored in the last home game at City Stadium in 1956. It was to be the last game the Packers would play at old City Stadium. 1957 brought the opening of New City Stadium and the first ripples in a new era for the franchise.

Back in California, Grace told Curly she did not want to live in Chicago during the football season. They decided that she would join him for short periods of time at their apartment, but she would stay at their home in Malibu Beach for most part of the season. It was the beginning of long periods of separation between the two that would eventually lead to marital problems. While they were together in the early 1950s, a good deal of their time was spent traveling across the country, visiting Europe and entertaining Hollywood friends at their large, elaborate Malibu Beach home.

Grace, a fairly well known socialite with 'class' before she ever met Lambeau, was recognized for her natural beauty — even then in her early 50s — and her calculating, manipulative manner. She had a mystical aura of beauty, a sweet feminine way of moving, talking and a natural way of presenting herself that was appealing to both men and women. Most notable were her brown eyes and when she talked to someone they felt like she cared deeply about them. Her granddaughter, Mary Hoyt Gough, recalled several incidents with Grace: "She always made me feel special, even though she was so glamorous. I remember she knit a sweater for me and I felt like it was the greatest thing in the world and exactly what I always wanted, just because she made it and how she gave it to me. She was really thrilled to be made a grandmother and when she heard the news ("It's a girl") she bought out a very nice department store and had a dozen boxes of clothing sent to my mother. Grace also loved German Shepherds throughout her life, caring for and breeding them. She gave me a German Shepherd when I was younger."

Lambeau thoroughly enjoyed the parties — often marathon events — that Grace put on for her friends. Grace would spend days primping before the party and sleep or stay in her bedroom resting for days afterward. Grace's older son, Warren Hoyt, did not like Curly and the two of them were never close. Warren did not approve of his mother's marriage to Curly, calling him "vain and egotistical." He insisted Curly enjoyed the association of Grace's Hollywood contacts and would introduce them to people from back east as 'his friends.' Warren accused Curly of giving Grace pep pills before leaving the house on nights when they were headed out on the town. Grace's nursemaid more or less confirmed this story when she later told granddaughter Mary Gough that Curly would give Grace 'pills' sometimes to perk her up. She said Curly would take them as well before certain occasions. Sadly, it wasn't long before Curly's indiscretions began to tear at their marriage. Often forgiving his wandering ways, Grace saw in Lambeau "a charming, colorful and handsome public figure who flattered her ego to no end, which she was extremely vulnerable to," according to Grace's granddaughter, Mary.

Summer, 1950. Lambeau left California and returned to the Cardinals' training facilities in Lake Forest, just north of Chicago, to begin preparing the team for the football season ahead. Ironically, his new team would meet the Packers in an exhibition game in mid-August at City Stadium. Much to the chagrin of the Packer board, Packer fans presented Lambeau with various tokens of esteem prior to the game attended by more than 20,000. The underdog Packers beat the Cardinals 17 to 14. While Lambeau's return was celebrated by some of the Packer fans, others were heard taunting him from the stands as he roamed the sidelines at the visitor's bench. He admitted later, "It was a very strange feeling coaching from the visitor's side of City Stadium." In addition, some of the Packer players were quoted in the *Press-Gazette*. Ed Neale said after the game, "I'd like to see Lambeau's face now," and Ted Fritsch said, "That's the way to welcome Curly home." Lambeau would suffer three more embarrassing losses to the Packers as a visiting coach before he would finally beat his old team as the Washington Redskins coach in 1953.

It was obvious to some of the Cardinal players early on that Lambeau was less intense and passionate about coaching a team other than the Packers. Jerry Davis, a three-year veteran defensive back and punt returner who had been with the Cardinals during their championship years, recalled Lambeau's first year: "He came at a bad time. Very few people got along with him. Lambeau didn't know them and they didn't know Lambeau. There was hardly any coaching from Lambeau at all. He wasn't really an in-depth coach, I'll tell you." Lambeau left little doubt about his surprising lack of interest in team discipline starting with training camp. His practices were short and often unorganized. He turned over much of the coaching to his assistants, particularly Cecil Isbell. Davis would say, "He left most of the work up to the assistant coaches, and then he wouldn't let them do it. He was butting in or butting out with them. Cecil started drinking and he got to be a pain in the ass."

Lambeau would often miss practices altogether. During the week, he would be gone for a couple of days in a row and even the assistants wouldn't know his whereabouts. Phil Bouzeous, equipment manager for the Cardinals from 1947 to 1958, remembered a particular incident: "Before the season started, we had a practice on a Saturday morning at Lake Forest and he came up to me after practice and said, 'Phil, I have to go into Chicago.' No sooner did he say that, he got in his car and left the premises. Everybody took off. Saturday night there wasn't a player in the place having dinner. But that's the type of guy he was. There were a lot of incidents about Curly, but you could see that he just couldn't handle it any more."

Charlie Trippi, in his fourth year with the Cardinals in 1950, thought Lambeau had lost his enthusiasm for the game. "We got Curly probably at the end of his coaching career. I don't think he had the enthusiasm he had when he was with Green Bay. When he coached us he was more or less a social coach than anything else,"

Trippi recalled. After starring at the University of Georgia, Trippi led the Cardinals in rushing three consecutive seasons and was the most popular player not only with his teammates, but also with the fans and the Chicago press. He thought Lambeau was just going through the motions: "I liked Curly as a person, but his coaching philosophy changed a great deal when he came with us. His assistants did all the work. Isbell was a good coach. I liked Cecil. I thought he was a very knowledgeable person and capable of being a good football coach." Clearly, Lambeau had nowhere near the passion for the Chicago Cardinals that he had for his Packers. The preparation, discipline, organization and motivation he put into the Packers seldom surfaced while he coached the Cardinals.

A week before the Cardinals would open their season, the Ronzani-led Packers were battered by the Detroit Lions in Green Bay, 45 to 7. The following Sunday, the Cardinals were to meet last year's NFL champions, the Philadelphia Eagles. Lambeau oozed confidence and told the *Tribune*, "There isn't a team in the league that has better personnel than the Cardinals and I know we will prove it tomorrow." Lambeau's projections fell a little short. The Eagles humbled the Cardinals by the identical score the Packers endured in their opener, 45 to 7. Author Joe Ziemba described the slaughter: "With Lambeau brimming with confidence and Hardy firmly in place at quarterback, the Cards eagerly anticipated the season opener at Comiskey Park with their heated rivals from Philadelphia. Against the Eagles, perhaps the term 'nightmare' might be too positive a word to describe what Hardy endured that afternoon. In the harrowing 45 to 7 loss to Philadelphia, Hardy was forced into a league-record eight interceptions and also lost a pair of fumbles for a total of ten individual turnovers! With substitute quarterback Frank Tripucka injured, Hardy gallantly played the entire game and never was left off the hook by the swarming Eagles defenders. 'They (the Eagles) rolled over an impotent and inept Cardinal eleven,' stated writer Harry Warren of the *Tribune*."[120]

Standing along the sidelines around the home team bench, Lambeau felt strange in spacious Comiskey Park watching his new team getting their brains kicked in. Home to the Chicago White Sox, Comiskey was really first and foremost a baseball park. The old stadium, built in the early 1900s with its double deck completely surrounding the field, could seat nearly twice that of Green Bay's wooden bleachers of 25,000. The player's benches were much further from the stands in Comiskey than City Stadium, so even though more than 40,000 could be at a Cardinals' game, the crowd noise never seemed as loud as it did in City Stadium.

After the embarrassing opening day loss, the Cardinals reversed their poor initial performance and beat the Baltimore Colts 55 to 13 the following Sunday. The 1950 season followed that pattern for the Cardinals, swaying back and forth in terms of wins and losses. For instance, in their return visit to Philadelphia, the Cardinals pulled a 14 to 10 upset to the same team they lost to early in the season. The team wound up with a disappointing 5-7 record and chants of "goodbye Curly" could be heard echoing through Comiskey Park toward the end of the season.

During the off-season, the Cardinals and the NFL faced another challenge when players began jumping to play pro ball in Canada. The lure was simple: the players would play in small markets, but garner big paychecks. The Cardinals lost several key players to the new Canadian league, including Lambeau's first-string quarterback, Jim Hardy. Though Lambeau was able to coax Hardy back to the Cardinals before the season started, he then traded him to the Lions. Lambeau had decided to put the versatile Charlie Trippi in that position. "Lambeau evaluated his offensive options and decided to go with Trippi as the Cardinals' quarterback in 1951. Trippi had earned acclaim in just about every position possible during his service with the team, so the move seemed logical to Lambeau."[121] Off the field, the front office had also been restructured prior to the 1951 season. Bennigsen left the Cardinals while Violet Bidwill's new husband Walter Wolfner became managing director. The two Bidwill sons, Charles 'Stormy' Bidwill and William V. Bidwill, were named president and vice president, respectively.

The team got off to a poor start, jump-starting the rumor mill about how long Lambeau would remain the Cardinals' coach. "Cardinals General Manager Walter Wolfner stated that, despite the team's ugly 1-3 record, 'I have no intentions of changing coaches at this time.' Wolfner, not widely regarded as a 'football' person around the league, probably didn't do much for Lambeau — or the team — by that pronouncement so early in the season. But then things turned nasty. There were rumors that Wolfner was feuding with Lambeau, that Lambeau was feuding with assistant coach Phil Handler, and that very few members of the Cardinals' management were even on speaking terms. This internal fracas erupted when Lambeau publicly criticized the struggling Cardinals' offense as well as Trippi for his failure to call the right plays as the Cardinals threatened the Redskins' goal line the previous Sunday. The proud Trippi was incensed and accused Lambeau of 'passing the buck' when referring to the play calling for the Cardinals. Lambeau had stated that Trippi was 'on his own' when calling the plays and hinted that the situation was responsible for the close loss to Washington."[122]

In an article by Joe Agrella appearing in the *Chicago Sun-Times* the day after the game, Trippi's side of the story surfaced, *"Charlie Trippi, Chicago Cardinals' quarterback, Wednesday blasted the team's coaching staff for what he called 'buck passing' over the Card's defeat by Washington last Sunday. The Cardinals lost to the Redskins in Washington, 7 to 3, after failing to capitalize on five scoring chances. Trippi has been widely criticized for failure to call the right plays when the Cardinals were near the Redskin goal. Earl (Curly) Lambeau, coach of the South Side club, has said that Trippi 'was on his own' at those times. 'That isn't true,' said Trippi with some emotion. 'The Cardinal coaching staff called 90 percent of the plays against Washington. Sitko, Angsman, Stonesifer and others regularly came in with plays to use. I was pretty much on my own until the Cards reached the Washington 10 or 15 yard line. And then I got my instructions from the bench. In the last series of plays, when we lost the ball on the Washington side, Lambeau called the first three plays. Two of them were passes and the other was a running attempt. I called the fourth play. With fourth and six yards to go, I tried a pass which didn't connect.'"*

The open rift between Lambeau and Trippi, the team's most popular player, began to tear the Cardinals apart. Clearly, Lambeau was ineffective as head coach. His first assistant, Cecil Isbell, was drinking heavily and could no longer be counted on, and his other assistant coach, Phil Handler, was constantly undermining him. In one game, Handler and Lambeau argued on the sidelines as witnessed by a reporter for the *Sun-Times*. "Handler, in charge of line substitutions, switched ends in the last minute of play. When Lambeau disagreed with this substitution and sent the original end back into the game Handler roared: 'Who in the blankety-blank-blank is making the line substitutions?' 'I'm the head coach,' barked Lambeau. 'I'm running things here.' 'You are in a blankety-blank-blank,' snarled Handler."[123]

Late in the 1951 season, the Cardinals lost in an uninspired performance to the Cleveland Browns, 49 to 28, dropping to a 2-8 record. Wolfner told the *Tribune* he was losing patience with Lambeau: "Lambeau's made mistakes...we're not going to take any hasty action...there's no harmony among the coaches. They're still at loggerheads most of the time, not speaking to each other most of the time. They've had the material. Why, with the players we've got on this team, they ought to be fighting for the championship."[124]

Cardinal veteran Jerry Davis had his own thoughts about Lambeau's coaching during his second year: "Curly didn't know his ass from third base, really. I wasn't against him. I tried to play the way he wanted, but hell, a couple of times I had to change the damn defense and go out there and tell Curly we can't run this defense against the Giants."

John "Red" Cochran, a running back who had been with the Cardinals for several years, remembered the game against the New York Giants and Lambeau's casual approach to coaching: "The team went to New York to play (I didn't go because I was injured) and one of the players told me what happened. We had not anticipated the Giants using the A-formation and during the course of the game they switched into it and one of the players said, 'Curly, they're in the A-formation.' Curly replied, 'Don't tell the players, maybe they won't notice it.'"

With team discipline all but non-existent, squabbling broke out among the players and coaches. Respect for Lambeau totally evaporated. The end had arrived. On December 7, 1951, Lambeau resigned as the head coach of the Chicago Cardinals, but agreed to remain with the team for its two final games. "I had heard Mr. Wolfner was going to act and I decided to beat him to the punch," Lambeau told the Chicago *Sun-Times*. At his Lake Shore Drive apartment, Lambeau said: "I do not expect to leave Chicago until after the Cardinals' game with the Bears. I plan to go to Comiskey Park Sunday afternoon, buy a ticket, and watch the Cardinals play the Redskins. During the week, I will go to Green Bay and visit my mother, and return for the Cardinals' game with the Bears. I sincerely hope to continue in football, a sport I have been associated with for so long."

Wolfner didn't wait long to respond to Lambeau's resignation. The statement issued by Wolfner to the *Sun Times* was as follows: "Mr. Lambeau stated in his article to Arch Ward and I quote — 'I will continue to fulfill my obligations to the club to the best of my ability until my contract expires or until I am relieved of my command.' I am answering this quotation: The Chicago Cardinals Football club is accepting Mr. Lambeau's resignation as of now and he is hereby relieved of all duties. Other statements were made by Mr. Lambeau to Mr. Ward [and by the way denied by him later, but we believe Mr. Ward 100 percent]. I don't care to comment on these other statements at this time with the exception that the Cardinal front office has done and will do everything in the future to produce a winner for the Chicago fans. There has been a terrific lack of discipline on the ball club while Lambeau has been head coach, starting in training camp and continuing throughout the season last year and this year. We have suggested to Mr. Lambeau at various times during the season that he take the proper corrective measures — stating to him at all times that he was the head coach and the boss of the ball club. We were always unsuccessful in getting him to take any action whatsoever and all he did do was pass the buck, blaming his assistants or various players. The games won and lost during the last two years speak for themselves. This office has been under tremendous pressure from various sources, mostly from the fans, to relieve Mr. Lambeau of his duties, but we were hesitant in taking any such action as it is not the desire of this office to injure anyone. The Cardinals are in the market for a new head coach and we will be glad to receive applications from any qualified person. Whoever applies will be granted an interview and will be screened carefully. We hope that we can come up with the proper outstanding man who will produce a winner for the Cardinals and the football fans of Chicago. The assistant coaches will carry on until the end of the season."

Wolfner lashed out a day later with his opinion, "Lambeau lost control of his assistant coaches and his players as well. Lambeau hasn't even spoken to one of his assistants for the last three weeks. This feeling can be attributed to Lambeau's alibis after losing games. He always blamed his assistants for the defeats."

Lambeau quickly responded to Wolfner's remarks in the *New York Tribune:* "I've never blamed my assistants in my life. I've always shouldered full responsibility for any losses. There is hardly a coaching set-up in which there is complete agreement. But club owners certainly don't air this kind of thing in public. I felt I just didn't fit into the Cardinals' organization." Later, Lambeau told the Green Bay *Press-Gazette* that he had been contemplating resigning ever since Ray Bennigsen had left the club: "No man can do a satisfactory job if he constantly is harassed by front office second-guessing."

Lambeau told the *Chicago Tribune* he could work for Ray Bennigsen, but Wolfner, not a football man, got under his skin, "I liked Ray. He knew where a coach's authority began and where it ended. That situation has not prevailed since his resignation and I simply can't work under the current set-up and retain my self respect."

The *San Francisco Examiner* also quoted Lambeau, "A gridiron leader has little chance to build morale when management interferes with the normal relationship between a player and coach. This is true particularly when the office manager, through inexperience, has little knowledge of the problems that beset a coach."

Lambeau offered to coach the team in his two remaining games, but Wolfner told him to take a hike. The following day, the Cardinals, now under the leadership of Handler, dropped a 20 to 17 decision to the Redskins before a paltry crowd of just 9,459 at Comiskey Park. The team completed a 3-9 campaign by once again surprising the Bears, 24 to 14.

Arch Ward did his best to present Lambeau's side of the sorry situation for an old friend in his article in the *Tribune*: *"Earl (Curly) Lambeau, for more than 30 years one of professional football's most successful leaders, yesterday announced his resignation as head coach of the Chicago Cardinals. Lambeau said his resignation would become effective at the expiration of his contract, February 1. 'I regret leaving Chicago where Cardinal fans have supported us loyally and I am especially sorry to part company with the players, who have given me all the cooperation any coach could ask. However, I don't fit into the Cardinal organization,' he explained. Lambeau, whose Green Bay Packers won six National league championships in the 31 years he directed that unit, says he is confident he can coach as competently as ever, if he operates in the right environment. No man can do a satisfactory job if he constantly is harassed by front office second-guessing, he added. 'Football success is about 50 percent physical and 50 percent emotional,' he told us in his Lake Shore Drive apartment yesterday. 'A coach has little chance to build morale when management interferes with the normal relationship between him and players."*

Lambeau was flying to California before the *Tribune* hit the streets. He would spend the remainder of December on the family ranch in Thousand Oaks with Grace and her daughter, Jane. They spent Christmas at their Malibu Beach home and a week later the three of them headed for a month-long journey through France, Germany and Italy. The trip hardly provided Lambeau with a getaway from the daily stresses of life. Grace and Curly argued and bickered throughout the trip, she at him for his coldness toward her and he at her for her continuous mood swings. When they returned, Lambeau made calls to his old cronies hoping to find an open head coaching job with an NFL team. There were none. At least no one was willing to bring Lambeau in after the bad publicity at Green Bay and Chicago the last couple of years. Now 54 years old, it looked like this would be the first time in 33 years that he would not be coaching a football team.

Then, in late August, George Preston Marshall, longtime owner of the Washington Redskins, asked Lambeau if he would take over the team with the season opener only two weeks away. Lambeau agreed to take over the mediocre Redskins even though he knew the impetuous and egomaniac Marshall went through coaches at an astonishing pace.

Herman Ball had been retained as coach for the start of the 1951 season, even though his record the previous two years had been a sorry 4-12. After three straight losses — by a combined 115 to 31 points — he was replaced by former running back Dick Todd. The team responded, winning five of the remaining nine games. Impatient after two preseason losses, Marshall fired Todd and went to Lambeau. The Redskins probably had less talent than the Cardinals, but Lambeau was determined to put more effort into this job. He got an apartment in Washington, but Grace stayed behind in California and decided to make short visits when they were getting along.

Lambeau had known the flamboyant and eccentric Marshall for years and knew exactly what he was getting into. It was a match up of two of the most egocentric veterans in the NFL. Marshall had owned the Redskins since 1937, but he also dabbled in show business, having produced several theatrical shows in Washington. He also was an extremely successful and wealthy businessman who owned a chain of laundry stores before selling out in 1948.

"Marshall was a dashing fellow whose love of show business manifested itself in many ways. It was evident in his own failed fling at acting, in his first marriage to a former Ziegfeld Follies girl and in his second to silent screen goddess, Corinne Griffith. It was apparent in his invention of halftime extravaganzas worthy of

Hollywood and in his groundbreaking radio and TV broadcasts of football games. It was what mainly drove the NFL rules changes he engineered — to make sure nobody got bored with a gridiron performance. Marshall liked to live the part. One of his trademarks during football season was his full-length raccoon coat. Another was his always-at-the-ready chauffeured limousine. (He never acquired a driver's license, hated to fly and loved riding railroads.) Marshall's coaches, though, were not always so pleased with him. "When it came to interfering with them, he was the expert, often calling plays from his box or on the field and sometimes even making his own substitutions. As a result, coaches did not stay long. Six head coaches passed through his revolving door in the team's first 14 years in Washington."[125]

Leery about accepting the head coaching job with Marshall, Lambeau was nonetheless desperate to get back into football. "Besides," he thought, "birds of a feather stick together." It didn't take Lambeau long to charm the Washington press, the fans and Marshall's wife, former actress Corrine Griffith. She once wrote, "Curly Lambeau is six feet tall, weighs 200 perfectly proportioned pounds, no bulges...is one of the kindest men I have ever known, though one of the toughest when necessary...has blue-gray eyes, derives his nickname from a head of wavy hair, and is — to use Ki Aldrich's vernacular — 'a pretty thing.'"

Lambeau made old Sammy Baugh, the NFL's leading passer and punter for years, his assistant coach. Baugh, who had been the Redskins' quarterback for the previous 15 years, had broken his hand during the exhibition season and wouldn't be ready to play until late in the season. "Baugh could throw the ball like a bullet and with the ease of a man flipping a baseball. He could nail a running target half the length of the field away. He was college All-America in 1935 and 1936, completing 109 passes for 1,371 yards the latter year, upsetting undefeated Santa Clara in the season's final game, and then leading TCU (Texas Christian) to a Cotton Bowl victory. With the Redskins, he led the NFL in passing six times and set records that were to last for years — such as most seasons played, 16; most passes thrown, 3,016; most passes completed, 1,709; and most yards gained, 22,085. He spanned two generations and two eras of the sport. When he hung up his No. 33 jersey in 1952, he left a long string of collegiate and pro records. He was elected to the College Football Hall of Fame in 1951 and as a charter member of the Pro Football Hall of Fame in 1963."[126]

The Redskins had some talent on offense, but their defense was atrocious. Teams piled up an average of 25 points a game against them in 1951. Lambeau did put more effort into the 1952 season, but the results were not there. The Redskins finished 4-8. As fate would have it, the NFL 1951 schedule had Lambeau meeting two of his old teams, the Cardinals and the Packers, in the first two games of the season. The Redskins beat the Cardinals in Chicago 23 to 7, and then lost to the Packers in Green Bay, 35 to 20.

"That also was the first season for one of the Redskins' most endearing players, 5 foot, 7 inch quarterback Eddie LeBaron. LeBaron had been a Korean War hero, wounded twice and decorated for what his Marine commendation called "complete disregard for his own safety to rescue members of his own platoon…while his platoon was under persistent artillery and mortar barrage." LeBaron threw nine of his 14 touchdown passes that 1952 season in the final three games. But friction developed between him and Lambeau — and increased the following season when LeBaron was forced to share quarterback duties with first-round draft choice Jack Scarbath. Even though the Redskins finished 6-5-1 in 1953, LeBaron bolted to the Canadian Football League."[127] "I went to Canada in 1954 because I really didn't care to play for him," LeBaron recalled. "I didn't get along too well with Curly, I guess not too many people did," he added.

LeBaron said Lambeau had good assistant coaches, so he spent most of his time with the defense during his two years with the Redskins, "Basically, I think he spent quite a bit of time with the defense, at least as far as the theory of the thing in putting his defense in. As far as offense, I don't think he knew five plays, but occasionally he put in a play that had been successful for him along the way. He gave us a lot of leeway. Sometimes you like that, but in my last three or four games, I think I threw nine or ten touchdown passes and we were a hot team. Then, in our second to last pre-season game in my second year, I hurt my knee and was not at full speed. Things didn't go as well as early as we liked. We won a lot of games by close scores and we did very well for most of the time. We had a bunch of guys hurt and Curly didn't like people who got hurt. In fact, I roomed with three other kids who were all hurt. Lambeau hardly spoke to them. It was tough. He didn't recognize injuries; he didn't recognize the person after they got hurt. I think he had a good football mind, but he really didn't work at it."

"'I really didn't want to play for him anymore,' LeBaron said in the book *Redskin Country/From Baugh to the Super Bowl,* 'and I'm sure he didn't want me around either...I told Marshall I'd go to Canada or, if he stood in my way, I'd go into private business. He put up a fuss, but he knew people were unhappy. It wound up Gene Brito and I both went to Calgary. I guess he thought Curly was right and we were wrong.' Other players considered Lambeau good, but unlucky. 'The big problem with Curly was injuries,' said Gene Pepper, who played guard on offense and tackle on defense from 1950 through 1953. 'The blockers and runners were hurt just enough so we couldn't turn the damn corner on running plays.' But some other Redskins thought Lambeau stressed defense too much, 'Hardly ever gave any time to the offense.'"[128] Lambeau actually improved the Redskins the following year to a 6-5-1 record, winning four of their last six games. Marshall, who got into several shouting matches with Lambeau during the season, nonetheless was so pleased with Lambeau's results that he renewed his contract for another year.

In the meantime, Curly and Grace were drifting further apart. She seldom left their home in Malibu to visit him in Washington and repeatedly heard of his indiscretions with other women. When he returned to California at the end of the season in late December, she told him she'd had enough and wanted a divorce. They separated in March of 1954 and the divorce was finalized in August. They had been married a little over eight and a half years. She was 58 and Lambeau was now 56 years old. Their divorce papers indicate Grace made Curly file, but admitted to his adultery and his request for a large portion of Grace's personal wealth.

The divorce was costly to Grace as she lost nearly two-thirds of her estate. Lambeau, by contrast, would gain considerable wealth from his marriage and subsequent divorce from Grace. She testified that in the last several years of their marriage her husband seldom took her out socially and frequently was away on unexplained absences. She said she became ill and unhappy when he criticized her. The court approved a property settlement in which Grace waived alimony privileges in return for a half interest in an 840-acre ranch. She also retained title to a lemon grove in Ventura County and a home and furnishings in nearby Malibu. Shortly after their separation, Grace became ill and was bedridden for months. Lambeau had no further contact with Grace or her daughter Jane after the separation in March. The separation was especially hard on Jane. She had a strong affection for Curly and when he left, she would never see him again. It was not long after that Jane became manic-depressive and began needing special medication and medical attention. She would eventually have a partial lobotomy, receive shock therapy and be treated for schizophrenia. She remains in a mental institution to this day.

With his marriage dissolved and another messy divorce behind him, Lambeau returned from California to Washington for his 1954 season with the Redskins. Another incident would further tarnish his reputation and strip away the one thing he loved more than anything else — the power and prestige of a head coach in the NFL.

"As matters developed, Lambeau was gone before the 1954 season began. After an exhibition game in California, Marshall's wife, Corrine, saw some players carrying beer to their rooms and told Marshall. There was a rule against drinking in the clubhouse or the team hotel, but Lambeau backed the players because the game they had played was an exhibition. There was a loud argument and some shoving between Marshall and Lambeau."[129] The two almost came to blows at one in the morning in the lobby of the Senate Hotel in Sacramento. Marshall was irked because some Redskins were drinking beer after a 30 to 7 loss to the 49ers in an exhibition game. The next day, Marshall fired Lambeau. Although neither Lambeau nor Marshall would comment on the incident the next day, it was witnessed by several players of the San Diego baseball team who were there to play Sacramento. One of the Padres, pitcher Al Lyons, said Marshall pushed Lambeau who pushed back before General Manager McCann, who was standing nearby, stepped in and separated them.

Lambeau, who admitted the pushing incident, would not comment on it following a 10:00 a.m. conference he had with Marshall. "I have no animosity," said Lambeau. "It was just an unfortunate thing. It's part of the game. After all, Marshall owns the club. I wish the team well. They're a good bunch and I think they can do it," Lambeau said. The break-up was inevitable. It was simply two extremely proud men with self-inflated egos that were bound to explode at some point. That the two managed to get through two years was probably a minor miracle.

The next day, Lambeau headed south to the Thousand Oaks ranch granted in his divorce with Grace. This would have been his thirty-sixth season as an NFL head coach. Lambeau would never coach in the NFL again, but his coaching career was not quite over. As he drove to the ranch, Dean Martin's hit song, *Memories Are*

Made of This, came over the car radio and seemed appropriate at the time for Lambeau.

Lambeau spent the winter of 1955 in California and then drove to Green Bay to spend most of the summer with his mother, brothers, Rummy and Ollie and sister, Vee, and refurbish his cottage on the bay because he was thinking of selling it. While he was in Green Bay, Donald and Nancy divorced. The two had been married nearly twelve years and had four children. "I was pregnant with the fifth one when I got my divorce," Nancy related. When he found out about the divorce, Lambeau was so angry with Don he immediately changed his will. "Curly was dumbfounded. He changed his will the day I divorced his son. He divided his estate into eight parts for his five grandchildren, two brothers and his sister. He changed it that day. I remember leaving the court and was so surprised to see him there," Nancy recalled. "He had his estate going to Don. When I divorced Don, he changed it. When he saw that it wouldn't have gone to his grandchildren, it was one way of providing for them. He divorced three women, but it never occurred to him someone would divorce his son," Nancy said.

While in Green Bay that summer, Lambeau felt the resentment many of the people had for him. While they were not openly unkind or rude, he could sense the feelings for him had changed. It was, after all, a city of Catholics. Divorce and adultery were unacceptable. Some of his old friends from the Packer days were less than cordial. Sensing the coldness around him, for possibly the first time in his life, Lambeau felt depressed. He couldn't help pondering the ugly events of recent years. A seemingly endless parade of events and relationships turned sour. The ignominious departure from the Packers, his disastrous tenure with the Cardinals, his run-in with long-time friend George Marshall that caused him to get fired from the Redskins, his ugly divorce from Grace and the less-than-friendly people of Green Bay that had once called him their hero. And now his estranged son was divorced with five kids — his grandchildren. "The relationship I had with those kids will never be the same," he thought. For the first time in 36 years, he had no team to coach. He felt like a man without a purpose. It felt as though he was forsaken, outmoded and out-of-date. It would be the low point of his life. He felt like he was on the road to perdition. For awhile, he became a recluse, sitting in front of his television for days and nights on end, watching popular shows of the time like, *I Love Lucy,* the *Ed Sullivan Show, The $64,000*

Question, I've Got a Secret and the *Perry Como Show.*

That same summer, he received a call that would lift him from his doldrums. Lambeau heard from his old friend from the *Chicago Tribune,* sports editor, Arch Ward. The annual college All-Star football game was in trouble due primarily to the lopsided wins by the pros over the college kids in recent years. The game was not as competitive as it had been in earlier years. Ward wanted Lambeau to come to Chicago and coach the college All-Stars because he thought a pro coach could do a better job preparing them to face the pros. He wanted Lambeau to be the first.

Lambeau would later say he did not want to take the job, but did so because of his long friendship with Ward. Archibald Burdette Ward was known as "Arch" to his friends and co-workers. As sports editor of the *Chicago Tribune* in 1933, he invented the Major League All-Star Game and the College All-Star Game. Born on December 27, 1886, in Kankakee County, Illinois, Ward was orphaned at age twelve. He was placed under the care of Father Daniel Gorman, a priest who later became bishop of Idaho. Ward attended Loras College in Iowa and transferred to the University of Notre Dame, where he became publicity director for legendary football coach Knute Rockne in 1919 and 1920. After graduation, Ward spent four years as sports editor of the Rockford (Ill.) *Star* before beginning a 25-year run with the *Tribune.* "Ward was a cool guy," according to Jerome Holtzman, a longtime Chicago sportswriter. "He wasn't very big; probably about 5 feet, 9 inches and about 160 pounds. He wore glasses and was always nicely dressed. He was the highest-paid sports editor in the country at the time." Ward would not get to see the College All-Star football game that summer. At the age of 69, Ward died on July 9, 1955.

Ward always supported Lambeau through his columns in the *Tribune,* even after the debacle with the Cardinals, so Curly wasn't going to say no to coaching the All-Stars. Besides, he did not have anything else going on. The game's organizers went out and hired a staff of assistant coaches, each one with extensive experience in professional football. Lambeau's staff would include Heartly "Hunk" Anderson, Steve Owen, Hampton Pool, Tony Canadeo and Chuck Hafron. Lambeau began the training camp at Chicago's Northwestern University campus in late July during an extreme heat wave that hit the Midwest. Some of the players on that 1955 All-Star team included a cadre of quarterback candidates like George Shaw (Oregon), the nation's total offense leader in 1954;

Ralph Guglielmi (Notre Dame), unanimous All-America pick from the number four rated team; and Paul Larson (California), the leading passer of 1954 with 125 completions for 1,537 yards. Contenders for the running back positions included Dick Moegle (Rice), consensus All-America in 1954, and eternally famous for having been tackled by an Alabama player coming off the bench in the 1954 Cotton Bowl; Lindon Crow (Southern Cal); Alan Ameche (Wisconsin), consensus All-America fullback; and L.G. Dupre (Baylor).

Up in the line were such stalwarts as Sid Fournet (Louisiana State), consensus All-America tackle; Rosey Grier (Penn State); Bud Brooks (Arkansas), an All-America guard; Jim Salsbury (UCLA), standout guard for the number two rated team of 1954; and Larry Morris (Georgia Tech), a consensus All-America pick at center in 1953. Pass receivers included Jim Hanifan (California), the nation's leading pass catcher in 1954 with 44 receptions; and Max Boydston (Oklahoma), consensus All-America end for the nation's undefeated, number three rated team of 1954."[130] While Lambeau drove the college kids through an extensive training camp despite the heat, the pro team they were to meet backed off their training regime at their training camp in Hiram, Ohio.

"The Browns had taken the NFL title the previous December with a crushing 56 to 10 win over the Detroit Lions, after an incredible and supposedly final game performance by their legendary quarterback Otto Graham. Coming into the 1955 season, Graham was at home in retirement and the Browns had George Ratterman as his successor at quarterback. Ratterman was known to be an extremely capable passer, and Cleveland had a fleet of excellent receivers. Included in this dangerous offensive arsenal for the Browns were receivers Pete Brewster, Len Ford, Horace Gillom, Dante Lavelli, and Ray Renfro. The Cleveland running attack wasn't bad either, with names like Dub Jones, Maurice Bassett, Don Paul, John Petibon and Tom James."[131]

August 12, 1955 — a night to remember for Earl Louis Lambeau. 75,000 fans packed Chicago's Soldier Field to see Lambeau's All-Stars upset the highly favored Browns, 30 to 27. Lambeau was a winner again and back into the national limelight. Some of his lost self-esteem, which previously was never in short supply, had returned. Leo Fischer of the *Chicago American* credited Lambeau and his staff for a big share of the win, as they had "made a success out of the experiment of using ex-pros rather than college coaches." Lambeau's old friend, George Strickler, now back with the *Tribune* wrote, "It was a thoroughly beaten and surprised bunch of champions who lumbered off to the welcome seclusion of a stuffy dressing room." In later years, several members of the 1955 College All-Star team would go on to compile successful careers in professional football, the two most notable being Alan Ameche with the Baltimore Colts, and Rosey Grier with the Giants and the Rams. Others who put together nice pro careers included Stars' MVP winner Ralph Guglielmi, Max Boydston, Tom Bettis, George Shaw, Lindon Crow, L.G. Dupre and Dick Moegle.

Lambeau would coach the College All-Stars two more years, but the results were much different. The Browns shut out the All-Stars in 1956 by the score of 26 to 0 and the New York Giants in 1957, with assistant coach Vince Lombardi running the offense, whipped the All-Stars 22 to 12.

The third time coaching the All-Stars, the novelty had worn off for Lambeau. Ron Kramer, a standout end from Michigan was a member of the 1957 All-Star team, along with Paul Hornung, a graduate of Notre Dame, Henry Jordan from Virginia, Len Dawson from Purdue, John Arnett of Southern Cal, and Tom McDonald from Oklahoma. Kramer recalled Lambeau's coaching that team, "I don't recall any of us players took the game too seriously — including Lambeau. A lot of guys would stay out late at night and Curly didn't seem to care. In fact, he was out with different women as much as the players. We would see him out in places in Chicago. I remember him being quite the ladies man at the time. He would even come to practice all dressed up. If you didn't know Curly was the coach, you would swear that he was some executive, not the College All-Star coach." Kramer, the fourth overall pick of the 1957 draft, went on to star at tight end for the Packers in 1957 and then again from 1959 through 1964 after a stint in the Air Force. He was inducted into the Packer Hall of Fame in 1975.

In the summer of 1956, Lambeau sold his cottage on the bay and bought some property in nearby Door County. He purchased a 100 year-old summer home on eight acres of land in Fish Creek, about an hour and a half drive from Green Bay. The land stood at the mouth of Cottage Row, a picturesque road winding along the Bay of Green Bay shore south of Fish Creek, lined with large old summer homes that date back, in some cases, to the turn of the century. Lambeau's home, a rambling structure with five bedrooms, three bathrooms and porches on three sides, was built in the 1860s and enlarged a number of times.

The picturesque property would become his Wisconsin home from late May to early November every year until his death. He grew fond of his home in beautiful Door County, not just because of the comfortable old house, but the people seemed much friendlier and more accepting of the former Packer coach. Whether it was the charming countryside or the cordial populace, Lambeau would come to spend most of his time in Door County when he was not in California during the winter months.

Meanwhile, after firing Gene Ronzani (they called it a 'resignation') the Packer board hired Lisle "Liz" Blackbourn as head coach. Blackbourn had never coached in the pros, but had been a successful high school and college coach at Marquette before he took over the Packers in 1954. Over the next four years, Blackbourn and the Packers would not have one winning season, going 4-8, 6-6, 4-8 and 3-9. The board eased Blackbourn out in 1957 and promoted his assistant coach, Ray "Scooter" McLean, to the top spot. They gave him a one-year contract. That year, 1958, was a disaster. The Packers won only one game and wound up with the worst season in the NFL with a 1-10-1 record. McLean turned out to be a terrible choice by the Packer executive committee. Although the 1958 Packers were talented with players like Paul Hornung, Jim Taylor, Bart Starr, Jim Ringo, Max McGee, Bobby Dillon, Ray Nitschke, Jerry Kramer, Forrest Gregg, and Tom Bettis, McLean had no team discipline or strategy to utilize what he had. The club was in total disarray at the end of the season when the board fired McLean.

In the nine years since Lambeau had left the Packers, their record was a pathetic 32-74-2. They had won less than a third of their games and were once again on the brink of falling out of the NFL unless they could find a coach who could bring them back to at least respectability and a winning record. The executive committee once again began that search. The Packers had been playing their home games in their new stadium that held just over 32,000 since 1957 and the Milwaukee games in Milwaukee County Stadium, home of the Milwaukee Braves, since 1953. With larger seating capacity on their home fields, they needed a winning team.

Fortunately for the Packers, they now had a bright young man, Jack Vainisi, as business manager. He got heavily involved with the search for a new coach. Vainisi, board president Dominic Olejniczak, and now member of the executive committee, Tony

Canadeo, had stumbled across a potential candidate who was then the assistant coach for the New York Giants — Vince Lombardi. Since Canadeo and Olejniczak had seen Vince Lombardi at a coaching clinic and liked what they saw, the Packers began to look at him as a serious candidate. Vainisi followed up with a phone call to Lombardi to see if he would be at all interested in the Packers' coaching spot, as well as general manger. The answer was an emphatic "Yes." Canadeo and other members of the executive committee, as well as Vainisi, began to ask others around the NFL about Lombardi. Everything they heard was positive.

Lambeau may have been gone from the Green Bay scene, but he was certainly not forgotten. While the Packers were considering Lombardi, there was an active movement in Green Bay to bring Lambeau back as coach and general manager. The movement, headed by popular local sports announcer and magazine editor Fritz Van, had begun before the disastrous 1958 season was even over. After a 48 to 21 loss to the 49ers in San Francisco in the next to the last game of the year, board president Olejniczak was hung in effigy. The dangling dummy with Olejniczak's name on it was hung in front of the Packers' downtown office.

That left the door open for the "We Want Lambeau" campaign. Art Daley, *Press-Gazette* sports editor, wrote that Lambeau would not return to the Packers even if the job were offered. Van had a different version of Lambeau's desire to return: "When I called Curly at his home in California regarding the rumors of him not being interested in returning to the Packers he left no doubt he wanted to return" recalled Van. "I asked him if he ever said he was not interested in returning to the Packers," Van added, and Lambeau replied, "Well, Bob Kelly, who is a great friend of mine, was giving his views. He did not talk to me and he said that he felt sure that I would not return. Last night, George Davis, the sports editor of the *Mirror-Express,* said most likely I would return to the Packers. Now they're both friends of mine with different views, but neither of them contacted me. They're giving their opinions." Then Van asked Lambeau if the position were offered, would he take it? Lambeau replied, "Let's put it this way. If I could be in a capacity where I had authority to improve and correct situations that are necessary to make the Packers a power in the NFL again, then I would return. If I had the same authority that I had before December 1, 1947, I think I could do a job."

With that encouragement, Van promoted Lambeau's return on

his radio program and through his sports magazine. He arranged "Lambeau Rallies" where former Packer players spoke on Lambeau's behalf and distributed news releases regarding the drive. Polls were taken by independent merchants, including one by Van Domelen's that showed the fans wanted Lambeau by a 7 to 1 margin.

Lambeau came to Green Bay during the Christmas holidays to visit his mother and siblings. While he was there, he arranged a visit with Olejniczak to talk about his interest in the coaching spot. It was a short visit. Olejniczak was not interested. Lambeau left for California the next day. When the board of directors met, Lambeau's name wasn't even brought up. "I don't believe it," said a startled fan when approached by a newspaperman.

The drive to bring back Curly had proved to be an impossible dream for Fritz Van and his followers. Van summed it up in one of his future publications. "The Packers' president, executive committee and the board of directors ruled the team's destiny with an iron fist. The highly criticized president and board were perfectly capable of riding out the storm that our fervent forces had ignited. They alone would continue to run the show — public opinion be damned. To be sure, 1958 had been a terrible embarrassment to them, and for some there was a full decade of shame, but they were still in office and Curly Lambeau was still on the outside looking in. And that's the way they would keep it."

The Packers thought they had their man. A personal interview with Lombardi was arranged to take place at the NFL club owners and coaches college draft meeting in Philadelphia in late January of 1959. On January 22, Olejniczak and Canadeo met with the 45 year-old Lombardi in Ole's room at the Warwick Hotel for a lengthy discussion about the Packers' position. They asked Lombardi how he would run the team and what his expectations would be if he were offered the job. Neither side made any commitments, but Canadeo knew who he wanted the next Packer coach and general manager to be after that night. There were other men the Packers were considering, but it was Lombardi they were most interested in.

A few days later, Lombardi was flown to Green Bay where Canadeo and Dick Bourguignon met his private plane and drove him to meet with another member of the executive committee, Jerry Atkinson. On the drive to the H. C. Prange's department store on a cold, snowy day to meet Atkinson in his office, Bourguignon wanted to know if the New York Giants' owner, Jack Mara, would let him out of his contract with the Giants. Lombardi said Mara told him to "use his good judgment" that he had received from his Jesuit college days at Fordham University. Canadeo and Bourguignon were quick to point out they too were Jesuit educated, Bourguignon at Marquette and Canadeo at Gonzaga. "We have a lot in common," they told him. The meeting with Atkinson went well and a meeting with the full board was scheduled at noon the next day at the Northland Hotel to approve or deny the recommendation of the executive committee to hire Lombardi.

Appropriately, the board meeting was held in the "Italian Room" of the hotel. A makeshift press center was set up in the hotel guest room number 173 where nearly 20 media people sat waiting for the board's decision. Hours later, Olejniczak came into the smoke-filled press room and announced that the Packers had just hired a new coach and general manager to a five-year contract for $36,000 and then proceeded to read the bio on Vince Lombardi. And with that act, the Green Bay Packer board and executive committee would no longer have a chokehold on their coach. "I want it understood," Lombardi would tell the board of directors, "that I'm in complete command."[132] Lombardi made it clear he would call all the shots from here on. The board would become little more than a rubber stamp for Lombardi's dictatorial management of the Green Bay Packers.

11

Redemption

Upon returning to California after being snubbed by Packer president Dominic Olejniczak, Lambeau heard rumors about Vince Lombardi being named coach and general manager. He did not know much about him except that he was an assistant coach with the New York Giants and that he had coached against Lombardi in the 1957 College All-Star game. Actually, Lambeau felt somewhat relieved when the Packers finally made the official announcement a few weeks later. The more he thought about it, the more he realized that coaching the Packers was not something he really wanted at this stage of his life. Now almost 61 years old, he knew the job of transforming the putrid state in which the Packers presently wallowed would be a Herculean task. Besides, he thought of the dismal prospect of working with the Packer board. Lambeau knew coaching the Packers would not and should not ever cross his mind again.

It was time to relax and slow down a bit. Over the next few months, Curly busied himself with work around his ranch in Thousand Oaks and spent time with friends in Palm Springs. His short visits to this resort city in the desert surrounded by mountains became longer each year. In January 1962, Lambeau bought a home in Palm Springs, making it his permanent winter location. Over the next five years, he spent summer and fall at his home in Fish Creek located on Wisconsin's Door County peninsula.

While Lambeau was in Wisconsin during the summer and fall of 1959, it became obvious Lombardi was whipping the Packers into a new image — his own. The team's early success gave testimony to Lombardi's strong leadership skills and coaching genius over the next several years. Lambeau found himself, along with everyone else in Wisconsin, rejoicing in the Packers' resurgence to power and championship status. In the five years before his death, Lambeau would experience what might be called a catharsis of sorts. It was certainly a turning point in his life — whether it was no longer the pressure of being in the national spotlight or not having the stress and tension that go with being a celebrity, Lambeau's behavior gradually changed. Arrogance, vanity and selfishness began to melt away. Accounts from many who knew him in the 1960s agreed that he became less ostentatious, more mellow. The death of his younger brother, Rummy, that year also hit him hard. Though he didn't suddenly turn into a shy, timid and meek shell of his former self, there were succinct changes.

It seemed the more successful Lombardi and the Packers became, the more relaxed and subdued Lambeau became. The harsh spotlight of success was now on Lombardi. The Packers were champions again and Lombardi was the new hero. Lambeau became just another fan and seemingly no longer the subject of resentment for many of the failures of the 1950s Packers that had been linked to his departure. Even the oldest of Packer fans now saw the elderly Lambeau as the patriarch of the Packers. The venerable representative of a bygone era. The emphasis was on the present and the glorious Packer success. In some ways, it was much easier for Lambeau to just be himself at this stage of his life.

Bob Van Duyse, who owned Bob's Corner Bar, a tavern in Sturgeon Bay, remembers Lambeau during the early 1960s as "a regular guy."

"I had a bar for 15 years and quite a few Packers would come in. Curly would come in with his fancy cashmere coat in my workingman's bar and chat with the guys. He was a down-to-earth guy. He wouldn't have come into my tavern if he weren't. He would shoot the breeze with me and drink Early Times and water. He had this commanding, hearty voice and when he spoke, you listened," Bob recalled. Mary Jane Van Duyse also recalled Lambeau's sense of humor and his charming personality: "My favorite characteristic of Curly was his sense of humor. I remember one time we had a dinner party at our house and my sister-in-law's mother, Clara, was invited. She was in her late 60s and my sister-in-law was concerned how her mother would get along with Curly. He liked having a good time and she was a bit prudish. Well, Curly was his usual self at the party. He was in the kitchen fixing drinks and calling her Clara. By the end of the evening, he was saying, 'Clara you impress me so much…Clara this and Clara that.' Everyone was laughing. At the end of the evening she said, 'I never met anyone who got to my heart like he did.' He could charm anybody."

As the 1960s began, Lambeau's life would center around the more mundane — fishing in Door County, golfing in Palm Springs and, as it would turn out, the "adoption" of a certain Door County family that he would spend a great deal of time visiting. He would say, "I fish almost every day (from his trim 27-foot power boat nicknamed 'Lazy') when the fishing's good. It's hard to beat the smallmouth bass, although I also do a little walleye fishing. The smallmouth will fight you to the very end," he said. Strangely enough, with three Door County courses within easy distance, he confined his links activity to California. "I play a lot of golf in the winter — but I never seem to find time for it in the summer," he would say in an interview with Lee Remmel of the *Press-Gazette*.

The simple things in life now were Curly's delight. Fish. Golf. Socializing with friends and especially with an "adopted" family — a family that would become the one he never had. It all happened through a chance introduction from the Green Bay announcer and journalist, Fritz Van, who had spearheaded the campaign, "Bring Back Curly," to coach the Packers in late 1958. One fall evening in 1960, while the Packers under Lombardi's stern hand were on their way to capturing the NFL's Western Conference championship, Van, his wife Dorothy, his 27 year-old sister, Mary Jane, and her date were sitting at a restaurant bar in Sturgeon Bay. They were having a drink while waiting to be seated for dinner when Van noticed Lambeau sitting alone at the other end of the bar. Van got up and walked around the bar and brought Lambeau back to introduce him to his group. Lambeau recognized Mary Jane as the Packers' Golden Girl who performed as the head majorette, donned in a skintight costume of gold lamé during Packer halftime shows for the past six years. After some small talk, Lambeau invited them to be his guest for dinner at the Sturgeon Bay Yacht Club. During that evening, Lambeau invited them to his house in Fish Creek the next night.

The next evening, Van, his wife and Mary Jane joined

Lambeau at his Fish Creek summer home where they sat at the bar in his game room, ate his favorite cheddar cheese dip, had a few drinks and talked. Later he grilled steaks. This would be the beginning of a relationship between Curly and Mary Jane that would last until his death five years later. Mary Jane said: "The first time I met him I was extremely impressed. I thought he was so handsome. I could see why all the girls liked him. He invited my brother, his wife and me to go to his house the next day. That's how I got acquainted with him. It went on from there."

While Mary Jane was somewhat of a local star in her own right, she knew little of Lambeau other than the fact he had been coach of the Packers. She knew little or nothing of his private life and his previous three marriages other than having seen Marguerite around Green Bay from time to time. Without more knowledge of his past, she took him at present face value and how he was when with her. Lambeau saw Mary Jane as a shapely and attractive young woman half his age, yet mature in a way he found appealing. Never married, Mary Jane came from ardent Catholic parents who had lived her entire life in Sturgeon Bay. Her father, Francis, was a local entrepreneur of sorts. At one time or other he owned several businesses in Door County, including a beer distributorship, a tavern and a gas station.

When she met Lambeau, Mary Jane had developed a reputation as the leader of the Packer "Golden Girls," a group of young women who performed at halftime during the Packer home games in Green Bay and Milwaukee. She had her own dance and baton-twirling studio in Sturgeon Bay where she taught aspiring young majorettes. She had already won numerous national awards, including the National Baton Twirling Champion, the "World's Most Famous Drum Majorette" and the "Best Known Majorette in the United States," plus several beauty contests. She had also appeared in movie shorts, worked as a model and announced for television as the local weather girl on a Green Bay television station.

What Lambeau discovered in Mary Jane was an unpretentious, uncomplicated young woman with a simple outlook on life that he found extremely appealing at this stage of his life. They spent time together golfing and enjoyed many hours on his boat in the bay. Although dating someone less than half his age would initially send tongues wagging around Green Bay and Door County, over the next five years people became accustomed to often seeing the two together. After a while, it somehow did not seem so unusual.

Ron Kramer, the Packers' excellent tight end in the early 1960s recalled seeing Curly and Mary Jane together: "He and the Golden Girl used to come to the Northern Hotel Bar together. God, he was a natty dresser, and always looked exceptionally sharp. He always came over and talked to us. Paul Hornung and Max McGee were usually there when he came in. He would ask about the team, how we felt, and so forth. I thought he was a real nice guy. I don't know — he and Mary Jane seemed to be a natural fit — she was the Golden Girl and he was Mr. Packer!"

Within a few days of their initial meeting, Mary Jane invited Lambeau to meet her parents with whom she still lived. Lambeau and Mary Jane's parents hit it off immediately. The four of them would often sit around the kitchen table and talk for hours. Lambeau, the same age as Mary Jane's father, would often visit Francis "Fritz" on his own at his tavern or stop in at their house in Sturgeon Bay. They would talk fishing or the state of the Packers and became good friends. Initially, Mary Jane's mother, Gertrude, was apprehensive of Lambeau's dating and later his obvious affection for Mary Jane. She would tell Mary Jane, "Have a good time, but don't get serious. He's a divorced man and older, so don't let it go too far." As the years wore on and they continued their relationship, Gertrude would ease up on such advice. Lambeau ingratiated himself to the Van Duyse family and would become well liked by all — not just Mary Jane.

As time passed, Mary Jane grew fonder of Lambeau in spite of their age difference. She would recall, "Yes, I did have affection for him, but I had some confusion in my mind because while I really liked him, we all liked him. He was so good to me, he couldn't have been better." She dated no one else the entire five years they had their relationship. "Nobody my own age interested me after I met him," she explained. When asked if eventually she would actually love Curly, she said, "Yes, I loved him, but there were so many emotional problems with me at that time. I was doing a lot of work at the Packer halftime shows and it wasn't easy. Vince Lombardi was watching and very strict. I had a lot of things on my mind and had about 500 students in my dance studio. It was hard, really hard."

The woman Lambeau nicknamed "Champ" would not deny her strong attraction to Curly, "He called me 'Champ.' Always Champ. He called me that right from the beginning until right to the end. When I met him the first time, I was very impressed with him. Then he started coming to our house. I invited him to see the Golden Girls practice. He would give me ideas on what to do."

As they continued their close relationship through the years, Lambeau began to mention marriage. However, in spite of their age difference, the major obstacle was religion. The Van Duyse's were devout Catholics and there seemed no way to get around Lambeau's previous marriages and divorces if Mary Jane was to get married in the Catholic Church and keep her own faith intact. Mary Jane felt Curly still had strong feelings for the church. She recalled, "He was still a Catholic at heart. He wanted to get his life together and come back and marry me. He had a friend whose brother was a monsignor. He knew a lot of priests and entertained them when they would come to Door County. When my mother's sister died, we were at her house and everybody congregated in the living room to say the Rosary and Curly got down on his knees and said the Rosary with us."

In the fall of 1961, the Packers were on their way to an NFL championship and Lambeau landed his own weekly television show on a Green Bay station. It was called "*Ask Curly Lambeau.*" Mary Jane was labeled his "Girl Friday" and appeared on the half-hour program with him. She would field questions about the Packers from the viewers and Lambeau provided the colorful answer. He also predicted the outcome of the Packer game to be played the following Sunday. After the show, they would usually stop at the Stratosphere, a popular restaurant in Green Bay.

Mary Jane was also featured as the weather girl on another Green Bay television station at this time and for several years afterward. She would recall, "Curly asked me to be on his television show, '*Ask Curly Lambeau.*' as his Girl Friday. The show aired in Milwaukee and Green Bay and was a popular show. It always amazed me how well he could answer questions and predict the following Sunday game. Next, I became a television weather girl. When I would get home from the 10:00 pm show, Curly often would have the grill going at my parent's house to cook rib eye steaks, which were his favorite. My folks were always included."

There was one characteristic of Lambeau's that struck Mary Jane that had seldom showed itself in previous years: "He was a humble person when fans would approach him and say, 'Pardon me, but are you Curly Lambeau?' He would reply, 'You know, I've been accused of that before,' but he was always ready to sign an

autograph and would talk to everyone — especially children."
Mary Jane would also see a softer side of Curly — his love of
music. "Curly was a wonderful singer and constantly hummed. He
told me he sang in church as a boy. His favorite songs of the 1960s
were *Greenfields* and *A Summer Place* and he also enjoyed Ray
Conniff's music."

That same fall, Lambeau's life was again touched by fire. This
time, a blaze of unknown origin, whipped by 45 mile an hour
winds, completely destroyed his house in Fish Creek. Lambeau
was in Green Bay at the time of the fire. "He loved his beautiful
summer home in Fish Creek, which ironically caught fire when we
were in Green Bay. I was working as a tearoom model. My mother was there having lunch when suddenly Curly came running in
and asked if we could find a way back to Sturgeon Bay as his home
was on fire. It burned right to the ground. It really bothered him
because he had a lot of valuable trophies and awards that were
destroyed, but he was a survivor. He remodeled his guesthouse. It
was beautiful," Mary Jane remembered. The only item to survive
the fire was a large crucifix that he later gave to Mary Jane's
mother.

Lambeau would say: "For awhile I stayed at Thorp's resort,
across the street, trying to figure out what to do. Then somebody
suggested I fix up the old carriage house. I found the same car-
penter who had cleaned it out and converted it to a garage 50 years
ago — Milton Hedeen of Sturgeon Bay — and he told me if I put
in a new beam under the floor it would be sound as a dollar."
Lambeau was proud of the fact that he was able to retain and use
virtually all of the structure. They scrubbed and oiled the original
cedar walls, laid vinyl floor covering over the four-inch thick floor-
boards. The big carriage doors were replaced with two picture windows and a red front door. The new wall opposite the entrance was
hung with red wallpaper with a lively Las Vegas pattern and a big
mirror to reflect the outdoor scene. Lambeau took his color scheme
from nature's autumn hues — red, yellow, orange, beige and wood
tones. "The painters were here and they wanted to know what color
to paint the new bookshelves near the fireplace. I happened to be
standing near a window where I could see the big maple tree in full
color — it was October. I said, 'Let's work from nature,' and I went
out and brought in a leaf. That same evening, I had to decide on the
color of the kitchen cabinets. There happened to be a sunset that
was out of this world and I said, 'Let's make them that color.'"

The next year Lambeau added the stables to his home, making one box stall a bunk room "for fishing buddies," and throwing two other stalls together to make a television room where TV fans could gather to get away from conversation in the living room. Another stall plus the old shower where the horses were washed was used for storage and tools. Wood from stall partitions was used to fill in the open space above the big stall doors. The old watering trough was now a plant box; the heavy metal oat feeder an oversized ashtray; big black harness hooks were handy to hold guests' fishing gear. Eventually Lambeau intended to build a new house on almost the same site as the one that burned to the ground. He never got to carry out those plans.

Lambeau, who had a housekeeper and handyman to help keep the Fish Creek property in shape, seldom ate at home. When he did, he prepared his evening meal (usually steak) on an outdoor barbeque pit he built himself. The rest of the time he ate at Dick Weisgerber's C & C Club in Fish Creek, a spot within walking distance of his house. Weisgerber played with the Packers in the late 1930s and early 1940s when Lambeau was coaching. Often entertaining his old friends and former players at his carriage house, Lambeau's social group usually dined at the nearby C & C Club. They told and retold old stories of the Packers' glory days and compared them to Lombardi's Packer team.

After the 1961 season, Lambeau returned to the West Coast and purchased a home in Palm Springs. For several years, he had been spending the winters in Palm Springs at a motel owned by his long-time friends, Ray and Irene Harlow. His new home was conveniently located between two golf courses, the San Jacinto Country Club and the O'Donnel Golf Course, where he played on one or the other almost daily. Lambeau fell in love with Palm Springs and often invited his Midwest friends to visit during the winter months. Lambeau's neighbors and occasional golfing partners included Bing Crosby, Bob Hope and Jack LaLanne. Don Hutson was also living in Palm Springs in the winter and the two golfed together often. Until the end of World War II, Palm Springs was a sleepy resort where only the rich and famous went to relax, recuperate and have fun away from the glare of cameras and inquisitive news media. Lambeau found Palm Springs to be a "small town" by Southern California standards, especially in comparison to the Los Angeles area during the 1930s to the 1960s.

Though she visited Lambeau in Palm Springs while he still

lived at the motel, Mary Jane declined visits to his home. "When I first went out to Palm Springs, his friends had a motel and they had a party for us. I would stay at the motel. Then Curly bought the house. He invited me out an awful lot and I just didn't want to go. He said, 'Well, I know how you are, so every time I invite you out I will have a house full of people, all your friends, you won't be alone.' He always had a lot of people around."

In November 1962, Lambeau was inducted to the Wisconsin Hall of Fame. Initiated in 1951, the Hall of Fame was created to honor a person who made a significant contribution or compiled a record of achievement in sport and whose contribution benefited and enhanced sport in Wisconsin or elsewhere. Lombardi was there that evening at the Elks Club in Green Bay along with other Wisconsin sports dignitaries to honor Lambeau. Lombardi's appearance was for show only. He did not care for Lambeau and made this no secret to those close to him. While Lombardi hardly knew Lambeau from firsthand experience, he did not approve of his lifestyle. The stories of Lambeau's womanizing while married, his three divorces and now running around with a woman half his age clashed with Lombardi's life values. A devout Catholic who attended Mass daily, Lombardi had little tolerance for Lambeau's reputation away from the football field.

There was another reason Lombardi disliked Lambeau. After several years of phenomenal success with the Packers, Lombardi thought *he* should be the Green Bay patriarch — not Lambeau. Any reference by the media to Lambeau's success overshadowing his own accomplishments irked him to no end. Art Daley, sports editor of the *Press-Gazette* at the time recalls an incident between Lambeau and Lombardi: "Lombardi had no love for Lambeau. For instance, there was the time I called Vince early in the week and said that Curly had been named to the Hall of Fame. I told him I would like to get a picture of you and Curly together and I could set it up for Saturday. Vince said 'Oh no, I'm not going to do that!' Bill Heinz was in town writing the book, *Run to Daylight*. I talked to Bill and said we have to get a picture of the two together so he talked to Lombardi. On Saturday morning, Curly is all dressed up, has on his suit coat and tie. We asked Lombardi to put his topcoat on and then we took the picture. We had them shake hands, but Vince wasn't happy about it.

When the picture came out on the front cover of the 1965 Packer yearbook, Curly gave me compliments on it, but Vince told me it was the worst cover ever. He didn't like it. He was so mad at me. He wouldn't talk to me that entire season. After the season was nearly over, I saw Vince at the Oneida Country Club and he said that I was too nice a guy and he couldn't be mad at me anymore. He told me to come out to practice. I told him I couldn't get in because it was Friday and the stadium is closed. He said that he would have it ready. When I walked on the practice field all the players are snickering like hell. They knew what was going on. We shook hands and he said that he was sorry. Later on he told me that he just couldn't stand to share the limelight shown Lambeau."

Lambeau was now 64 years old, but still looked and acted much younger. While he had gained some weight since his youth, he still appeared fit. He watched his diet, colored his hair a bit leaving it a little gray, exercised regularly and continued to be extremely well-dressed when in public. In March 1963, the Los Angeles *Examiner* newspaper carried a column by Bud Furillo: "Curly Lambeau is a legend in Green Bay and a twister in Palm Springs. The man, who organized, played for and coached the Packers, lives the good residential life in the desert resort of resorts. To keep the breadbasket from turning into a bakery, Curly joins the twist parade two or three nights a week. The big Belgian is 64, but he moves around the dance floor like the age of 24. 'When it comes to exercise, twisting is better for me than golf,' claims the man who coached three successive world champions." Ironically, the twist was the very last thing Lambeau would be doing when he died nearly two years later.

Lambeau had begun work on his autobiography several years before; that could have been a sign of his sense of remorse for some of the indiscretions in his life. He called it *Forty Years of Mistakes*. It was lost when his Fish Creek home was destroyed by fire. He told friends that he had been working on it for two years and it would have been too much work to start over again. "I enjoy life too much to think of starting the book all over again," he would say later. If he had started the book over, an important chapter would have had to include his induction into the prestigious Pro Football Hall of Fame in September 1963.

When Lambeau first received word he had been selected for induction, he couldn't believe it. He would be enshrined with the very best professional football players and coaches in the long and illustrious history of the game. Players and coaches he had played with and against. The best of the best would be enshrined in this hallowed Hall located in Canton, Ohio. The Hall opened on September 7, 1963, and Lambeau was to be with an inaugural class of 17 enshrinees. The Canton Bulldogs' Jim Thorpe was among the original inductees, and a seven-foot high bronze statue of Thorpe now stands immediately inside the building's entrance. Modern-era players nominated for the Hall must be retired from the game for five years. Coaches must also be retired. Voting is performed by a 36-member panel composed of a media representative from each NFL city, one Professional Football Writers of America (PFWA) representative, and five selectors-at-large. This panel first designates a list of finalists before choosing honorees. Each inductee is honored not only with a bronze bust in the Hall's Enshrinement Gallery, but also in the Enshrinee Mementos Rooms.

Among the initial 17 inducted into the Hall was Lambeau's old friend and competitor, George Halas, who at 68 years old was still coaching the Chicago Bears. Also inducted in the inaugural class were three of his former players, Don Hutson, Johnny Blood and Cal Hubbard; and his former boss when he was with the Washington Redskins, George Preston Marshall. Unfortunately, Marshall could not attend because the Redskins owner, now only a shell of his former self, was a wheelchair invalid who had lost his memory. Lambeau's old friend and former public relations director, George Strickler, back with the *Chicago Tribune* wrote: "The legends and traditions of professional football came to life in five splendid hours here today when the elite of the sport, assisted by prominent leaders in business and government, dedicated the new million dollar National Professional Football Hall of Fame. Twenty high school marching bands, a parade three miles long, and the greatest outpouring of Cantonians in the memory of the oldest active police official culminated in an impressive open-air ceremony at which 17 of professional football's most honored figures were enshrined as charter members."

Lambeau and the other inductees would never forget the parade that is the third biggest annual parade in the country behind the Rose Bowl parade and Macy's Thanksgiving parade. It draws an estimated 250,000 to 400,000 people along the two-mile route. Real football fans, not people out for the sun or to be on TV, but real fans. They sit up to a dozen rows deep on the curbs and sidewalks of this town of 80,000 where George Halas sat on a running board in a Hupmobile auto showroom in 1920 to help organize the National Football League. Packed and applauding along the entire route, they sat in bleachers, folding chairs, on scaffolding, suspended from a crane and on top of motor homes. They hung out second-story windows of a parking garage and stood on roofs. A baby was in a stroller parked on the back of a dump truck. As the parade moved past city buildings, churches, bars, used car lots, pizza shops, beauty salons, the Irish Eyes Social Club and a pet shop, people called out the names of inductees. Some rushed the cars for autographs, pictures or just to shake hands, defying orders from National Guardsmen.

It was to be the pinnacle of Lambeau's illustrious career as player and coach in the National Football League. It would be an honor only a few of those in the game ever achieve. On his return from Canton, Lambeau stopped off in Sturgeon Bay to visit the Van Duyse family and downplayed the induction award. "When he came home from Canton, he came past my house and asked my mother, 'What should I use this plaque for?'" Mary Jane recalled.

In the few years before his death, Lambeau tried to patch up the poor relationship he had with his son, Don. They played golf together or met for dinner occasionally. Mary Jane recalled a time when they went to dinner with Don and his wife, "I don't know what was wrong between them, but one night Curly invited me to the C & C Club to meet Don. We met Don at the club and had dinner, but he did not have the personality and charisma Curly had."

Nobody knows if Curly ever succeeded in getting closer to Don. No one I interviewed knew if they actually patched up the hard feelings of the past. Mary Jane indicated that Don had visited Curly a few months before his death and that they had a good time playing golf together. Don remarried after his divorce from Nancy only to divorce a second time a few years later. Donald died in April 1984 in DePere, a suburb of Green Bay. His life in later years is somewhat of a blur and even his obituary was non-existent in the Green Bay *Press-Gazette.*

In the few months before his death, Lambeau would try to convince Mary Jane to marry him. Mary Jane was concerned they would not be able to get married in the Catholic Church. She encouraged him to see a priest, which he did on several occasions, but there is no evidence he received any hope having been divorced three times. Clearly, Lambeau knew he had no chance to get married in the church. His only hope for marrying Mary Jane was that she would change her mind.

He was still persistent and would eventually propose, presenting her with an engagement ring. Lambeau carefully selected a place to give Mary Jane the ring — a location that would produce maximum impact. The two of them were in Los Angeles in February 1965 where Mary Jane had been invited to perform during halftime at the NFL Pro Bowl game. Early that morning they both attended Mass at a Catholic church in Los Angeles. Mary Jane would recall the proposal: "The day he gave me the diamond ring I was so surprised. I knew he wanted to marry me, but we had agreed that we were going to wait until he could get a priest to allow us to marry in the church. It was all up in the air. First of all, I couldn't believe he was coming to take me to church. Then he handed me this box during Mass. I just looked at him. I told him how we had talked about it. I told him I didn't think I could accept it. He said, 'Keep it Champ, until we can work things out. I want you to have this ring.' He said even if I wear it for a party ring, he wanted me to have this diamond from him and that someday I will wear it proudly. I never really told anybody except my mother."

Friends of Lambeau, Marie and Ed Enright, would tell Mary Jane how much Curly thought of her. After his death, Ed Enright wrote to her and said, "I know how much Curly loved you and how much he wanted to marry you. In fact, Mary Jane, when he proudly showed us his home he said, 'Ed, wouldn't it be wonderful if Mary Jane would marry me and we could live here. Hell, I wouldn't need to return to Door County if I had Mary Jane.' So you see our friend, you had a regular guy in love with you." Enright would add a postscript to his letter, "Curly told me honestly that he loved Mary Jane more than any other girl in his life." Mary Jane was optimistic that something just short of a miracle would happen to make it possible for them to marry.

After the Pro Bowl game, Mary Jane returned to Sturgeon Bay and Lambeau drove to his home in Palm Springs. He wrote to her every week and would repeat how much he loved her, missed her and wished she would visit him in Palm Springs. He told her he was not dating other women in California. "I don't think I would know how to act if I dated another girl," he wrote in one letter. Lambeau would return to Wisconsin in late April of 1965. One of the first things he did when he got to Green Bay was to buy a new boat and new Cadillac convertible. The boat he asked to have transferred to the public dock in Fish Creek and then drove his new red Cadillac to visit Mary Jane and her family in Sturgeon Bay.

On April 26, 1965, he would receive his last official honor from his hometown while still alive. He and five other former Packer members of the Pro Football Hall of Fame — Don Hutson, Cal Hubbard, Mike Michalske, Johnny Blood and Clarke Hinkle — were honored at the fourth annual Elks Sports Banquet in Green Bay. Nearly 500 were in attendance to pay homage to Lambeau and the five Packers who played for him. Lombardi was there and when he made his speech to the audience, he said, "These are the men who made the National Football League, who made it the great sport that it is today and gave it its color. Our present day players should be ever thankful to these men and those like them who gave them the game…and gave them the huge salaries we pay today." Lambeau would tell those at the banquet he was proud to have coached the five who were now in the Pro Football Hall of Fame and said, "I know for sure these five could make it in the National Football League if they were playing today."

It would be the last time he was publicly quoted. Five weeks later, on June 1, 1965, he would be dead from a sudden heart attack. He was 67 years old. As fate would have it, he would die in the Van Duyse's front lawn with Mary Jane at his side.

He and Mary Jane were to dine out that night at a restaurant in Sturgeon Bay and he had driven down from Fish Creek in his new Cadillac convertible. While waiting for Mary Jane to get ready, Lambeau removed his white sport coat and said to Mary Jane's father, who was mowing the lawn, "Let me take a turn at that. I need a little exercise." He took the push mower from Francis and began to cut the grass in front of their home. After five minutes or so he stopped and said, "Look at the new dance I've learned," and began to do the twist.

About that time, a neighbor, Herb Reynolds, came walking up the sidewalk. He stopped and began to talk to Lambeau. "I told him he was working up quite a sweat and he wiped his brow with his handkerchief. Then he said, 'I feel kind of sick' and fell over on the grass," Reynolds said. An immediate call was made for a doctor, an ambulance and a priest, but, "I knew he was dead as I held him in my arms," Francis Van Duyse said. Just as Curly fell, Mary Jane was standing on the front porch of the house. She ran down and knelt by his side and kept saying, "Curly, Curly….I love you." She said different emotions welled up in her, "I can't explain how sad I was. I was so mixed up because I hadn't married him and there he was. All I ever worried about is that I would hurt him. I didn't want to do that because I loved him."

She would recall the shock of Lambeau's sudden death on that warm June evening, "He was in great physical shape except about two months before he died he complained he had an upset stomach. The night that he died at our house was all so surprising because we were getting ready to go to dinner. My dad was waiting for Curly and mowing the lawn. Herb Reynolds, a well-known photographer in our little city, was across the street and we all waved to him. Then Curly said, 'Look what I learned in Palm Springs' and he's doing this crazy twist with the lawnmower and my dad is saying, 'Curly, don't do this.'"

Suddenly, unexpectedly Lambeau was gone. St. Paul's words of warning may have echoed through the warm night air, "For you yourselves know well that the day of the Lord will come like a thief in the night."[133] Curly might have taken to heart the wise observation of Seneca, written almost twenty centuries ago: "It is not that we have so little time, but that we have wasted so much of it."[134]

Newspapers around the nation proclaimed Lambeau's death the following day. A large banner headline splashed across the front page of the *Press-Gazette*. Art Daley wrote, "Curly Lambeau is dead. The founder of the Packers…the big Belgian…the incurable optimist…the guy who never lived in the past…died while talking with Herb Reynolds on the front lawn of the Francis Van Duyse residence in Sturgeon Bay."

Arthur Daley, well known sports columnist of the *New York Times* who had covered many of the games the Packers played against the Giants, wrote: "There are two important dates in the history of Green Bay. The metropolis was founded by Jean Nicolet in 1634, the Green Bay Packers by Curly Lambeau in 1919, and any vote by the townspeople as to the relative importance of these two events would probably find Lambeau winning by a landslide."[135]

George Halas, who as the Chicago Bears' coach, competed against Lambeau on the field of play as though each game was a matter of life or death, wrote his own open letter to the *Press-Gazette: "There's a limit to everything. Life ends. Curly Lambeau is gone. It's a world of turns. Curly gave me some of my greatest battles when he had the Green Bay Packers. He did a tremendous job. I doubt if the league would exist today without the likes of Lambeau. Lambeau's death was a terrible shock. He was one of the builders of the National Football League. Not only did he help by always fielding a team, but he was able to get financing to help others. And don't forget he had some great teams at Green Bay throughout the 20s and into the 30s. I saw him at the league meeting and he looked fine. Sure, Curly is gone. Others will go. Me, too. I guess. But we'll leave you all something. A great game. Don't ruin it. I can go on and on. I can talk about great players I've had and great coaches in the league. But it doesn't make much difference. Curly Lambeau did his job. I'm doing mine. Others are doing theirs. It's a great game and it'll get better. Let's thank the likes of Curly Lambeau.*"

When the *Chicago Tribune* interviewed Halas the day after Lambeau's death, he said, "It's such a terrible shock. We've had such a fine relationship. I last saw him earlier this year at the league meeting in Palm Desert, California. He drove me over to the golf club and I commented on how great he looked. He said he felt fine. Without him, pro football simply wouldn't exist as it does today. He had to be dedicated to the game. Only somebody who really loved it would have continued with conditions as bad as they were in 1930, 1931 and 1932."

Oliver Kuechle, sports editor of the *Milwaukee Journal* and close friend of Lambeau, wrote: "Few men anywhere have ever done as much for their hometowns as Lambeau has for his."[136]

People all over the nation began to express their feelings. Messages of sympathy came in from Don Lambeau, Curly's brother Ollie and his sister, Mrs. Francis Evrard. Other messages urged the renaming of City Stadium to "Lambeau Stadium" or "Curly Lambeau Memorial Stadium." Two wires were received from Notre Dame, from Edward (Moose) Krause, athletic director, and the other from the Rev. Edmond P. Joyce, S.C. executive vice president of Notre Dame. Father Joyce's message read: "On behalf of the entire Notre Dame family we extend our profound sympathy to the family of this great sportsman and athletic leader. A special Mass will be held tomorrow (Saturday) morning in Sacred Heart Church (on the Notre Dame campus) for the repose of his soul."

His sudden death left many of his contemporaries in shock. Packer President, Dominic Olejniczak and others would say, "The city of Green Bay and the state of Wisconsin will have to be eternally grateful to Curly because in my opinion we would not have professional football were it not for his untiring efforts and personal sacrifices. No one man has made a greater contribution to the city, to the state or to the league than Curly has made." NFL Commissioner Pete Rozelle expressed sorrow at Lambeau's death, calling him "one of the true pioneers of the game and certainly a great part of what the National Football League is today is directly traceable to him." Don Hutson, Lambeau's greatest player and long time friend, was "too broken up" to comment immediately. "Don and Curly were very close," Mrs. Hutson said, adding, "This has hit him pretty hard." Tony Canadeo, Lambeau's lone hope for rushing yardage during the losing years, said, "What he has done for Green Bay borders on the miraculous. He brought a small town into the big leagues. I know when anyone thinks of Green Bay, they also think of Curly." Buckets Goldenberg, Lambeau's former all-pro guard from Wisconsin, said, "His death comes as a great shock to me. I had just seen him last week. Certainly present day coaches, owners and players all owe Mr. Lambeau a great debt of gratitude." Ted Fritsch, Lambeau's fullback from 1942 to 1949, said, "I remember the first years under him. I was always mad at him because he was always on my back about being overweight. I understood his demands later and it helped me in my coaching."

In Canton, the NFL flag in front of the Pro Football Hall of Fame hung at half-mast the day after Lambeau's death. His plaque in the main hall, a cold metal testament to his greatness, was adorned by a floral wreath.

Saturday morning, June 6, beneath overcast skies, Curly's funeral was held at the Shauer & Schumacher Funeral Home. Hundreds jammed into the funeral home while hundreds more stood outside as it began to rain. In addition to his son, five grandchildren and his brother, Ollie, sister Vee and their spouses, many of Lambeau's old friends were inside — Ed Schuster, Charles McWey, Vic McCormick, Ray Evrard, Carl Mraz, Art Daley, Dominic Olejniczak, Mike Murphy, Ollie Kuechle, John Rose, C.A. Gross, Max Murphy and Mayor Donald Tilleman. George Halas headed a list of other NFL team representatives including Ollie Haugsrud and Jim Finks of the Vikings; Bert Bell Jr., of the Colts; Bud Erickson of the Lions; Dan Rooney of the Steelers; and Wally Lemm of the Cardinals.

Also present were Gene Ronzani, who had followed Lambeau as Packer coach in 1950, Lisle Blackbourn, who followed Ronzani and Phil Bengtson, an assistant coach with the Packers at the time. Lombardi did not attend.

Mary Jane, her father, Francis, and brother, Fritz, sat in the second row during the funeral. Mary Jane, who unashamedly wept, remembered the service, "I know what I wore because I remember my mother telling me that people were going to be looking at me.

I wore a black dress and had a little black lace scarf over my head."

Monsignor John Gehl, longtime pastor of Xavier Cathedral Catholic Church stood before Lambeau's flag-draped casket and closed his eulogy with, "...and may God leave him with a winning score." Father Gehl said he felt it was "fitting and proper" to speak of the Packers' founder "on this occasion" after conducting Catholic rites with his assistant, the Rev. Mark Schommer, who tried out with the Packers in 1954. Father Gehl expressed sympathy to Lambeau's family on behalf of the Cathedral parish, but added, "not only does the family sustain a loss but the entire city of Green Bay and the state of Wisconsin suffers a loss." The Cathedral pastor paralleled Lambeau with Father Allouez and General Langlade for shaping the history of Green Bay and then suggested "something fitting should be done in Curly Lambeau's memory. I do think that our stadium or arena should be called by his name. This would be proper." Father Gehl added, "I have traveled over much of this country and because of this man everyone knows of Green Bay. I'm sure that if our industry spent millions of dollars to advertise Green Bay they could not approach the benefits that Curly Lambeau has provided Green Bay."

As the mourners filed out of the funeral home, they were led by the pallbearers — Don Hutson, Dick Weisgerber, Johnny Blood, Arnie Herber, Buckets Goldenberg, Charley Brock and George Strickler. All except Strickler were men who had played for Lambeau as a Packer. Strickler was now the assistant sports editor for the *Chicago Tribune* and was a close friend of Lambeau for years.

Fritz Van would recall leaving the funeral home with Mary Jane and their father, "I don't remember much of the service, but what really stands out in my mind is when we left the funeral home through the side door and seeing the throngs of people gathered. I don't know if you would call it a hush, but you could see people had been really talking." A long line of cars traveled to Allouez Cemetery in the pouring rain. At the gravesite, a large tent had been erected to allow some to avoid the heavy rain. Hundreds of others stood with umbrellas while the Legion Guard sounded taps and Father Gehl made his final remarks. It was damp. It was dark. It was depressing.

One of those at the gravesite was Mary Jane who recalled, "Everybody was looking at me. I was feeling so sad. But the one man that came out with me was Johnny Blood. He loved Curly so much."

Lambeau was not loved by everyone. There were those who condemned his past lifestyle and others who disliked him for different reasons. But Lambeau would die at a time when he had finally returned to favor with the citizens of Green Bay. It was 15 years since his shameful departure from the Packers. The unsavory circumstances surrounding his departure were now all but forgotten. With his honor now restored, Lambeau was recognized as the founder and leader of the Packers for those 30 plus years.

Lambeau may not have "conquered the world" as he so proclaimed in his senior yearbook at Green Bay East High School, but he was certainly triumphant in his "world" of football.

12

The Legacy

ike a thief in the night, death had come. Suddenly. Swiftly. Now, Curly Lambeau belonged to the ages. But how would he be remembered? What would be his legacy? Within a week of Lambeau's death, there was a movement in Green Bay to honor him in some defined manner. By early July, a seven-member citizen committee was named by the City Council to study a recommendation on a proposal from the Council for a museum-type building near City Stadium. Another option, renaming the stadium itself in Lambeau's honor, had been discussed by the City Council. But they dismissed the idea as "a trite and bush league way of memorializing the first coach of the Green Bay Packers." A memorial museum, they reasoned, would be much more fitting. An added attraction for the summer tourists that visit the stadium — a memorial-type building would be just the ticket. One of the committee members told the *Press-Gazette,* "They enjoy looking at the stadium and the turf, but we have nothing to portray the history and founding of the Packers." Alderman Earl Katers said the memorial building idea "would be something like the Kennedy Library" and that "just to name something after a man who died doesn't accomplish anything." He said it was important, from the standpoint of national publicity, to retain the identity between the people of Green Bay and the stadium. Thus, the museum idea went under the microscope of an appointed group of committee members including Charles Brock, chairman; Arnold Herber, vice-chairman; and Andy Uram, all former Packers; Haydn Evans, WBAY; Ben Laird, WDUZ; John Torinus of the Packer executive committee; and David A. Yuenger, *Press-Gazette.*

Howls of protest against the council's museum plan were swift and robust. Fans, media and former players made clear their preference for re-naming the stadium.

Len Wagner, a sports reporter for the Green Bay *Press-Gazette* wrote in his column the day after the Council's announcement: *"The Stadium Commission feels that renaming the stadium Lambeau Field is 'trite' and 'bush league.' Gentlemen, if honoring an individual by naming America's most beautiful football stadium after him is bush league, just what is to be considered major league? Consider for a moment the number of newspaper stories that will be read across the country year after year referring to a Packer victory in Lambeau Field. Or consider the number of radio listeners and television viewers who year after year would hear sportscasters greeting them with 'Hello everybody from Lambeau Field in Green Bay...' This is a trite honor?"*

The *Press-Gazette* soon followed up with an editorial promoting honoring Lambeau by renaming City Stadium stating, "Lambeau Field is the proper name." Even the Packers' executive committee made the official statement that it was in favor of renaming the stadium "Lambeau." In his official statement on behalf of the executive committee, Dominic Olejniczak, president of the Packer Corporation, said, "The Green Bay Packers executive committee recommends to the City Council and the Stadium Commission unanimous approval of naming City Stadium in honor and memory of Curly Lambeau, whose foresight and success played a most vital role in firmly establishing Green Bay as a power in the National Football League." Executive committee approval of the recommendation was unanimous, Olejniczak said. The other six members of the committee were Attorney Fred Trowbridge, Leslie Kelly, John B. Torinus, Tony Canadeo, Jerry Atkinson, and Richard Bourguignon.

Not everyone agreed with re-naming the stadium Lambeau Field. A prominent objector was one Vincent Thomas Lombardi. Lombardi told those who were closest to him that he didn't like the idea of playing in a stadium named after Lambeau. As he exclaimed to one, "Hell, if they want to change the name why don't they call it Lombardi Field." Lombardi may have been jesting, but it was no joke that he strongly disliked Lambeau, the way he lived his life and his disregard for his Catholic religion.

As the idea of renaming the stadium gained momentum from numerous sources, the City Council reversed its plan for the museum and recommended that City Stadium be renamed to honor Lambeau. The council members tossed their 'recommendation' to the Stadium Commission for further action. On August 2, the Stadium Commission approved the name change and the following day, after eight weeks of avoiding a vote and the offering of a substitute proposal, it took the Council just three minutes and five seconds to rename the stadium for E. L. (Curly) Lambeau, the founder and first coach of the Packers who died June 1. There was no Council debate. The only Council comment was the opinion of Alderman Francis Hessel that Lambeau Stadium would sound better than Lambeau Field on television.

City Stadium, in name, would be no more. The Packers' home field had carried the name for nearly 40 years. The original City Stadium with its wooden bleachers was built behind East High School in 1925. Additional bleachers were added through the years until it reached a maximum seating of 25,000 in 1946. In those days it was considered as having the best playing surface and the only field dedicated strictly to football in the NFL. All the other teams played in major league baseball parks. After World War II, City Stadium gradually faded from its once proud position as one of the favored fields in the NFL to an inadequate and obsolete installation. Its limited capacity made it increasingly difficult for the Packers to schedule top teams at home.

By the mid-1950s, the Packer executive committee determined the need for a new stadium to seat around 33,000. Some board members doubted that Green Bay would ever be able to sell that many tickets for a game. Causing even more debate was the question of where to build the new stadium. Green Bay's east side, where the Packers built their tradition, was an area that had some support. Others started a movement to build it on the west side of town. To avoid further infighting, the Packer board hired an outside firm to make an impartial study of possible sites for the new stadium. The Osborn Company came up with a totally new site on the far southwestern outskirts of the city which was then almost exclusively farmland, but it was also adjacent to what was to become the outer beltline, Highway 41, around the city on the west side. It was a site that also had very fine access into the city. Not only was this site ideally located, it consisted of a sloping piece of ground, which was made up of very firm clay soil. The Osborn Company recommended moving large quantities of this earth from one side of the hill to the other in order to form a natural earthen bowl. The engineers pointed out that at least the lower half of the seats then could be constructed below ground level without the need for expensive supports. It also would allow fans to enter the stadium through openings at about midpoint, and thus they would not have to climb up or down more than half the total rows of seats. Immediately, Green Bay city officials and the entire Packer organization supported the new plan. It had been the concept from the beginning that the city would construct the stadium and the Packers would enter into a 20-year lease, which would guarantee repayment of at least 50 percent of the servicing cost of the bond issue that would provide the construction funds.

With estimated costs for building the new stadium set at $969,000, a referendum to approve the issuance of bonds from Green Bay citizens was necessary. The *Press-Gazette* pushed for a "yes" vote and numerous citizen groups were organized to get the referendum passed. In a well-attended pep rally at the Columbus Club on the weekend before the vote, George Halas came to Green Bay and told Packer fans that the only way they could continue to compete in the NFL was to build the new facility. The "yes" vote was carried by more than a 2 to 1 margin. Stadium construction began in 1956 with the new facility dedicated at a game with the Bears in September 1957. Among the celebrity faces in the crowd that day were Vice President Richard Nixon and television star James Arness of "Gunsmoke" fame. There had been a weekend of festivities in Green Bay, including a giant parade featuring Miss America, Marilyn VanDerBur, as the grand marshal. The Packers did their part to make the dedication a memorable event, whipping the Bears, 21-17. City Stadium went through several additions over the next several years to reach just under 51,000 when it was officially renamed Lambeau Field in a brief ceremony prior to the first pre-season game against the New York Giants on August 14, 1965. The Packers would defeat the Giants 44 to 7 to set the tone for future games at Lambeau Field. Over the next three years, the Packers would lose only three games at Lambeau, while the team was recording three straight NFL championships.

Len Wagner was correct when he wrote in his *Press-Gazette* column in 1965 that Lambeau Field would be mentioned every fall in newspapers across the country, and that the name would be broadcasted to thousands by radio and television announcers greeting listeners and viewers with, "Hello everyone from Lambeau Field in Green Bay." Now the longest-tenured facility in the National Football League, Lambeau Field, unique and incomparable, easily ranks as one of the most recognized and envied locales in all of professional sports. This fact received special recognition in 1999 when *Sports Illustrated* named it the eighth-best venue in the world to watch sports — and the lone NFL stadium to make the magazine's list of 20.

Lambeau Field has become almost mystical with its storied games and magical moments. Bud Lea, a retired sports columnist who covered the Packers for many years, recently wrote the following: "Lambeau Field comes equipped with memories. There's the south end zone where Bart Starr sneaked in for the winning touchdown against the Dallas Cowboys in the 1967 Ice Bowl. There's the visiting bench where Mike Ditka blew a gasket after instant replay officials ruled Don Majkowski had not stepped over the line of scrimmage after firing the winning touchdown pass to Sterling Sharpe to beat the Chicago Bears 14 to 13 in 1989. There are the Lambeau Leaps, where Green Bay's touchdown heroes jump into the stands."

On one of my visits to Green Bay to obtain material for this book, I drove through several hours of rain and fog. The fog had now turned into a hazy mist as I turned down Lombardi Avenue and past Lambeau Field. There it was, almost like seeing it in a dream, this huge mausoleum rising up from the ground, shrouded in a magical haze. "The land of legends," I murmured as I slowly drove past, thinking of all the great players and games played in that historic stadium. Laden with lore and tradition, based around hand-to-hand struggle, elemental and brutal in its finality, football played in this coliseum atmosphere is what the game is all about. It is fitting that the stadium bears the name — Lambeau — of one of the greatest the game of football has ever known.

CURLY LAMBEAU'S NFL RECORD

	W	L	T	Pct.	Place	Playoff
1919 GB*	9	1	1			
1920 GB*	10	1				
1921 GB	3	2	1	.600	7 NFL	
1922 GB	4	3	3	.571	8 NFL	
1923 GB	7	2	1	.778	3 NFL	
1924 GB	7	4	0	.636	6 NFL	
1925 GB	8	5	0	.615	9 NFL	
1926 GB	7	3	3	.700	5 NFL	
1927 GB	7	2	1	.778	2 NFL	
1928 GB	6	4	3	.600	4 NFL	
1929 GB#	12	0	1	1.000	1 NFL	
1930 GB#	10	3	1	.769	1 NFL	
1931 GB#	12	2	0	.857	1 NFL	
1932 GB	10	3	1	.769	2 NFL	
1933 GB	5	7	1	.417	3 NFL	
1934 GB	7	6	0	.538	3 NFL	
1935 GB	8	4	0	.667	2 NFL	
1936 GB#	10	1	1	.909	1 NFL	1-0
1937 GB	7	4	0	.636	2 NFL	
1938 GB	8	3	0	.727	1 NFL	0-1
1939 GB#	9	2	0	.818	1 NFL	1-0
1940 GB	6	4	1	.600	2 NFL	
1941 GB	10	1	0	.909	2 NFL	0-1
1942 GB	8	2	1	.800	2 NFL	
1943 GB	7	2	1	.778	2 NFL	
1944 GB#	8	2	0	.800	1 NFL	1-0
1945 GB	6	4	0	.600	3 NFL	
1946 GB	6	5	0	.545	3 NFL	
1947 GB	6	5	1	.545	3 NFL	
1948 GB	3	9	0	.250	4 NFL	
1949 GB	2	10	0	.167	5 NFL	
1950 ChiC	5	7	0	.417	5 NFL	
1951 ChiC	2	8	0	.200	6 NFL	
1952 Was	4	8	0	.333	6 NFL	
1953 Was	6	5	1	.545	3 NFL	
	226	**132**	**22**	**.624**		**3-2**

* Statistics not included in NFL records

\# NFL Champions

LAMBEAU'S CHAMPIONSHIP AND PLAYOFF GAMES

The first championship game in professional football was played in 1932, when the National Football League was divided into a Western and Eastern Division. Curly Lambeau took his Packers into four NFL championship games in 1936, 1938, 1939 and 1944. In 1941, Lambeau's Packers played the Chicago Bears in an NFL Western Division playoff game for the right to play in the NFL championship game.

Between 1935 and 1944, Lambeau would reach the pinnacle of his coaching career. His Packers would win 75 percent of all their regular NFL season games, win the Western Division championship four times, finish second five seasons and take three world championships. The Packers' record during this remarkable span was 73-21-4. No other NFL coach came close to matching Lambeau's success during this period.

During the time between 1936 and 1944, Lambeau was at this coaching best. He had matured into a seasoned pro football strategist, motivator and recruiter. He found the players he wanted, negotiated their contracts, set up exhibition games, handled team travel arrangements, and basically ran the Green Bay Packer organization.

1936 NFL CHAMPIONSHIP GAME
Green Bay 21, Boston 6
December 13, 1936 at New York
Attendance: 29,545

George Preston Marshall, who owned the Eastern Division champions, the Boston Redskins, planned on moving the team to Washington D.C. the next year because of poor attendance so he arranged for the game to be played in New York instead of Boston. Lambeau wanted to avoid the cold December weather in Green Bay, so he took the team to New York for their workouts several days before the game. They stayed at the Victoria Hotel and practiced at the Polo Grounds the first two days, then moved to Central Park to run through their workouts. It rained hard in New York for two days before the game, making the playing field a sloppy, muddy mess on game day, even though the sun was shining brightly at kickoff. It wasn't much of a contest. The Packers won easily.

Lou Gordon of the Packers recovered a fumble near midfield at the start, and on the first Green Bay play from scrimmage Herber passed 42 yards to Hutson for a touchdown. The game was less than three minutes old. Earnest (Pug) Rentner boomed through for a yard for the Redskins' lone score in the second period. Smith missed the kick and the Packers held a slim 7 to 6 lead at the half. The Packers got a touchdown in each of the remaining periods. Milt Gantenbein took an eight yard toss from Herber for the third-period score and Bob Monnett got the last one on a two-yard plunge. Not only were the Redskins playing without the benefit of hometown support, they had lost their ace back, Cliff Battles, early in the first period because of an injury. To make matters worse, their starting center, Frank Bausch, was thrown out of the game for fighting in the third quarter.

| **Green Bay** | 7 | 0 | 7 | 7 | - | 21 |
| **Boston** | 0 | 6 | 0 | 0 | - | 6 |

Green Bay - Hutson 48 passes from Herber (E. Smith kick)
Boston - Rentner 2 run (kick failed)
Green Bay - Gantenbein 8 pass from Herber (E. Smith kick)
Green Bay - Monnett 2 run (Engebretsen kick)

TEAM STATS

Green Bay		Boston
7	First Downs	8
67	Rushing Yardage	39
23	Pass Attempts	26
9	Pass Completions	7
.391	Completion Percentage	.269
153	Passing Yardage	77
2	Interceptions	1
10	Punts	7
34	Punting Average	35
4	Punt Returns	5
27	Punt Return Yards	58
2	Fumbles	5
1	Fumbles Lost	2
3	Penalties	4
15	Penalty Yardage	25

1938 NFL CHAMPIONSHIP GAME
New York Giants 23, Green Bay 17
December 11, 1938 at New York
Attendance 48,120

The Packers would once again win the Western Division championship with an 8-3 record in 1938, and earned the right to the playoff game against the Eastern Division champions, the New York Giants. Newspapers again hyped up the playoff game as "David" Green Bay, smallest city in the NFL, going against "Goliath" New York, the largest. Don Hutson, injured the previous week, was still limping, but Lambeau had hoped that he would be available to play.

When they arrived in New York, the team checked into the Victoria Hotel and within hours had started their practice session in Central Park. Hutson would not work out since his injured knee kept him from practice, but Lambeau had him spend time with the team in an attempt to keep his injury a secret from the Giants.

The Packers all but pushed New York out of the Polo Grounds on game day, but the Giants, coached by Steve Owen, won the NFL title, 23 to 17, when a pair of first-period Packer punts were blocked and turned into scores. The largest crowd ever to see a championship game up to that time, 48,120, saw a bruising battle that belonged statistically to the Packers. The Giants turned one of the blocked kicks into a 13 yard field goal, and a few minutes later New York's Tuffy Leemans ran six yards for a touchdown. That gave the Giants a nine-point edge before the game hardly was underway. The Packers retaliated at the start of the second quarter on a 50 yard pass-run play that started with a pass from Herber to Carl Mulleneaux, who carried the ball into the end zone. Lambeau from the sidelines, dressed in his tweed overcoat and dark fedora, would send Hutson onto the field from time to time to serve as a decoy, but the Giants ignored him because of his limp, and the strategy failed to work. The Packers dominated the game statistics as they collected 14 first downs to 10 for the Giants and gained 164 yards to 115 on the ground. In the air, the difference was even greater, the Packers piling up 214 yards to 97 for the Giants.

Green Bay	0	14	3	0	-	17
NY Giants	9	7	7	0	-	23

New York Giants - FB Cuff 14
New York Giants - Leemans 6 run (kick failed)
Green Bay - C. Mulleneaux 40 pass from Herber
   (Engebretsen kick)
New York Giants - Barnard 21 pass from Danowski (Cuff kick)
Green Bay - Hinkle 1 run (Engebretsen kick)
Green Bay - FB Engebretsen 15
New York Giants - Soar 23 pass from Danowski (Cuff kick)

TEAM STATS

Green Bay		New York
13	First Downs – Total*	16
7	- By rushing	10
4	- By Passing	6
2	- By Penalty	0
2	Fumbles – Number	4
0	- Times Lost Ball	2
2	Penalties – Number	3
10	- Yards Penalized	20

* *Includes Touchdowns*

INDIVIDUAL STATISTICS

New York	No.	Yds.	Avg.	Green Bay	No.	Yds.	Avg.
				RUSHING			
Soar	21	65	3.1	Hinkle	18	63	3.5
Leemans	13	42	3.2	Monnett	4	29	7.3
Barnum	3	8	2.7	Herber	3	22	7.3
Danowksi	1	4	4.0	Isbell	11	20	1.8
Karcis	3	3	1.0	Laws	4	20	5.0
Cuff	2	-7	-3.5	Jankowski	3	14	4.7
	43	**115**	**2.7**	Uram	2	-1	-0.5
				Miller	1	-3	-3.0
					46	**164**	**4.6**

New York	No.	Yds.	Avg.	Green Bay	No.	Yds.	Avg.
				RECEIVING			
Soar	3	41	13.7	Becker	2	79	39.5
Howell	2	3	1.5	Mulleneaux	2	54	27.0
Barnard	1	20	20.0	Uram	1	24	24.0
Barnum	1	20	20.0	Isbell	1	22	22.0
Leemans	1	5	5.0	Scherer	1	19	19.0
Perry	0	8	-	Gantenbein	1	6	6.0
	8	**97**	**12.1**		**8**	**214**	**26.8**

			PUNTING			
Danowski	6		39.5	Herber	3	41.3
Gildea	1		55.0	Hinkle	2	18.5
Barnum	1		33.0	Isbell	1	0.0
	8		**40.6**		**6**	**26.8**

PASSING

	Att.	Comp.	Comp Pct.	Yds.	Int.	Yds/Att.	Yds/Comp.
NEW YORK							
Danowski	11	7	63.6	77	0	7.0	11.0
Leemans	2	1	50.0	20	1	10.0	20.0
Barnum	1	0	0.0	0	0	0.0	0.0
Soar	1	0	0.0	0	0	0.0	0.0
	15	**8**	**53.3**	**97**	**1**	**6.5**	**12.1**
GREEN BAY							
Herber	14	5	35.7	123	0	8.8	24.6
Isbell	5	3	60.0	91	1	18.2	30.3
	19	**8**	**42.1**	**214**	**1**	**11.3**	**26.8**

1939 NFL CHAMPIONSHIP GAME
Green Bay 27, New York Giants 0
December 10, 1939, at Milwaukee
Attendance 32,278

As Western Division champions, the Packers were again scheduled to meet the Eastern Division first place team, the New York Giants, in early December. This playoff game would be played at Milwaukee's State Fair Park and charge a top of $4.40, an unprecedented high in professional football. State Fair Park was sold out two days after tickets were put on sale. A crowd of 32,279 was on hand for the rematch, including 6,000 in seats on the automobile racing track.

The Packers played inspired ball and shutout the Eastern champions, 27 to 0. It was Lambeau's fifth world championship. So rugged was the Green Bay defense that the Giants gained only 70 yards rushing all afternoon, and their gains via passes, also minimized by a cold 35-mile-an-hour wind, came to 98 yards. About the only satisfaction the New Yorkers got was that once again they held Hutson scoreless. But it was his catch of a 15 yard pass from Herber that set up the first touchdown. The score came on a Herber-to-Milt Gantenbein toss of six yards. Cecil Isbell threw 20 yards to Joe Laws for another marker in the third, and Ed Jankowski plunged a matter of feet for the third. Paul Engebretsen and Ernie Smith each kicked a field goal.

The crowd braved a cold, cloudy, blustery day to attend the game, giving the Packers a record gate of more than $80,000 as Green Bay recorded the first shutout in a NFL championship game. Members of the New York press complained about what they called deplorable conditions. What raised their ire so was the rickety press box atop the grandstand at State Fair Park. As the press box swayed in 35-mile winds, the writers feared for their lives. They also complained about a 'monumental traffic jam' after the game, and took pity on fans seated on folding chairs set up in the racetrack. 'For a day at least, professional football dipped back into its unsavory past and did itself uncalculated harm' wrote an indignant Stanley Woodward of the New York *Herald Tribune*.

New York	0	0	0	0	-	0
Green Bay	7	0	10	10	-	27

Green Bay - Gantenbein 7 pass from Herber (Engebretsen kick)
Green Bay - FG Engebretsen 29
Green Bay - Laws 31 pass from Isbell (Engebretsen kick)
Green Bay - FG E. Smith 42
Green Bay - Jankowski 1 run (E.Smith kick)

TEAM STATS

Green Bay		New York
13	First Downs – Total*	9
7	- By rushing	5
4	- By Passing	3
2	- By Penalty	1
2	Fumbles – Number	1
0	- Times Lost Ball	0
4	Penalties – Number	5
50	- Yards Penalized	21

Includes Touchdowns

INDIVIDUAL STATISTICS

Green Bay	No.	Yds.	Avg.	New York	No.	Yds.	Avg.
				RUSHING			
Uram	10	38	3.8	Leemans	12	24	2.0
Isbell	14	28	2.0	Miller	2	19	9.5
Hinkle	13	23	1.8	Soar	4	14	3.5
Laws	3	20	6.7	Richards	7	12	1.7
Jankowski	7	14	2.0	Cuff	3	7	2.3
Jacunski	1	11	11.0	Barnum	4	4	1.0
Herber	2	3	1.5	Kline	1	1	1.0
Hutson	1	3	3.0	Owen	1	-2	-2.0
	51	**140**	**2.7**		**34**	**79**	**2.3**

Green Bay	No.	Yds.	Avg.	New York	No.	Yds.	Avg.
			RECEIVING				
Hutson	2	21	10.5	Shaffer	2	16	8.0
Craig	2	6	3.0	Falaschi	2	6	3.0
Jacunski	1	31	31.0	Leemans	1	37	37.0
Laws	1	31	31.0	Gelatka	1	24	24.0
Gantenbein	1	7	7.0	Barnum	1	6	6.0
	7	**96**	**13.7**	Cuff	1	5	5.0
					8	**94**	**11.8**

PUNTING

Hinkle	5		22.6	Danowski	4		42.5
Herber	2		34.5	Barnum	2		36.0
	7		**26.0**		**6**		**40.3**

PASSING

	Att.	Comp.	Comp Pct.	Yds.	Int.	Yds/Att.	Yds/Comp	Yds. Lost/Tackle
GREEN BAY								
Herber	8	5	62.5	59	3	7.4	11.8	1-6
Isbell	2	2	100.0	37	0	18.5	18.5	
	10	**7**	**70.0**	**96**	**3**	**9.6**	**13.7**	**1-6**
NEW YORK								
Danowski	12	4	33.3	48	3	4.0	12.0	1-9
Miller	6	3	50.0	40	1	6.7	13.3	
Leemans	4	1	25.0	6	1	1.5	6.0	
Barnum	3	0	0.0	0	1	0.0	0.0	
	25	**8**	**32.0**	**94**	**6**	**3.8**	**11.8**	**1-9**

1941 NFL WESTERN DIVISION PLAYOFF GAME
Chicago Bears 33, Green Bay 14
December 14, 1941, at Chicago
Attendance 43,425

In the first divisional playoff game in NFL history, the Packers and Bears had to play a game at Wrigley Field to determine the Western Division champion and the right to play the New York Giants for the world championship. Hundreds of Packer fans crowded around the train station along with the Packers' famed Lumberjack Band on the Saturday before the game to give the team a noisy send off.

The next day, on a cold and windy December Sunday, the Packers were no match for the powerful Bears before a crowd of 43,425 at Wrigley Field. They lost, 33 to 14. The sub-freezing temperatures and strong winds contributed to a loosely played game with eight fumbles, seven interceptions and a total of 15 penalties called on both teams. Two weeks after the attack on Pearl Harbor, the NFL got a taste of problems in the offing at the league's championship game. Just over 13,300 fans turned out at Chicago's Wrigley Field. There were about 43,000 empty seats as the Bears bludgeoned the Giants, 37 to 9.

Green Bay	7	00	7	0	-	14
Chicago Bears	6	24	0	3	-	33

Green Bay - Hinkle 1 run (Hutson kick)
Chicago Bears - Gallarneau 61 punt return (kick blocked)
Chicago Bears - FG Snyder 24
Chicago Bears - Standlee 3 run (Stydahar kick)
Chicago Bears - Standlee 2 run (Stydahar kick)
Chicago Bears - Swisher 9 run (Stydahar kick)
Green Bay - Van Every 10 pass from Isbell (Hutson kick)
Chicago Bears - FG Snyder 26

1944 NFL CHAMPIONSHIP GAME
Green Bay 14, New York Giants 7
December 17, 1944, at New York
Attendance 46,016

Finishing the year at 8-2, the Packers won the Western Division and met the New York Giants for the championship. The Giants' quarterback was the former Packer, Arnie Herber, who Lambeau said was washed up when he cut him in 1941. He had come out of retirement to lead the Giants to an 8-1-1 record.

As Lambeau and his Western Division champions readied to leave for Charlottesville, Virginia for a week of pre-title game practice in warmer weather, American B-29's were bombing Japan. In a companion strike, nine ships and a Japanese troop convoy were sent off Leyte. Gasoline and food ration cards were still in effect as were transportation problems, which delayed the Packers' departure for Charlottesville. They were delayed a day trying to get their train out of Green Bay. When they finally arrived in Virginia for a week of pre-game workouts, they had two workouts a day, squad meetings and films of the previous Giants' games every day. Lambeau had good reason for spending so much time in preparation. His team had lost to the New York Giants four weeks earlier, 24 to 0, before a large crowd in New York of 56,481 fans. This championship game was played on December 17, 1944 and drew 46,000 at the huge Polo Grounds. Back in Wisconsin, Packer fans had the choice of two radio broadcasts of this game. Harry Wismer was broadcasting the game on WTAQ and Russ Winnie, the voice of the Packers, was describing action over Milwaukee's WTMJ.

Lambeau decided to put Don Hutson in as more of a decoy and stuck with the running game. Their young fullback, Ted Fritsch, scored both Green Bay touchdowns. The Packers beat the Giants, 14 to 7. Joe Laws also chewed up a lot of yards on the ground, gaining 72 yards in 13 carries in this game. "I only used two plays for myself that day," said Laws. "I used a half-spinner in the middle and a trap over the guard. I'd keep my eye on Larry Craig, the Packers' blocking back, and then whichever way he took the guy he was blocking I'd go the other way. At our quarterback meeting the night before the game Curly said we're going to throw all caution to the wind. You have permission to call anything you want."

A large crowd of Packer fans crowded around and on the tiny Chicago Northwestern depot platform once again to meet the team after their championship victory. The celebration went on through the evening and into the early morning hours by some of the more rambunctious fans. This season marked the last time the Packers would win a world championship until a coach by the name of Lombardi would lead Green Bay to a championship game 17 years later. This season would also be the year before the Packers' decline from power in the NFL. No one knew it at the time, but the glamour years for Curly Lambeau were over. The championship of 1944 would be Lambeau's last hurrah.

Green Bay	0	14	0	0	-	14
New York Giants	0	0	0	7	-	7

Green Bay - Fritsch 1 run (Hutson kick)
Green Bay - Fritsch 28 pass from Comp (Hutson kick)
New York Giants - Cuff 1 run (Strong kick)

TEAM STATS

New York		Green Bay
9	First Downs – Total*	13
6	- By rushing	10
2	- By Passing	3
1	- By Penalty	0
2	Fumbles – Number	2
0	- Times Lost Ball	0
11	Penalties – Number	4
80	- Yards Penalized	48

INDIVIDUAL STATISTICS

New York	No.	Yds.	Avg.	Green Bay	No.	Yds.	Avg.
				RUSHING			
Cuff	12	76	6.3	Fritsch	18	59	3.3
Livingston	12	22	1.8	Laws	13	72	5.5
Paschal	2	4	2.0	Comp	7	42	6.0
Sulaitis	1	-1	-1.0	Duhart	7	15	2.1
	27	**101**	**3.7**	Perkins	2	-4	-2.0
					47	**184**	**3.9**

				RECEIVING			
Liebel	3	70	23.3	Hutson	2	46	23.0
Cuff	2	23	11.5	Fritsch	1	28	28.0
Livingston	2	21	10.5		**3**	**74**	**24.7**
Barker	1	0	0.0				
	8	**114**	**14.3**				

				PUNTING			
Younce	10		41.0	L. Brock	6		36.8
				Fritsch	4		41.0
					10		**38.5**

				PUNT RETURNS			
Cuff	3	29	9.7	Comp	4	46	11.5
Livingston	1	2	2.0	Laws	3	37	12.3
	4	**31**	**7.8**	Duhart	1	5	5.0
					8	**88**	**11.0**

				KICKOFF RETURNS			
Cuff	1	24	24.0	Laws	1	9	9.0
Livingston	1	22	22.0				
Herber	1	17	17.0				
Sulaitis	1	16	16.0				
	4		**19.8**				

				INTERCEPTION RETURNS			
Younce	1	5	5.0	Laws	3	28	9.3
Livingston	1	0	0.0	Duhart	1	0	0.0
Hein	1	-3	-3.0		**4**	**28**	**7.0**
	3	**2**	**0.7**				

PASSING

	Att.	Comp.	Comp Pct.	Yds.	Int.	Yds/Att.	Yds/Comp	Lost/Tackle
New York								
Herber	22	8	36.4	114	4	5.2	14.3	3-16
GREEN BAY								
Comp	10	3	30.0	74	3	7.4	24.7	2-21
Brock	1	0	0.0	0	0	-	-	
	11	**3**	**27.3**	**74**	**3**	**6.7**	**24.7**	**2-21**

Sources: *The Football Encyclopedia, The Complete History of Professional Football from 1892 to the Present* and *Total Football II, The Official Encyclopedia of the National Football League*

FOOTNOTES

ONE – Requiem For An Original

1 Lambeau, More Than a Name by Cliff Christl appeared in the *Voyager*, Winter/Spring 2001

TWO – "Conquer the World"

2 Rockne of Notre Dame, The Making of a Legend by Ray Robinson
3 Rockne by Jerry Brondfield
4 A Notre Dame magazine, The Sports Immortals Museum Collection, Joel Platt, Director
5 A Notre Dame magazine, The Sports Immortals Museum Collection, Joel Platt, Director
6 The Fighting Irish Football Encyclopedia by Michael Steele
7 The Green Bay Packers-The Story of Professional Football by Arch Ward
8 The Fighting Irish Football Encyclopedia by Michael Steele
9 Collection of letters from Packer City Antiques, Marv Niec, assistant archivist Packer Hall of Fame
10 Collection of letters from Packer City Antiques, Marv Niec, assistant archivist Packer Hall of Fame
11 The Packer Legend by John Torinus
12 Packers vs. Bears by Glenn Swain
13 The Green Bay Packers-The Story of Professional Football by Arch Ward

THREE – Trials of the Twenties

14 Rockne by Jerry Brondfield
15 Rockne by Jerry Brondfield
16 Pro Football Hall of Fame
17 The Coffin Corner Newsletter-Magazine of the Professional Football Researchers Association
18 The Coffin Corner Newsletter-Magazine of the Professional Football Researchers Association
19 Birthplace of a Commonwealth, A Short History of Brown County, WI by Jack Rudolph
20 Birthplace of a Commonwealth, A Short History of Brown County, WI by Jack Rudolph
21 Milwaukee Journal-Sentinel October 27, 2001, article by Cliff Christl
22 Milwaukee Journal-Sentinel, October 27, 2001
23 The Packer Legend by John Torinus
24 Pigskin by Robert Peterson
25 History of the Green Bay Packers – The Lambeau Years, Part One by Larry Names
26 Packers vs. Bears by Glen Swain
27 The Chicago Bears by Richard Whittingham
28 Mudbaths and Bloodbaths, the Inside Story of the Bears-Packers Rivalry by Gary D'Amato and Cliff Christl
29 History of the Packers – The Lambeau Years, Part One by Larry Names
30 Milwaukee Journal, June 7, 1965

31 History of the Packers – The Lambeau Years, Part One by Larry Names
32 The Packer Legend by John Torinus
33 Packers vs. Bears by Glenn Swain
34 The Packer Legend by John Torinus
35 Packers vs. Bears by Glenn Swain

FOUR – Fame

36 Packers vs. Bears by Glenn Swain
37 Vagabond Halfback by Ralph Hickok
38 Recorded interview from *What a Game They Played* by Richard Whittingham
39 Vagabond Halfback by Ralph Hickok
40 The Green Bay Packers, Pro Football's Pioneer Team by Chuck Johnson
41 Packer Legend by John Torinus
42 The Green Bay Packers, Pro Footballs Pioneer Team by Chuck Johnson
43 What a Game They Played by Richard Whittingham
44 Vagabond Halfback by Ralph Hickok
45 Mudbaths and Bloodbaths by Gary D'Amato and Cliff Christl
46 Mudbaths and Bloodbaths by Gary D'Amato and Cliff Christl
47 Illustrated History of Pro Football by Robert Smith
48 Packers vs. Bears by Glenn Swain
49 What a Game They Played by Richard Whittingham
50 Vagabond Halfback by Ralph Hickok
51 Vagabond Halfback by Ralph Hickok
52 Vagabond Halfback by Ralph Hickok
53 History of the Packers, Pro Footballs Pioneer Team by Chuck Johnson
54 Packer Legend by John Torinus
55 Packer Legend by John Torinus

FIVE – Tarnished Luster

56 Mudbaths and Bloodbaths by Gary D'Amato and Cliff Christl
57 What a Game They Played by Richard Whittingham
58 Mudbaths and Bloodbaths by Gary D'Amato and Cliff Christl
59 What a Game They Played by Richard Whittingham
60 Milwaukee Journal, Oliver Kuechle 1970
61 What a Game They Played by Richard Whittingham
62 What a Game They Played by Richard Whittingham
63 What a Game They Played by Richard Whittingham
64 What a Game They Played by Richard Whittingham
65 What a Game They Played by Richard Whittingham
66 Vagabond Halfback by Ralph Hickok
67 Vagabond Halfback by Ralph Hickok
68 Vagabond Halfback by Ralph Hickok
69 Vagabond Halfback by Ralph Hickok
70 Vagabond Halfback by Ralph Hickok
71 Vagabond Halfback by Ralph Hickok
72 The Catholic Catechism by John A. Hardon, S.J.
73 Letter provided by Packer City Antiques, Marv Niec, assistant archivist
    Packer Hall of Fame
74 What a Game They Played by Richard Whittingham
75 What a Game They Played by Richard Whittingham

76 *Green Bay Packers, Pro Footballs Pioneer Team* by Chuck Johnson
77 *The Coffin Corner* Newsletter-Magazine of the Professional Football
   Researchers Association
78 *The Coffin Corner* Newsletter-Magazine of the Professional Football
   Researchers Association
79 *The Coffin Corner* Newsletter-Magazine of the Professional Football
   Researchers Association
80 *What a Game They Played* by Richard Whittingham

SIX – Image of Greatness

81 Appeared in the September 29, 1957 program for the Packers-Bears game
82 *What a Game They Played* by Richard Whittingham
83 *The Packer Legend* by John Torinus
84 *Football's Stars of Summer* by Raymond Schmidt
85 *Football's Stars of Summer* by Raymond Schmidt
86 *The Green Bay Packers Pro Footballs Pioneer Team* by Chuck Johnson
87 *The Green Bay Packers, Pro Footballs Pioneer Team* by Chuck Johnson
88 *Packers vs. Bears* by Glenn Swain
89 *Packers vs. Bears* by Glenn Swain
90 *Green Bay Packers, Pro Footballs Pioneer Team* by Chuck Johnson
91 *Milwaukee Journal* December 18, 1994

SEVEN – The Last Hurrah

92 Notes from the Packer Hall of Fame, courtesy of Tom Murphy, archivist
   Packer Hall of Fame
93 Contract courtesy of Marv Niec, Packer City Antiques, assistant archivist
   Packer Hall of Fame
94 *Football's Stars of Summer* by Raymond Schmidt
95 *Of Mikes and Men* by Curt Smith
96 Information obtained from the Packer Hall of Fame
97 *The History of the Green Bay Packers - The Lambeau Years, Part Two,* by
   Larry Names
98 *Packer vs. Bears* by Glenn Swain

EIGHT – Fall From Grace

99 Leonard Matlin, *Signet,* a division of Penguin Putnam, Inc.
100 *Football's Stars of Summer* by Raymond Schmidt
101 *Football's Stars of Summer* by Raymond Schmidt
102 *The Packer Story* by Arch Ward
103 *Football's Stars of Summer* by Raymond Schmidt
104 *Football's Stars of Summer* by Raymond Schmidt
105 *Pigskin – The Early Years of Pro Football* by Robert Peterson
106 *Packers vs. Bears* by Glenn Swain
107 *The Packer Legend* by John Torinus
108 *The Green Bay Packers, Pro Footballs Pioneer Team* by Chuck Johnson
109 *The Green Bay Packers, Pro Footballs Pioneer Team* by Chuck Johnson
110 *The Green Bay Packers, Pro Footballs Pioneer Team* by Chuck Johnson
111 *Downfield* by Jerry Poling

112 Packer Legends In Facts, 75th Edition by Eric Goska
113 The Green Bay Packers, Pro Footballs Pioneer Team by Chuck Johnson
114 Packer Legends in Facts, 75th Edition by Eric Goska

NINE – Shameful Finish

115 Filmed interview provided by Packer Hall of Fame, courtesy of Tom
   Murphy, archivist
116 The History of the Green Bay Packers - The Lambeau Year, Part Three by
   Larry Names
117 The History of the Green Bay Packers - The Lambeau Years, Part Three by
   Larry Names
118 Milwaukee Journal June 2, 1965

TEN – Road to Perdition

119 The History of the Green Bay Packers by Larry Names
*120 When Football Was Football, The Chicago Cardinals and the Birth of the
   NFL* by Joe Ziemba
121 When Football was Football by Joe Ziemba
122 When Football was Football by Joe Ziemba
123 Chicago Sun Times
124 When Football was Football by Joe Ziemba
125 The Redskins Book by Shirley Povich
126 The Redskins Book by Shirley Povich
127 The Redskins Book by Shirley Povich
128 The Redskins by Shirley Povich
129 The Redskins by Shirley Povich
130 Football's Stars of Summer by Raymond Schmidt
131 Football's Stars of Summer by Raymond Schmidt
132 Lombardi, His Life and Times by Robert W. Wells

ELEVEN – Redemption

133 Thessalonica 5:22
134 Seneca, Debrevitate Vitae 1,3
135 New York Times, Monday, June 7, 1965
136 Milwaukee Journal, June 2, 1965

David Zimmerman is a successful businessman and author of fourteen books, including *In Search of a Hero, the Life and Times of Tony Canadeo.* He lives in the Milwaukee area with his wife, Peggy, and their children and has been an avid Packer fan since attending his first game as a youngster in 1949.

For inquiries, contact:

EAGLE
BOOKS

P.O. Box 253
Hales Corners, WI 53130
414-425-2370 ext. 114